BROUGHT TO YOU IN LIVING COLOR

75 YEARS OF GREAT MOMENTS IN TELEVISION & RADIO FROM NBC

BROUGHT TO YOU IN LIVING COLOR

75 YEARS OF GREAT MOMENTS IN TELEVISION & RADIO FROM NBC

MARC ROBINSON

FOREWORD BY TOM BROKAW   PREFACE BY BOB WRIGHT   INTRODUCTION BY KELSEY GRAMMER

JOHN WILEY & SONS, INC.

Produced by: Top Down Productions, Encino, CA
Design by: Bocu & Bocu, San Gabriel, CA

This book is printed on acid-free paper.

This publication is designed to provide accurate
and authoritative information in regard to the
subject matter covered. It is sold with the understanding
that the publisher is not engaged in rendering
professional services. If professional advice or other expert
assistance is required, the services of a competent
professional person should be sought.

ISBN 0-471-09016-6

Printed in the United States of America.

10 9 8 7 6 5 4 3 2 1

ACKNOWLEDGMENTS

The creation of any published book is a collaborative act, and for no volume is that statement more true than for this one. First thanks go to NBC's Chairman and CEO Bob Wright, and to his wife, Suzanne, for their interest in and support of this project. Kassie Canter, Senior Vice President of Corporate Communications at NBC, provided the book's title, as well as a perceptive eye and a great deal of indispensable guidance. William Bartlett, Director of Corporate Communications, abandoned his departmental colleagues for many months to ensure that the quality of this historical record matched that of NBC's broadcasting tradition. Broadcast historian Alec Cumming created the "tome" that served as the genesis of the book; and he stuck with the project to the end, acting as a researcher, interviewer, writer, and resident expert on all things NBC.

A distinguished group of professionals offered their personal recollections, including Neal Baer, Merrill Brown, Tom Brokaw, Fred Collins, Katie Couric, John Damiano, Dick Ebersol, Randy Falco, Bill Griffeth, Sue Herera, Ron Insana, Peter Jankowski, Andrew Lack, Matt Lauer, Warren Littlefield, Rick Ludwin, Lorne Michaels, Robert Morton, Conan O'Brien, Jane Pauley, Tim Russert, Willard Scott, Barry Schindel, Thomas Schlamme, George Schlatter, Neal Shapiro, Sidney Sheldon, Lilly Tartikoff, Pamela Thomas-Graham, Grant Tinker, Jack Welch, John Wells, Brian Williams, and Bob Wright.

Many people within NBC were instrumental in ways large and small. From NBC Entertainment's publicity department, Rebecca Marks, Curt King, Jennifer Skorlich, and Cathryn Boxberger were especially gracious and helpful, while Brian Robinette contributed some brilliant writing, along with a thorough review of crucial sections of the manuscript. NBC Entertainment executives Ted Frank, Sheraton Kalouria, and Rick Ludwin kept the entertainment narrative on the right path, while Bill Wheatley at NBC News, and Jon Miller and Steve Ulrich at NBC Sports, generously shared their time and expertise. Among others deserving mention for their assistance are Deborah Ader, Ernie Angstadt, Cameron Blanchard, Lisa Connell, Michelle Jaconi, Kara Keenan, Brian Kiley, Ann Kolbell, Wendy Kravitz, John Lavet, David Lipsius, Gillian Lusins, Nancy Nathan, Kim Niemi, Mary Paris, Carrette Perkins, Ryan Osborn, Frank Radice, Cory Shields, Kevin Sullivan, and Jamie Warren.

Historians and curators who helped us untangle myth from reality in the early decades of this story include Michael Biel of Morehouse College, Sam Brylawski of the Library of Congress, Mortimer Frank of the Julliard School of Music, Jane Klain and Ron Simon of the Museum of Television & Radio, and Alex Magoun of the David Sarnoff Library. Independent scholars who provided expertise include Steve Dworkin, Joe Mackey, Elizabeth McLeod, and Ed Reitan.

The good people at John Wiley & Sons deserve a great deal of thanks for their perseverance and commitment, especially Joan L. O'Neil, Vice President and Publisher, professional and trade division, Senior Editor Jeanne Glasser, Managing Editor Robin Factor, Senior Project Supervisor Ruth Acosta, Associate Manufacturing Manager Andrea Price, Editorial Program Coordinator Bonnie Neel, and Prepress/Imaging Technicians Ian A. Smith, Clint Lahnen.

Special thanks to Stephen Battaglio, for stepping in with some crucial last-minute guidance; to Robert J. Juncosa and Robert D. Juncosa; and to Ray Whelan, Jr., and Jon Green at Globe Photos for their generous support.

The production team did an extraordinary job: Annie Huang and Peter Huang of the design firm Bocu & Bocu, who contributed the beautiful design of the book and produced all of the layouts; Digby Diehl, who contributed superbly to the writing; Media Clearance Coordinator Gudrun Olafsdottir, who found and cleared so many wonderful images; Bob Woods, who lent his research and writing expertise to many of the sports sections; and Nick Clemente, who managed some of the project and consulted on all of it.

Special thanks also to Debra Englander of John Wiley & Sons, Dick LeRoy, Joe Garner, Marc Firestone, Bob Lieberman, Stephanie and Kara Rubenstein, and most of all, to Zachary Robinson, for all of their support.

CONTENTS

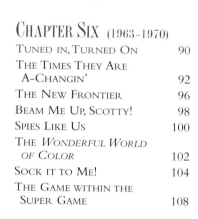

A Salute to NBC's Affiliates

With its glorious history, the NBC network has been the source of unforgettable moments for generations of Americans. But let's pause a moment on that word, "network." In a literal sense, a network is a fabric of interwoven cords that are knotted or secured at the points of intersection. In the case of a broadcaster such as NBC, the fabric is its national programming, and the secure knots throughout are the more than 200 individual stations across the nation that transmit this programming to their local audiences.

But NBC's affiliates do much more than broadcast our national programming. They play a vital role in their cities and towns, televising local news and sports, supporting their communities through public-service and philanthropic efforts, and helping citizens come together around commonly held goals.

Without these affiliated stations, there would be no network, no national broadcaster, and no National Broadcasting Company. Thus, on the occasion of NBC's seventy-fifth anniversary, we would like to acknowledge and salute our affiliates, that, indeed, made—and continue to make—NBC possible.

The symbiotic relationship between national broadcasters and affiliates goes back to NBC's origins. We have television affiliates today (KSDK in St. Louis and WCSH in Portland, Maine, to name two) that were with us as radio affiliates on November 15, 1926, when NBC first went on the air. Seventy-five years later, through massive transformations in every facet of our society, they are still with us—still serving St. Louis and Portland residents with local news and public-service programming, while presenting the high caliber of entertainment, news, and sports programming that only a national network has the resources to provide.

Indeed, it is precisely this blend of NBC's national identity and resources with the distinct personalities of its local affiliates that makes NBC such a valuable organization to its viewers. We are constantly aware that the whole is much more than either of our separate parts—and that the network-affiliate relationship is what best serves the American public.

NBC's legacy of a strong television affiliate body dates back to David Sarnoff and his famous speech in 1947 urging our radio affiliates to apply immediately for television licenses. But there has been a remarkable line of officers to make the General's vision a reality. Men named Paxton, Lynagh, Yager, Elkins, and Sander, to name some of NBC's Affiliate Board chairmen, constitute a "who's who" of broadcasting history unmatched by any other network.

NBC is itself the proud owner of thirteen affiliated stations, including some with incredibly rich traditions: WMAQ in Chicago, for example, which became NBC's first all-color station in 1956, and WNBC in New York, the nation's first commercial television station, which first hit the airwaves on July 1, 1941.

We salute and thank the current and past members of our Affiliate Board, as well as all the other broadcasting professionals at local stations who have been part of NBC's history over the past seventy-five years.

Randy Falco

RANDY FALCO
President,
NBC Television Network

John Damiano

JOHN DAMIANO
Executive Vice President,
Affiliate Relations

FOREWORD

TOM BROKAW
Anchor and Managing Editor,
NBC Nightly News with Tom Brokaw

One of my favorite stories from my mother's family history involves my grandfather, Jim Conley, a studious man who was a farmer on the treeless South Dakota prairie in the 1920s. He worked hard, farming mostly with a team of horses and rudimentary machinery on that remote place far from the nation's metropolitan centers.

One year, for Christmas, his father-in-law gave him enough money to buy one of the new crystal radio sets. My mother recalls him sitting up half the night at the kitchen table with the radio headsets on, listening through the static to KDKA in Pittsburgh. He became a radio addict, forgoing sleep to listen to late-night broadcasts of music, comedy, news—whatever was on the air, most of it on the new NBC network.

I often think of him when I sit at my high-tech NBC News desk, broadcasting to millions of viewers. What I do now is simply an extension of what so enthralled him seventy-five years ago. This electronic network, first radio and then television, became the connective tissue for a vast land of diverse interests and met a common need for entertainment, news, and information.

Through the Great Depression and World War II, a time of great stress and uncertainty for America, radio was a critical source of information and solace. Franklin Roosevelt became the first electronic president, as he used the radio airwaves as an instrument of democracy, speaking to citizens everywhere at once on matters of national urgency in his wonderfully reassuring and theatrical voice.

As someone born in 1940, I began life as a child of radio but then had a pioneering experience with television. Until I was fifteen we lived in an area of South Dakota so remote we couldn't get a television signal. So when we moved to a larger town I was stunned by this new window on the world sitting in the corner of our tiny living room. It was a simple black-and-white set, but what wonders it contained.

My mother and I were hooked on David Garroway's keen intelligence and easy charm on *Today* in the mornings. We stayed home Sundays to watch his *Wide Wide World* broadcast, seeing places we never expected to visit in person.

For me, however, *The Huntley-Brinkley Report* was the boyhood equivalent of an aspiring baseball player seeing Joe DiMaggio or Jackie Robinson for the first time. That newscast brought the news of the world into our home with such grace and clarity that it fueled my ambitions to one day be a journalist. At the end of the NBC News coverage of the memorable and very tight 1960 election night, when John F. Kennedy's victory wasn't secure until the following morning, my goal was clear: become an NBC News correspondent and chase the big stories around the world.

And so I set off on what has been a remarkable journey through the latter half of the twentieth century on the always accelerating curve of broadcast journalism. From the coverage of the civil rights movement to the assassination of John F. Kennedy to the early days of space exploration, television news was suddenly a vital nerve center for a nation that thrives on the shared experience.

As America rolled into the social turmoil of what we now call simply "the sixties," again it was television news images that shaped so much of the debate: images from Vietnam, from Haight-Ashbury in San Francisco, from the 1968 Democratic Convention in San Francisco to the first reports of something called "Watergate" in Washington through to the first resignation of a sitting president in our history.

I was White House correspondent for NBC News during Watergate, and I remember thinking when it was all over how proud I was to be part of a medium that provided a daily recitation and analysis of the facts. The Founding Fathers could not have anticipated that one day something called "television" would be critical to the timely flow of important information to the citizenry during a constitutional crisis.

Of course, television news was not just a camera trained on America. The world has always been our beat, but never more so than during the heady days of the 1980s when the Soviet Union and Communism began to collapse. Fortunately, the technology of television was evolving as rapidly as historic events were unfolding. The use of satellites and video cameras allowed Americans to not only witness the collapse of Communism as it happened, but also to listen in on the many discussions that followed on how the new world would evolve. On the night the Berlin Wall fell, I was able to broadcast directly from the wall as East Germans scrambled over that barrier to freedom directly behind me. It was one of the most dramatic and important moments in the twentieth century, and it was there on NBC, live and in living color, as we used to say. That was just the beginning of what turned out to be a technological explosion of dizzying proportions. I call it the "Big Bang" of television news, in which a whole new cosmos was formed out of a combination of cable proliferation, satellites, and computers. Suddenly, the world was wired as it never had been before, and there was a ceaseless quest for something to fill all of those hours that were now available on all those channels.

On September 11, 2001, we had more unforgettable images and stunning developments than we ever could have imagined to fill all of those screens. Television news performed magnificently across the spectrum of networks and cable outlets. America was under attack, and American citizens were able to witness the horror of it, hear firsthand accounts from survivors, mourn with those who lost loved ones, hear the president rally the nation, consider the analysis of experts, and share common grief with friends and strangers alike. I have never been more proud of my colleagues and my association with NBC News than I was that day.

NBC has come a long way since those early days of radio. We now have so many more parts: NBC, the television network; the NBC-owned stations; MSNBC, the all-news cable network; CNBC, the business-news network; and a diverse portfolio of online properties. But our fundamental mission has not changed since that long-ago time when my grandfather listened to that tiny two-tube radio in his isolated farmhouse.

Broadcasting is a great resource in a nation of so much geographical, ideological, and economic diversity. In times of crisis or frivolity, everyone has equal access to information, education, and entertainment. That's a powerful equation for people in a free society, wherever they live. NBC has been proud to perform that service in America for seventy-five years, and it is a commitment it will keep to its audience as we move forward in a new century.

PREFACE

SUZANNE AND BOB WRIGHT
*Bob Wright is Vice Chairman & Executive Officer, GE,
and Chairman & Chief Executive Officer, NBC*

Commercial television began on July 1, 1941, when the Bulova Watch Company paid NBC's New York station $9 to have a Bulova clock appear on-screen as an announcer read the time. Fortunately, American viewers today have much more compelling programming to watch—and NBC has improved its rates.

This book is not about the evolution of the broadcasting business as much as it is a celebration of the shared experiences, transmitted via NBC's radio and television network, that make up our nation's collective memory. But before we embark on this historical journey, I'd like to point out that this volume, and these memories, could not exist without the efforts of various partners. These include, most importantly, our 200-plus affiliates, some of which have been with us since we first went on the air. Among our other key partners are the production companies that make programs for us, the advertisers who pay for them, the media-buying groups and advertising agencies that buy air time and create ads for their clients, and the talent agencies that help us find the right actors and actresses to make a show come alive.

Advertisers on broadcast television have created images and phrases as indelible as anything seen as part of network programming. If you watched television in the 1960s, you undoubtedly remember Dinah Shore singing "See the U-S-A in your Chev-ro-let." In fact, for every memorable TV catch-phrase ("Sock it to me!") there is no doubt an equally compelling advertising slogan

("You deserve a break today").

The earliest producers of programming for radio and then television were not broadcasters such as NBC but the advertising agencies themselves. In 1926, the same year that NBC was founded, a Philadelphia agency called Young & Rubicam relocated to New York City in order to be closer to NBC and the center of the new broadcast-network business. Within a few years, Young & Rubicam would be the source of popular radio programming such as Fred Allen's show on NBC, *Town Hall Tonight* (which had as its producer a young man named Pat Weaver, who would later revolutionize television).

After World War II, when network television was just beginning to take off, ad agencies (or consumer-product companies themselves) were again the main sources of programming. In 1950, for example, the top six television shows (all on NBC) were connected with then (and still) famous brand names: *Texaco Star Theater*, *Fireside Theatre* (from Procter & Gamble), *Philco Television Playhouse* (Philco radios), *Your Show of Shows* (Admiral refrigerators), the *Colgate Comedy Hour*, and the *Gillette Calvacade of Sports*.

Indeed, many of NBC's most vital advertisers today have relationships with NBC that date from the beginnings of television, if not earlier: in addition to Procter & Gamble, these include General Motors, Ford, Johnson & Johnson, Philip Morris, and Chrysler. Meanwhile, names that have faded from the screen have been replaced by vibrant brands such as Toyota, Pfizer, McDonalds, Honda, Pizza Hut, Taco Bell, and KFC.

Today, the actual buying of air time for these national advertisers is usually handled by media-buying groups such as Magna Global, Omnicom, Starcom, Mediavest, Mediacom, and Media Edge. While some of these entities are of recent vintage, they all have roots that extend deep into broadcast history by virtue of their relationships with the renowned advertising agencies, such as Young & Rubicam, McCann Erickson, Grey Advertising, Leo Burnett, Benton and Bowles, and BBDO, that NBC has worked with throughout the years.

Major consumer-products makers are today no longer in the business of producing television shows (with the exception of Procter & Gamble). Increasingly, we produce our own shows, but NBC and its audiences are also indebted to quality production studios such as Warner Bros., Studios USA, Paramount, Carsey Werner, Universal, and Touchstone. We are equally indebted to talent agencies such as William Morris, Creative Artists, ICM, Endeavor, and UTA.

All of these partners share in the credit of the achievements highlighted in the following pages, for each of them plays a crucial role in enabling us to present a bounty of free, compelling, high-quality programming that the pioneers of this industry could hardly have imagined. You can't buy an ad on NBC for $9 anymore. But whatever the price, advertisers and marketers in the twenty-first century continue to be well served by broadcast television, as are millions of viewers across the nation.

1943

1954

1956

1959

1975

1980

1986

INTRODUCTION

KELSEY GRAMMER
aka Dr. Frasier Crane

The National Broadcasting Company is celebrating its seventy-fifth birthday. For three-quarters of a century, it has both documented and shaped the unfolding canvas of contemporary culture. It was and is the first of its kind. From the early days of radio to the television programming of today, NBC has provided this country, and even the world, with an evolving collection of shared memories and images. Certainly there are other networks and broadcasters that followed, but this shared national experience did not exist before the National Broadcasting Company.

O. B. Hanson, the engineer who designed NBC's Radio City studios, stated in 1932, "Radio is as fabulous as Prince Housan's magic carpet of Arabian Nights fame—more so as it can fly completely around the world seven times in one second." Seven times in one second! The mere thought of it is mind-boggling. Imagine what he might have written about television.

Technologically, both radio and television are beyond my meager comprehension of science, but as a marvel of communication and entertainment, I believe they are as significant to recent history as the Gutenberg press was to its time centuries ago. For the last seventy-five years, NBC has chronicled and characterized that history—shared and even shaped it. The history of NBC is, then, *our* history, and its story belongs to each and every one of us.

My own memories of NBC and its programming abound and are indelible. The recollections can be turned over like the pages of this book. It was Jack Benny in an appearance on *The Tonight Show* with Johnny Carson who said, "I always play up to my audience." That simple phrase has defined my life's work. I will never forget the impact Orson Welles made on me when he recited Shakespeare on *The Dean Martin Show*, or how I admired Bob Hope for the gift of laughter he brought to us and to our men and women overseas. Before *Rowan & Martin's Laugh-In*, the two comedians had a "summer replacement" show that aired in Dean Martin's slot. There was a recurring skit they did as two spies, first exchanging passwords and then ridiculous bits of information. That skit always began with the words, "I've got the yo-yo," and then, "I've got the string." Obviously, it made an impression on me. There was also a weatherman routine on the show that featured a relatively unknown George Carlin! To this day, I sing the *Bonanza* theme whenever I am in a hurry; well, not the words of course, no one actually knows the words. There *are* words, you know.

All right, maybe some of my memories are not yours. There are several more celebrated landmarks of television that we all share because of NBC. We traveled to the "final frontier" with the original *Star Trek*, we cried with (even if a football fan cursed) *Heidi*, donned pastel clothes with Crockett and Tubbs while cruising Miami, memorized classic scenes of *Saturday Night Live*, patrolled the mean streets of *Hill Street Blues*, revived the situation of comedy with *Cosby*, litigated with the libidinous legal eagles of *L.A. Law*, pulled for the lives and doctors of *ER*, became *Friends* with six

charming New Yorkers in oversized apartments—and fought from both sides of the aisles with the impassioned politicos of *The West Wing*.

If you're like me, you may even have hoisted a few (or a few too many) in a bar where "everybody knows your name"—or crossed verbal swords with a cerebral Seattle radio psychiatrist whose penchant for the polysyllabic makes him the paradigm of pomposity.

And we will never forget the legacy that precedes us. We stand on the shoulders of giants such as Arturo Toscanini in *Live from Studio 8H*, whose celebrated recordings of the Beethoven symphonies are considered by many the finest ever made. In the early days of television, we said hello to Howdy, guessed the secret "woid" for Groucho, tipped our coffee mugs to J. Fred every morning on *Today*, hailed Sid Caesar, started something big with Steve Allen, and cozied up on the couch in our cardigans with Perry Como. Chet Huntley and David Brinkley brought us the evening news. Their candor and unique perspective are hallmarks

in the industry to this day.

Not all of the giants were "on the air." There were those who played their roles behind the scenes: creative geniuses such as Sylvester "Pat" Weaver, Grant Tinker, and Brandon Tartikoff; industry leaders such as "the General," David Sarnoff; forward thinkers such as Bob Wright, who successfully navigated NBC through the challenges of cable competition and audience fragmentation. There would have been no Super Bowl without NBC's broadcast validation of an upstart sporting confederation known as the American Football League in the early 1960s. Shows such as *Cheers* and *Seinfeld* might never have flourished without the support of the network executives who believed in them.

The halls of NBC—either in the vertical monolith known as "30 Rock" in New York or in its more horizontal counter-part in Burbank—are alive with memories; memories that extend from the fourth floor in New York where Lowell Thomas broadcast the news to the sixth-floor corner office where Weaver penned his philosophical memoranda to

the Burbank complex where the images of past greats such as Bob Hope, Johnny Carson, and Redd Foxx are etched on the massive "elephant doors" and stand as towering sentinels outside the studios where they once held court entertaining America and the world.

There are events too that tower in our collective conscience as brought to us by NBC. There was the Cuban Missile Crisis and the tragic death of a young President Kennedy, and then our disbelief as we watched Jack Ruby gun down Lee Harvey Oswald during an exclusive NBC live broadcast. I will never forget the day Anwar Sadat was assassinated, or the rising tide of dissent during the Vietnam War that defined a decade and redefined our nation. And there is no one alive today who will ever forget September 11 and the subsequent groundswell of resolve and love of country that will surely define our future.

Whether sobering or silly, catastrophic or carefree, NBC's memories are ours for the sharing. I feel privileged to invite you to rediscover them on the pages herein.

THE BIRTH OF THE NATIONAL

As the 1920s began and the brutal shock of World War I began to fade, entertainment was becoming increasingly democratized. The advent of record players for the home brought popular singers into people's living rooms, and Hollywood's explosive growth brought major stars into everyone's local movie theaters. Electronic technology was inspiring new forms of artistry and creating an increasingly expectant national audience.

Another intriguing electronic gizmo—radio—wasn't, however, quite ready for prime time. Invented by men with names like Marconi, Fessenden, and DeForest, and put into practice by intrepid amateurs, "the wireless" was a form of communication with obvious potential, even if no one had yet figured out how to produce programming that was both professional and commercially viable.

As early as November 1916, a young Russian immigrant and radio fanatic named David Sarnoff had proposed to executives at American Marconi a "Radio Music Box" that would bring entertainment and information into the home. "This proposition would be especially interesting to farmers and others living in outlying districts removed from cities," Sarnoff wrote. "By the purchase of a 'Radio Music Box,' they could enjoy concerts,

EXPERIENCE

lectures, music, recitals, etc., which may be going on in the nearest city within their radius."

Sarnoff's employers scoffed at the idea, but when he presented it again in 1920—after American Marconi had been bought by General Electric and renamed the Radio Corporation of America (RCA)—his superiors began to realize that the pesky memo

writer was something of a prophet. By late 1920, "broadcasting" was becoming a reality, put into motion by Westinghouse, whose KDKA in Pittsburgh had (arguably) pioneered the form. And in 1922, American Telephone and Telegraph's radio stations began to "network," broadcasting radio programs over multiple stations linked via AT&T's "long lines."

But by the mid-twenties, AT&T decided it wasn't interested in producing content for a national audience. Executives at General Electric and Westinghouse (which had joined forces with GE in RCA), however, were very interested. They also understood that unless professional, well-crafted entertainment and information could be presented to the

American public, only hobbyists would want to buy a radio. So the two companies joined forces to create a new subsidiary for RCA that would be dedicated to bringing top-quality broadcasting to towns both big and small, from coast to coast. That subsidiary, announced to the public in August 1926, was called the National Broadcasting Company.

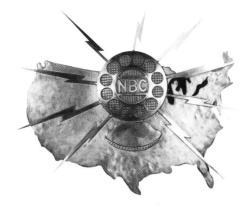

LIVE FROM NEW YORK... IT'S A RADIO NETWORK!

"Think of it! Ten or maybe even twelve million persons may be hearing what takes place in this ballroom tonight."

With this, NBC's first president, Merlin H. Aylesworth, opened the four-and-a-half-hour gala inaugural broadcast of the National Broadcasting Company. The date was November 15, 1926, and more than a thousand of New York's most glamorous society and show business figures had gathered in the Grand Ballroom of the Waldorf-Astoria Hotel (on the site where the Empire State Building now stands). The spectacular program, carried by twenty-five affiliate stations in twenty-one cities, was heard as far west as Kansas City.

It was estimated that half of the nation's approximately five million radio sets were tuned in as an unprecedented (if mainly highbrow) array of talent came before the NBC microphones. Walter Damrosch conducted the New York Symphony Orchestra, Metropolitan Opera star Titta Ruffo sang, and, from Chicago, soprano Mary Garden sang "Annie Laurie." The crowd-pleasing vaudeville team of Weber and Fields performed their broad comedy, while the famed Goldman Band played patriotic music. Will Rogers poked fun at President Coolidge in a remote pickup from his backstage dressing room in Independence, Kansas. The dance bands of Ben Bernie, Vincent Lopez, B. A. Rolfe, and George Olsen played long into the night. The remotes, the stars, the scale of the event were designed to create a buzz, and to impress whoever might be tuning in. After all, this was a *National* Broadcasting Company, coming right into your home!

Radio had come a long way in a short time. Only six years earlier (November 2, 1920, to be precise) this new medium had taken its first tentative steps, when Westinghouse's Frank Conrad "broadcast" the 1920 Harding-Cox election results to a handful of listeners and

hobbyists in Pittsburgh. While historians continue to debate whether Conrad's KDKA was really the first commercial radio station, it was certainly the first widely publicized one.

By 1924, "radio broadcasting" was a full-fledged fad. Average folks were beginning to put radio sets in their living rooms, but what they heard often left much to be desired. The airwaves were a chaotic mess, with 1,400 stations on the air, and many of them giving anybody who walked into the studios a chance to show off their "talent." With no consistent scheduling and raw, uneven programming, the novelty began to wear thin. By 1926, the number of stations had dwindled to 620.

The official formation of NBC as a broadcast network, with regularly scheduled and well-produced programs, energized the radio industry. Rarely had people in smaller cities and towns had the opportunity to listen to the kind of big-city entertainers NBC presented. The result was a boom in radio sales and listeners. (It did take some time, however, for the network to gear up its programming. After the excitement of the inaugural broadcast, the next evening's lineup included such fare as *Auction Bridge Lessons* and the *Jolly Buckeye Bakers*.)

On January 1, 1927, announcer Graham McNamee presided over NBC's first coast-to-coast network broadcast— the Rose Bowl football game from Pasadena. On that same day, a second set of NBC radio stations, known as the Blue network, began broadcasting to a new group of affiliates. (The stations that debuted a month and a half earlier were called the Red network. The names came from the color of the pencils used by the radio engineers who drew up the national maps.)

On October 1, 1927, a rapidly growing NBC moved into state-of-the-art, acoustically designed, art deco rooms at 711 Fifth Avenue in New York City.

Radio days were upon us.

(Opposite) Singer Jessica Dragonette, seen here at NBC's Fifth Avenue studios, began hosting her own show on NBC in 1929. She was the operetta-singing star of the *Cities Service Concerts.* *(Above, left)* Humorist Will Rogers and the comedy team of Weber and Fields *(below)* performed on the inaugural gala. *(Above, right)* In NBC's master control room, Chief Engineer O. B. Hanson (standing) prepares to give the signal to start NBC's debut broadcast.

"Beginning tonight you will receive a new thrill in radio..."

— NBC President Merlin H. Aylesworth

LAUGHTER IS THE GREAT UNIFIER

Network radio arrived just when America most needed to laugh. The stock market had plummeted, thousands of banks and businesses had gone under, and twelve million people were unemployed. In the midst of the Great Depression, radio provided a welcome escape. Even if you didn't have a nickel for a movie, you could stay at home, turn on the radio, and—momentarily, at least—leave your troubles behind.

AMOS 'N' ANDY

One of the most famous (and, eventually, controversial) situation comedies of all time was also, arguably, the *first* situation comedy of all time. The pioneering *Amos 'n' Andy* was heard on the Blue network in 1929, after launching (as *Sam 'n' Henry*) three years earlier on Chicago's WGN. The show did for radio what Milton Berle would do for television twenty years later: captivate the nation, boost receiver sales, and prove the commercial viability of network radio. For fifteen minutes a night, broadcasting live from a small radio studio at NBC's Chicago affiliate WMAQ, Amos and Andy would entangle themselves in messes of love and friendship, all the while failing at one "can't miss" business scheme after another. The show was such a huge hit in its 7:00 p.m. time slot that the phone company reported a sharp drop in calls while it was on the air and many theaters moved back their openings to 7:30. Even President Coolidge reportedly insisted that all White House activities cease during *Amos 'n' Andy* time.

The two main characters owned a broken-down car and the "Fresh Air Taxicab Company of America Incorpolated." The hard-working Amos would rhetorically ask "Ain't dat sumpin'?" at the slightest provocation. Andy considered himself the brains of the operation and spent most of his time taking credit for Amos's ideas, "restin' his brain," and "workin' on da books." It wasn't long before listeners everywhere were repeating those phrases and many others—inside jokes everyone could recognize and share.

The only thing was, Freeman Gosden (Amos) and Charles Correll (Andy) were white, and they played the lead characters with southern black accents. As American society changed, *Amos 'n' Andy* would increasingly come under fire for stereotyping African-Americans. Only recently have historians begun to acknowledge the writing and performing genius of Gosden and Correll—and the genuine love and respect they had for their characters.

FANNY BRICE *(Above, right)* Mischievous brat Baby Snooks was a wonderful radio invention. Comedienne Fanny Brice created this comically unlovable kid as part of her act for the Ziegfeld Follies. She began performing the character on radio in 1936, and Baby Snooks stayed on the air, on one show or another, until her creator's death in 1951. Barbra Streisand paid tribute to Brice in *Funny Girl*, and Lily Tomlin's Edith Ann character was inspired by Snooks.

(Opposite) A promotional photo of Charles Correll as Andy *(left)* and Freeman Gosden as Amos *(right)*. Of course, they performed the radio show without greasepaint. *(Top)* Bob Hope.

EDGAR BERGEN & CHARLIE McCARTHY *(Right)* Two of the biggest stars in network radio were a ventriloquist…and his dummy! *The Chase and Sanborn Hour* kept millions of listeners roaring with laughter from 1937 to 1948. The dummy, Charlie, cheerfully insulted anyone within earshot, even stars as revered as Frank Sinatra, Lana Turner, and Dorothy Lamour (pictured here). As for W. C. Fields (also pictured here), he and Charlie clashed frequently. Fields once threatened to turn wooden Charlie into venetian blinds. The dummy's response: "That makes me shudder." One of Charlie's best lines from his feud with Fields was: "Pink elephants take aspirin to get rid of W. C. Fields."

GEORGE BURNS & GRACIE ALLEN *(Left)* George and Gracie were vaudeville headliners before appearing on CBS Radio in 1932; they moved to NBC in 1937 and switched back and forth between the two networks with the highly successful *Burns and Allen Show* until they went to television in 1950. George played the incredulous, cigar-smoking straight man to contrast with Gracie's blissfully oblivious comedic style. One of their most famous gags revolved around Gracie's alleged lost brother. To the delight of audiences, Gracie would barge into other shows seeking the mythical lost brother. When the press discovered that Gracie had a real brother, an accountant in San Francisco, the sudden spotlight was so upsetting to him that he sent Gracie a terse note ("Can't you make a living any other way?") and went into hiding.

GRACIE ALLEN'S
Dizzy - lutions
for 1942
1. I wont confuse George
2. George wont confuse me
3. We'll only confuse each other

ABBOTT & COSTELLO *(Right)* Bud and Lou first performed their classic burlesque routine, "Who's on First," on the *Kate Smith Radio Hour*, and they gained tremendous fame for their inimitable vaudeville/slapstick teamwork with frequent appearances on *The Chase and Sanborn Hour*. After becoming film stars with *One Night in the Tropics* and *Buck Privates*, they got their own NBC program in 1942 and were a big hit. *The Abbott & Costello Show* raised huge amounts of money for the War Bond Drive, yet the two would suffer financial problems and personal battles throughout their career. A bemused Joe DiMaggio looks on as the boys go to bat.

 "Our program has been cut off the air so many times, the last page of the script is a Band-Aid!" — FRED ALLEN

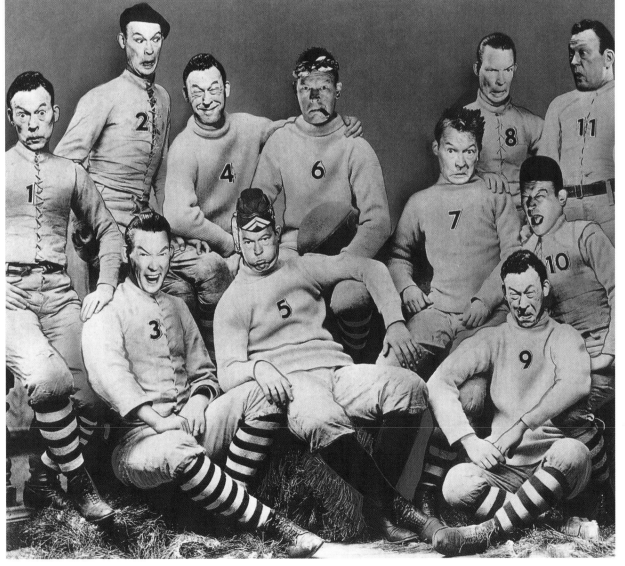

ED WYNN *(Above, with sportscasting legend Graham McNamee as his straight man)* Ed Wynn was a zany, pun-loving star on his Texaco-sponsored *The Fire Chief*, here wearing his fire chief hat advertising gasoloon (a word created when McNamee misread a script). Wynn insisted on performing his show in costume before a live audience at NBC's New Amsterdam Theater. Despite his legendary stage fright, the audience inspired Wynn's best clown instincts, and he thrived. Other vaudeville stars—such as Bert Lahr, George Jessel, and the Marx Brothers—were not nearly as successful adapting their talents to the new medium.

FRED ALLEN *(Left)* If you listened to early radio, you probably know Fred Allen, a vaudevillian with a curmudgeonly wit and a gift for clever insults. Beginning in 1932, he hit the spot for so many people that almost three out of every four radios—over twenty million— were tuned to his show in its first few seasons. Fred wrote most of the sketches, many of which included his squeaky-voiced wife, Portland Hoffa. He satirized the times with "Allen's Alley," which were staged man-on-the-street interviews with wacky Americans from all slices of life (average American John Doe, Senator Beauregard Claghorn, and New England farmer Titus Moody, to name a few). Fred's most lasting legacy is probably his penchant for trying to humiliate NBC executives for meddling with his show, which tended to run long. ("This is the season when NBC executives swim upcarpet to spawn!") The tactic has become somewhat of a tradition at NBC. As programming executive Rick Ludwin says, "You have to have a thick skin to work here or you won't last long."

NETWORK NEWS BEGINS

In the early days of radio, full-fledged broadcast news organizations didn't exist. Though political commentary was heard, big stories such as political conventions and ticker-tape parades were covered, and sensational news-readers such as Walter Winchell became household names, there was no such thing as a network news department—not until an unlikely figure came onto the scene: a five-foot-tall, cigar-chomping public relations man named Abe Schechter.

As radio gained momentum, newspapers were increasingly threatened. Newspaper executives began to question their practice of publishing radio program information, and the Associated Press reconsidered its decision to provide radio stations with wire stories. The situation came to a head in 1933, when the American Newspaper Publishers Association passed a resolution requiring that radio program logs be printed solely as paid advertising and the Associated Press began refusing to feed stories to radio outlets.

In response, Schechter, himself a former journalist, brought NBC into the newsgathering business. As the network's first news director, he became a one-man newsroom, digging up stories on his own.

Schechter made sure all affiliates knew to call him when news was breaking. By working the phones and invoking the name of newscaster Lowell Thomas, Schechter often got the story—even when print reporters were being stonewalled. Cashing in on his publicity contacts, he rewarded the affiliates with tickets to sporting events or, better yet, Rudy Vallee broadcasts. Abe Schechter left NBC during the war to become the senior public relations officer for

"OH, THE HUMANITY!"

The tragic explosion of the *Hindenburg* on May 6, 1937, is one of the most memorable events in the history of radio news. Herbert Morrison, a reporter for Chicago NBC affiliate WLS, was on the ground to cover the landing. Suddenly, his description of the routine docking turned to an anguished cry: "Oh, the humanity!" The network had never before aired prerecorded material, believing that to air anything not live—especially news—would be rejected by the public as fraudulent. But so powerful was Morrison's reaction that NBC replayed the coverage—the first on-the-spot, prerecorded network news segment.

General MacArthur. Eventually, he returned to NBC and was instrumental in developing the *Today* show.

No single event did more to convince the nation of radio's power as a news medium than the Munich crisis in September 1938. As Hitler's hostile intentions toward Czechoslovakia became clear, NBC delivered particularly extensive coverage. Nearly 500 broadcasts, relayed via shortwave, were heard from Europe during the eighteen days of the crisis, which culminated on September 29 when Germany, England, France, and Italy signed the official agreement that would spell the end of Czechoslovakia.

The crisis also marked the most brilliant scoop in the history of radio news, when NBC correspondent Max Jordan read the official text of the agreement to listeners forty-six minutes ahead of the competition and before many of Jordan's rival reporters in Munich even had the news. The network outshone the competition in technology, as well. During much of the crisis, atmospheric conditions prohibited direct transmission of shortwave signals from Munich, but NBC rigged a system that bounced the radio waves from Germany to Africa, then to South America, and finally to New York. So while CBS listeners often heard static from Europe, NBC was able to give the nation on-the-spot reporting and analysis of what was at the time the greatest political drama of the twentieth century.

In 1927, when Charles Lindbergh arrived in Washington after his historic transatlantic flight *(above, second from right, with unidentified other luminaries)*, NBC treated listeners to continuous on-the-spot coverage, showing American audiences the depth of coverage a network could deliver. The day after Lindbergh's toddler son was kidnapped in 1932, NBC staff announcer Ben Grauer read a poignant message from Anne Morrow Lindbergh to the kidnappers, giving the recipe for the baby's special formula. After Bruno Hauptmann was arrested and charged with kidnapping, radio provided blanket coverage of what was—to that point, anyway—the trial of the century.

WHEN RADIO WAS THE NEWS

In the beginning, the places where radio could take us was news in itself. NBC broadcast from a number of unlikely venues, including an aircraft in flight in 1929, a bathysphere 2,200 feet under Bermudan waters in 1931, Auguste Piccard's hot air balloon over the Dakotas in 1932, and while parachuting earthward *(opposite, top)* in August 1929. More substantively, at David Sarnoff's insistence, NBC broadcast innovative programs such as the *University of Chicago Roundtable*, during which leading educators and experts discussed social and political issues of the day, and *America's Town Meeting of the Air*, a revolutionary show that gave regular folk the chance to ask questions of the nation's most important politicians and intellectuals.

(Above) The Babe and Graham McNamee. (Right) NBC made transatlantic shortwave broadcasts of the 1936 Olympics from Berlin, where Jesse Owens won four gold medals under Hitler's nose.
(Far right) Like Owens, Joe Louis decimated his German counterpart to record a huge moral win for all of America. Here, he squares off in the prefight meeting with German boxer Max Schmeling before their 1938 rematch in New York City.

Sports Is the Biggest Drawing Card

The history of sportscasting is almost as old as the history of broadcasting itself. In 1921, not long after pioneering station KDKA made what is thought to be the world's first sportscast (the April 11, 1921, Johnny Ray–Johnny Dundee fight), Julius Hopp, J. Andrew White, and David Sarnoff orchestrated a much bigger event—the broadcast of the Jack Dempsey–Georges Carpentier prizefight. General Electric borrowed the world's most powerful radio transmitter from the U.S. Navy (a deal

(Above) Jesse Owens and Ralph Metcalfe at the 1936 Olympics. *(Right)* O. B. Keeler broadcast the U.S. Amateur Golf Championship from the Beverly Country Club in 1931. He had his own "caddy," an NBC engineer with new technology, the pack transmitter.

quietly arranged through former Assistant Secretary of the Navy Franklin D. Roosevelt), and though the equipment overheated and literally melted down, it worked just long enough for an estimated audience of 30,000 to hear Dempsey's fourth-round knockout victory. So began the long, tempestuous love affair between the electronic media and big-time sports.

More history was made when WEAF's Graham McNamee (along with legendary sportswriter Grantland Rice) announced the 1923 World Series— arguably inventing the art of baseball play-by-play in the process. This series was the first-ever heard as a radio "chain" (i.e., network) broadcast. (The Yankees beat the Giants 4 games to 2.) It was the third "Subway Series" in a row—but the first to be played at Yankee Stadium.

McNamee pioneered a chatty, informal style, punctuated with colorful, dramatic descriptions of action on the field—more thrills than stats. Soon, McNamee and his partner, Phillips Carlin, would master the two-man sportscasting technique still used today. Over time, a distinguished group of sportscasters joined

their ranks, including Clem McCarthy, Red Barber, Tom Manning, and Bill Stern.

Meanwhile, in the mid-1930s, a young sportscaster (specializing in track and football) known as "Dutch" was regularly heard on NBC affiliate WHO in Des Moines, Iowa. Occasionally, his games would be picked up for the entire network—giving Ronald Reagan his first national exposure.

SPORTS FIRSTS

NBC brought many national sports events to the public for the first time. Clem McCarthy called the first broadcast of the Kentucky Derby in 1929. The network started its long legacy of Olympic broadcasts with the 1932 games in Los Angeles, where twenty-one-year-old Babe Didrikson set world records. In 1937, Bill Stern aired the first radio sports show, *Colgate Sports Newsreel*, which ran through 1951 with a mix of sports figures and celebrities as guests.

In 1927, for the legendary rematch between Jack Dempsey and heavyweight champ Gene Tunney, NBC linked the Red, Blue, and Pacific stations—sixty-nine in all—as Graham McNamee and Phillips Carlin breathlessly broadcast the fight. In the seventh, Dempsey sent Tunney to the mat, but the referee refused to count until Dempsey withdrew to a neutral corner. Tunney got to his feet by the count of nine and went on to win the fight on a decision.

RADIO CITY

NBC'S CASTLE IN THE AIR

O. B. Hanson designed the NBC studios with television in mind, even though in the early 1930s no one knew when or how television would develop. Hanson did know that television would require a great deal of electric lighting, so he provided for this with (as he described it) "a system of flood and spotlights that rivals the summer daylight." The studios are as busy as ever today. Studios 3A and 3B house *NBC Nightly News* and *Dateline NBC*, respectively. Studio 3K, once the home base for NBC's top-secret TV experimentation, is now the province of NBC Sports. Conan O'Brien hosts his late-night talk show from Studio 6A.

And Studio 8H? The world's largest radio studio when built, in addition to being Arturo Toscanini's home, it has served as mission control for NBC's election coverage and as the source of innumerable live dramas and variety shows. Today, Studio 8H is famous for being the origin of the ninety most hilarious minutes in television: *Saturday Night Live*. Yankees owner George Steinbrenner loaned the studio's seats to *SNL* executive producer Lorne Michaels with the understanding that they would be returned when the show was canceled. More than a quarter-century later, *Saturday Night Live* and 250 bleacher seats from Yankee Stadium are still firmly ensconced in 8H.

In the midst of the Depression, oil baron John D. Rockefeller, Jr., was busy transforming twelve decrepit acres in midtown Manhattan into the world's largest commercial development. The venture was either bold or foolhardy— Manhattan was awash with vacant office space. But it was fortuitous for NBC, since by the early 1930s the broadcaster had already outgrown its studios at 711 Fifth Avenue.

Seeking a marquee tenant after the Metropolitan Opera withdrew from the project, Rockefeller struck a deal with RCA's new president, David Sarnoff, and altered the initial concept of the development: with RCA and NBC as anchor tenants, the complex, informally known as Radio City, would be the central home of the fledgling radio and television industry. In 1931, when architects unveiled the scale model of the fourteen-building art deco monument, the centerpiece was the seventy-story RCA Building at 30 Rockefeller Plaza. RCA moved into its new headquarters in the fall of 1933, and the first broadcast went out on November 11, almost exactly seven years after the inaugural gala at the Waldorf.

NBC Chief Engineer O. B. Hanson laid out thirty-five studios, built, as Hanson wrote in a 1932 article, "like thermos bottles, bottles within bottles." To keep out noise and vibrations, the studios "floated" above the building floor on felt-padded steel springs, while the ceilings and walls were insulated with several inches of rockwool. Observation galleries gave visitors a chance to see behind the scenes, and the NBC Studios would become—and remain— a famous tourist destination.

Variety shows with mass appeal aired on the Red network. The Blue network generally carried more cultured fare, such as broadcasts from the Met (hosted by Milton Cross in Seat 44). Broadcasts on both networks ended with the words, "This is the National Broadcasting Company," at which point the announcer would strike the three tones of the NBC chimes: G-E-C. Although historians differ, some claim the notes stand for the General Electric Company— the parent company of RCA and NBC until 1932, and, since 1986, NBC's parent company.

(Above) 30 Rock in the 1930s. (Left) David Sarnoff wanted to sell radios, but he also wanted to use the miracle of broadcasting to uplift and enlighten the American public. With Arturo Toscanini and the NBC Symphony Orchestra, he would do both. Toscanini was the world's most famous conductor, even to those who didn't know classical music. The maestro was known for his fervent opposition to fascism. In 1931, he refused to play a fascist hymn and was beaten by a group of Mussolini's goons. In 1933, he rejected Hitler's invitation to conduct at the Bayreuth festival. On December 26, 1936, he made a bold appearance, conducting the inaugural performance of the Palestine Symphony Orchestra, comprised of refugee European Jews, for free. The NBC Symphony Orchestra was assembled from the best musicians from around the world, who were eager to play with Toscanini. Toscanini and the orchestra became a cultural phenomenon, with requests for seats reaching as high as 50,000 per month.

A Revolution in Politics

(Below, left) In 1936, NBC covered Franklin Roosevelt's bid for reelection. In the newsroom, vote tallies were updated by hand as the returns came in. *(Below, right)* In front of 30 Rock, NBC placed an illuminated map so passersby could follow the state-by-state results. Roosevelt won by a landslide.

At one point, Roosevelt *(opposite)* was voted radio's most popular personality, besting even Jack Benny.

Before World War I, the nation's political campaigns were waged largely in the press. Whistlestop campaigns notwithstanding, few voters had the opportunity to hear their political candidates. The rise of radio in the twenties changed all that.

In 1923, seven stations were linked to carry the first-ever broadcast of the opening of Congress; President Coolidge's remarks were heard as far west as Dallas. A year later, eighteen stations linked to cover the contentious Democratic National Convention—giving many Americans their first taste of just how rowdy the democratic process can be. (The convention produced the nomination of John W. Davis after 103 roll-call votes.)

These early "chain" broadcasts were somewhat haphazard and definitely experimental. But by 1928, it was a different story. The Red and Blue networks, now forty-eight stations strong, provided NBC's first coverage of both national conventions. In the campaign between Herbert Hoover and Al Smith that followed, radio put Smith at a disadvantage. Voters in middle America found his New York accent unpleasant (he pronounced "radio" as "raddio") and greatly preferred Hoover's midwestern tones. Radio not only covered the election, it made a difference in who became president.

If radio gave a boost to Hoover over Smith, it virtually catapulted New York Governor Franklin D. Roosevelt into the Oval Office. FDR was the first office-seeker to use the radio to political advantage. Eloquent but not stuffy, Roosevelt was an appealing mix of patrician and populist. Radio was the ideal medium for this upbeat candidate with a sense of humor—the more so because no one could see his crutches or wheelchair on the air. Saddled with the legacy of the Depression, Hoover was overmatched.

In 1933, as Chief Justice Charles Evans Hughes was

"You know, Orson, you and I are the two best actors in America." — FDR, UPON MEETING ORSON WELLES

swearing him in, Roosevelt didn't respond with the traditional "I do." Instead, he repeated each phrase of the oath of office in his own voice, loud and clear. FDR knew who his real audience was—the American people sitting by their radios. In his first address immediately after the

swearing-in, Roosevelt sought to reassure a frightened and dispirited country that there was hope, and that he had a plan for dealing with the nation's economic woes. The inaugural rallying cry, "The only thing we have to fear is fear itself," may well be the first political sound bite.

Eight days into his presidency, FDR held his first radio "fireside chat" with the nation. With a calm, avuncular manner, he spelled out his plan to get us out of the Depression—in words anyone could grasp.

In his first hundred days in office, Roosevelt kept talking to

the American public as he sent a blizzard of New Deal proposals to Capitol Hill. He continued his folksy "fireside chats" throughout his four terms. He spoke as if he were sitting in the living room like one of the family, and Americans came to see him in that light.

A NATION SWINGS TO THE MUSIC

The crooners crooned, the jazzers jazzed, the dancers danced, and the music, more often than not, sure did swing.

The joyful sounds of the thirties and forties were, in many ways, a uniquely American response to the Depression and the storm clouds of war. The era's pop stars, jazz icons, and big bands expressed an unprecedented youthful energy, ambition, excitement, and freedom. This was music and broadcasting as public, democratic art—music shared over the airwaves, shared with friends…but probably not shared with Mom and Dad.

The arrival of network radio had profoundly changed the star-making machinery of the day. Literally overnight, performers such as Bing Crosby, Ella Fitzgerald, and Glenn Miller were made stars via network coast-to-coast hookups. A well-timed radio performance had the power to take unknown songs, singers, and bands right to the top of the recording charts. Remotes from hotels and nightclubs across the land picked up the sounds of young America, loud and clear. Teenagers embraced this music with a particular passion. They were drawn as

"If you gotta ask, you'll never know."

— LOUIS ARMSTRONG, ANSWERING THE QUESTION, "WHAT IS JAZZ?"

well to the swing dances—Jitterbug, Lindy Hop, Shag, and Shim Sham—which emphasized personal freedom, athleticism, and sexuality.

There was more to the music revolution of the times than just the swing bands. Listeners dialed in to the sophisticated café society tunes of Eddy Duchin's orchestra, the unthreatening jazz of the Clicquot Club Eskimos, and the languid crooning of Russ Columbo. There was music for all ages, including the long-lasting *Bell Telephone Hour* (1940–58), with its light classical music and pop performers.

When Benny Goodman was first heard nationwide on the *Let's Dance* program, a show that ripped through the nation on Saturday nights for six months in 1934–35, the swing band craze was truly under way, with Goodman its brightest star. Although his newly formed band shared the *Let's Dance* spotlight with the popular slow-dance stylings of Kel Murray and the Latin-tinged sound of Xavier Cugat, Goodman's jazzed-up and danceable pop/swing hybrid became the focus, especially as the music played long into the night. (The program, broadcast live from New York, was actually five hours long, in order to give each time zone in the country a three-hour show!)

Soon, Glenn Miller, Artie Shaw, Les Brown, and countless other swing combos populated NBC's airwaves; the network boasted in 1939 that it was already presenting music from some forty-nine different bands.

One of the most popular and best-remembered pop music series of the era was *Your Hit Parade*, a show that introduced the concept of "hit songs" climbing up or falling down the "charts." Every week, singers such as Frank Sinatra, Dinah Shore, Snooky Lansen, the Andrews Sisters, and Doris Day would perform the hit numbers of the moment. Practically all of the music programming on radio today, particularly "hits" radio, owes a debt to this concept. The show continued to be popular on NBC television in the fifties with the format unchanged.

(*Above*) The Glenn Miller Orchestra was a regular on NBC from 1938 until 1942, when Miller joined the U.S. Army Air Corps as a captain, and assembled a new band to entertain the troops overseas. On a flight over the English Channel to Paris on December 15, 1944, Miller's plane crashed and was never recovered. (*Far left, bottom*) Tommy Dorsey, known as the "Sentimental Gentleman of Swing," created tender moods for love song ballads. Benny Goodman (*below, and opposite with singer Peggy Lee*) deserved the title King of Swing—his historic 1935 broadcasts introduced that music to a generation.

BING CROSBY *(Below)* As Crosby's biographer Gary Giddins put it, "By the time Bing was ready for radio, radio was waiting for the voice made to showcase the closeness it could provide." William Paley had signed him to CBS for a huge amount of money in 1931, but in 1935 he came to NBC as host of *Kraft Music Hall* and stayed for eleven years. (He would have stayed longer at NBC had the network allowed him to pretape his shows, but the network's all-live policy was still in place as late as 1946.) Though he became one of Hollywood's biggest film stars, radio conveyed his personal warmth in a way that made Americans love him and his music. No one knew better how to convey security, love, melody, and good humor through a microphone—and to a vast audience—than Bing.

TOMMY DORSEY & FRANK SINATRA *(Above)* Frankie Boy was just another kid from Hoboken, N.J., imitating Bing Crosby—until 1935, when he and his group (the Hoboken Four) won first prize one evening on NBC's *Major Bowes' Amateur Hour*. His rise to stardom was unstoppable when he joined Tommy Dorsey's band, performing many classic big-band remotes from the Meadowbrook nightclub in New Jersey. (Dorsey and Sinatra's big hit together: "I'll Never Smile Again.") Sinatra later took a regular weekly spot on *Your Hit Parade* from 1947 to 1949, followed by the five-day-a-week *Lucky Strike Light Up Time* (1949–50) and a series of his own shows, including *The Frank Sinatra Show*, which aired through 1955.

DUKE ELLINGTON *(Left)* Sir Duke first came to national fame in a series of weekly broadcasts which were heard around the country from 1927 to 1931 from Harlem's Cotton Club over radio station WHN. The Cotton Club was a prestigious, although segregated, entertainment venue at Lexington and 142nd Street, and it provided Ellington with the financial stability to build a band of extraordinary musicians for whom he composed such famous songs as "Take the A Train," "Sophisticated Lady," "Mood Indigo," and "Satin Doll." The Ellington band was heard frequently on the radio from the Savoy Ballroom and Café Zanzibar in the thirties and forties. It also performed regularly for NBC, including thirteen appearances on *Today*, until Ellington's death in 1974.

SWING TIME AT THE SAVOY The Savoy Ballroom, a large, pink dance hall that was built during the Harlem Renaissance of the 1920s, filled an entire city block between 140th and 141st streets on Lenox Avenue. It was the birthplace of the Lindy Hop (named in honor of Charles Lindbergh) and the location of many NBC musical broadcasts (the network maintained a regular line for pickups from the dance hall). *Swing Time at the Savoy* was a brilliant, if short-lived, 1948 radio variety show that saluted and highlighted black musicians' contributions to American culture. With shows written by Langston Hughes, and with appearances by W. C. Handy, Billie Holiday *(below)*, Ella Fitzgerald *(far right)*, Count Basie *(right)*, and the Ink Spots, *Swing Time at the Savoy* was an undeniable highlight of live music on radio. Regarded as the most important performer in the history of jazz, Louis "Satchmo" Armstrong (not pictured) headlined the first black-oriented NBC variety series, *The Fleischmann's Yeast Harlem Revue*, which aired at 9:00 p.m. on Friday nights in 1936 and 1937. Armstrong shared the spotlight with comedians Eddie Green and Gee Gee Pearson. Although no recordings exist from this series, the show helped cement Satchmo's reputation as America's ultimate ambassador of music.

RUDY VALLEE *(Below)* The saxophone-playing crooner hosted *The Rudy Vallee Show* from 1929 to 1939. Known as "The Vagabond Lover" (after one of his movie roles), Rudy was the quintessential crooner. He knew exactly how to softly and intimately sing for the radio audience, understanding (unlike many stage performers of the era) the need for a low-key, relaxed style of presentation. Even when Vallee's show lost some of its popularity in the late thirties, Rudy kept up a reputation for "discovering" talent, including Eddie Cantor, Edgar Bergen, Alice Faye, Beatrice Lillie, and Milton Berle.

ROCKEFELLER
PLAZA

NBC

NBC IS RED, BLUE, AND...WHITE

By the end of the thirties, with the nation slowly but surely moving out of the Depression, radio was reaching heights of popularity barely imaginable at the time of NBC's birth in 1926. By now, almost every home had a radio; not only had radios become affordable, they had become indispensable as a household utility, just as David Sarnoff had cannily predicted in 1916. Radio had truly become a magic box of news, sports, music, and entertainment, and a national hearth around which we gathered, as the world became ever smaller and more accessible.

NBC had a hearty competitor in CBS, the Columbia Broadcasting System, founded in 1927 by William Paley. The two companies battled for the biggest stars, the most glamorous shows, and the best news coverage. Performers and commentators often jumped from one network to the other, searching for bigger paychecks and better time slots. Even so, NBC's Red and Blue networks dominated the Golden Age of Radio, with comedy classics such as *Fibber McGee and Molly* and *The Jack Benny Program*; daytime dramas such as *One Man's Family*, *Ma Perkins*, and *Portia Faces Life*; kids' shows such as *Little Orphan Annie*, *The Tom Mix Ralston Straight Shooters*, and *Jack Armstrong*; and innovative mysteries such

as *Lights Out*, *The Shadow*, and *The Inner Sanctum*. All these shows, with the help of skilled writers, smart directors, and brilliant sound-effects specialists, created pictures with sound and built imaginative universes of drama, laughter, and pitch-perfect American entertainment.

Yet David Sarnoff, head of RCA and NBC, was not entirely focused on the mastery and wonders of his radio networks. Instead, he was spending considerable time and money on mysterious goings-on in a locked studio on the third floor of 30 Rockefeller Plaza. There, television broadcasting was being invented. Just as NBC had started as a way to sell radios, the experimental broadcasts of W2XBS were designed to sell "television" to a curious public becoming accustomed to the bewildering speed of American whiz-bang ingenuity. It's hard now to imagine what people were thinking as they squinted into those tiny TV monitors at the 1939 World's Fair, but if they thought they were looking at the future, they were right. (For example, in the late thirties, NBC showed off its brand-new mobile television unit, pictured above, in front of 30 Rockefeller Plaza.)

Sarnoff's television dreams, however, had to be put on hold. As of December 7, 1941, the nation was at war— and NBC was more than ready to fight the good fight.

TELEVISION GOES PUBLIC

On April 20, 1939, RCA President David Sarnoff stood before an NBC camera and pronounced: "Now we add radio sight to sound. It is with a feeling of humbleness that I come to this moment of announcing the birth in this country of a new art so important in its implications that it is bound to affect all society. It is an art which shines like a torch of hope in a troubled world. It is a creative force which we must learn to utilize for the benefit of all mankind."

The occasion was an announcement of NBC's first regularly scheduled television service, which would have its official kickoff ten days later, at the opening ceremonies of the 1939 World's Fair. Sarnoff read his lines at Flushing Meadows, a former marshland east of New York City chosen as the site of the fair and its "World of

Tomorrow," which was designed to give citizens a glimpse at a utopia based on science, technology, and exciting new consumer products. Presumably, every television set in the New York area was tuned in—all two hundred or so.

Sarnoff's announcement was significant despite the tiny viewing audience. After all, there was no better promotional opportunity than the World's Fair, with its millions of visitors streaming into the RCA Pavilion adorned with TV sets encased in transparent Lucite. (With television sets costing about a third as much as an automobile, the programming and technology still primitive, and World War II approaching, it would be another ten years before television would become a true mass medium.) At the fair itself, the TV demonstration was a hit, with visitors dazzled by the broadcasts emanating from Studio 3H in Rockefeller Center. Radio was magical enough; being able to see distant images as well was astonishing indeed.

The exhibit came after years of research. Sarnoff had begun bankrolling Vladimir Zworykin's pioneering work in television in 1929. By 1931, NBC had taken over RCA's experimental station W2XBS, which broadcast test

(Above) A program from the 1939 World's Fair expresses the futuristic notions of the time. Television sets in the RCA Pavilion *(right)* were just one part of the vast window on the future. On a fairground dominated by the Trylon and the Perisphere— a 700-foot triangular tower and a huge sphere enclosing Democracity, a futuristic projection of life in 2039—sixty nations and many large corporations took turns trying to dazzle the crowds with technological wonders. General Motors offered a vision of freeways in 1960 and Kodak previewed film that could produce color pictures.

images—but only to RCA engineers. A few years later, visitors touring Radio City saw prototype sets and were offered a chance to view themselves on-screen, as NBC tentatively started to develop programming for the new medium. On June 7, 1938, W2XBS (Channel 1 on the dial) televised stage star Gertrude Lawrence in scenes from the Broadway hit *Susan and God*.

In 1941, the FCC approved commercial use of television, and awarded W2XBS the first commercial license. On July 1, the station became WNBT, which presented the nation's first commercial broadcasting day. Programs included the *Sunoco Newscast* with Lowell Thomas, coverage of a Dodgers-Phillies baseball game (sponsored by General Mills), and a radio/TV simulcast of *Truth or Consequences*, sponsored by Ivory soap.

On December 7, 1941, WNBT announcer Ray Forrest interrupted the Sunday afternoon telecast of the film *Millionaire Playboy* to tell the small audience of the invasion of Pearl Harbor. By then, many RCA scientists and engineers had already been diverted from television to the war effort.

They were instrumental in developing radar and in improving the depth charge, an important weapon against U-boats in the Atlantic. RCA personnel also played a key role in inventing an infrared "sniperscope," deployed with devastating effect against Japanese forces hiding in bunkers on Okinawa.

With Sarnoff and RCA's engineers preoccupied—not to mention the rest of the nation—the effort to sell the American public an exciting new entertainment technology would have to wait for the war's end.

Despite continuous improvements, television was far from ready for prime time. The heat of TV lighting was still hot enough to melt candles and boil root beer. Perhaps worse, cameras did not "read" light flesh tones, and early performers—such as Eddie Albert, (*above*, with unknown woman)—had to wear garish green makeup and black or purple lipstick, which made for some odd encounters in the 30 Rock commissary.

AMERICA GOES TO WAR

With the advent of radio, war came with a soundtrack. For the first time, Americans were able to listen to reports sent directly from battlefields and distant capitals, wondering and worrying as the bombs fell. Long before Pearl Harbor, NBC had broadcast both the rantings of Adolf Hitler and the eloquent, defiant words of Winston Churchill—brought live to American listeners via RCA's reliable shortwave transmissions. (This was decades before the miracle of satellite broadcasting in the mid-sixties.)

On June 22, 1940, just a month after the British Army evacuation from Dunkirk, reporter William Keirker broadcast an eyewitness account from a World War I–era railway car at Compiègne: France had fallen; Britain was alone.

On December 13 of that year, correspondent Fred Bate was heading from NBC's London office to the BBC Broadcasting House to make his nightly newscast back to the States. Without warning, the Broadcasting House was hit by a parachute mine, and Bate was nearly killed by falling debris. He was found wandering through the building's rubble— badly burned yet still clutching his script, looking in vain for his studio. Sent back to the States to recuperate, he soon returned to London, eventually becoming one of the era's legendary radio journalists.

A little less than a year later, at 2:30 p.m. ET on December 7, 1941, announcer Robert Eisenbach reported that Japanese forces had bombed Pearl Harbor. At 4:00 p.m., the network aired a one-hour news special, featuring a live report from NBC affiliate KGU in Honolulu describing the damage. (Electing to stay with regular programming, CBS aired only brief bulletins throughout the day.)

(Above) The gang from *The Jack Benny Program* heads off to entertain the troops in a government limousine. (*Left to right*) Bandleader Phil Harris, singer Dennis Day, announcer Don Wilson (standing) and Eddie "Rochester" Anderson. (*Opposite, top*) The Japanese surrender to General Douglas MacArthur aboard the USS *Missouri* at the end of World War II. (*Opposite, bottom*) Jimmy Stewart in uniform and Mercedes McCambridge are on the air for the war effort.

☆ FOURTH CHIME ☆

"This is NBC, the National Broadcasting Company." Those words were followed by three tones, G-E-C, heard at station-break intervals on the hour and half-hour. The NBC three-note chime became a registered trademark of the network in 1950 (and the first audible trademark filed with the U.S. Patent Office). Starting back in 1933, a fourth chime was occasionally heard— initially as an internal paging system for NBC employees. After the *Hindenburg* exploded in 1937, it became an "all hands on deck" call—a signal to local stations to keep the lines open for urgent, breaking news. Broadcast on December 7, 1941, it was sent out again in the early-morning hours on June 6, 1944, this time followed by the dot-dot-dot dash of Morse code, meaning V for Victory—the invasion of Normandy had begun.

Under David Sarnoff the network threw itself into the war effort. Beginning in 1942, *The Army Hour*, produced jointly by the U.S. Army and NBC, aired every Sunday afternoon with firsthand reports from military personnel on duty—everyone from privates to top brass. Americans across the country heard Jimmy Doolittle describe his daring raid on Tokyo and Claire Chennault explain how his Flying Tigers were hauling supplies over the "Hump" (the Himalayas) to China. Sarnoff himself became a general in the Army Signal Corps and was responsible for coordinating D-Day communications and directing the use of European shortwave facilities.

NBC also put its international shortwave transmitters—the "White network"—at the disposal of the armed services under the direction of the Office of War Information.

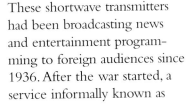

"All our facilities and personnel are at your instant service. We await your commands."

— David Sarnoff, RCA President and NBC CEO, radiogram to President Roosevelt, December 7, 1941

These shortwave transmitters had been broadcasting news and entertainment programming to foreign audiences since 1936. After the war started, a service informally known as the "Voice of Freedom" (later to become the Voice of America) was broadcast in ten different languages. The broadcasts offset German propaganda in occupied countries and brought news of the U.S. commitment to the war effort.

As events unfolded, the legendary H. V. Kaltenborn provided lucid commentary from the NBC studios in Radio City. W. W. Chaplin began reporting from Normandy shortly after the landing on D-Day, broadcasting from a truck in an apple orchard of a seventeenth-century chateau. Merrill Mueller reported from the deck of the battleship *Missouri* as the Japanese foreign minister signed the final instrument of surrender. This was a time when instant reportage mattered deeply, and NBC's power as a news organization grew tremendously.

Hope didn't play it safe—his overseas trips often took him near the front lines. He once quipped: "The closer we got to enemy fire, the louder the laughter. If it started getting hysterical, I knew it was time to dive for a foxhole." Pretty girls were always part of his shows, with Joey Heatherton *(upper left)*, Frances Langford *(bottom left)*, and Lana Turner in the lower right doing their patriotic best for the boys. Privately, he admitted that he was devastated by the realization that so many young men in his audiences would never see home again. Hope vividly remembered one impromptu show he performed by a tree stump for a group of marines headed for Guadacanal. The next day, most of the boys in that audience were killed.

THANKS FOR THE MEMORIES

No entertainer is more closely associated with the American GI than NBC's premier comedy star, Bob Hope. He gave of himself tirelessly for decades, performing five, six, or seven shows a day, and then going to visit the "boys" in hospital wards. In the process, he became a symbol of America that was more recognizable than Coca-Cola.

Performing for American men and women in military service all over the globe, Hope saw himself as a missionary of humor, bringing comfort and a taste of home with his perfectly delivered American irreverence. His genius was in knowing how to ridicule officers, powerful folk, and presidents without pushing too hard. In a simple gesture with enormous resonance for his audience, Hope would invite soldiers to step up to the microphone and say a few words to their families back home.

Hope made his first appearance on NBC in 1933 on *The Rudy Vallee Show*. By 1938, he was starring in his own broadcast, *The Pepsodent Hour*, and had frequent run-ins with network censors due to his risqué double entendres and innuendos. But his popularity grew as he perfected his urbane, smooth-talking persona. He and pal Bing Crosby constantly "crashed" each other's shows; whenever they did, the ratings would go through the roof.

On May 6, 1941, Hope did his first remote radio program in front of men in uniform, broadcasting from the March Field Army Air Force Base in Riverside, California, to a wildly enthusiastic audience. Hope could easily blend the comedy of everyday life into military situations. His ability to poke fun at authority was a huge hit with military audiences. "Definition of the most dangerous man in the world?" he smirked. "A second lieutenant with a map."

For the duration of World War II, Bob Hope was "on the road" in earnest—all but 9 of his 144 programs during the war originated from an Army, Navy, or Marine outpost somewhere in the world. His first trip overseas to entertain troops in action took place in 1943, when he visited England, Iceland, North Africa, and Sicily. His traveling show wasn't just entertainment but a living reminder of the way of life our boys had left behind.

Hope's efforts on behalf of servicemen and -women didn't stop when the war ended— instead they continued for another half a century. After V-J Day, the USO began sending Hope to entertain troops far from home at Christmastime, and he continued doing so through the Berlin Airlift, and the wars in Korea, Vietnam, and the Persian Gulf. His NBC televised specials, broadcast in January after the Christmas season, were huge successes. He won an Emmy for his 1966 Christmas special from Southeast Asia. The 1970 Christmas special was the highest-rated program in television history to that date. In 1997, Bob Hope—"America's number-one soldier in greasepaint"—was designated an honorary veteran of the armed forces, the only civilian to be accorded that honor.

Hope was a patient and generous autograph signer, and he particularly remembers this young woman *(above)* from the British Army Auxiliary in World War II: "I'd do anything for a girl in uniform. She wanted an autograph from a big name, so I signed, 'Laurence Olivier.'" *(Below)* Hope frequently wisecracked that the golf clubs were part of his uniform.

ON THE BRINK OF TELEVISION

Almost as soon as it had been announced, the exciting new world of television was yanked out of the hands of enthusiastic consumers (at least out of the hands of wealthy consumers; TV sets in 1941 were still very expensive). For the duration of World War II, consumer television set production was halted, and New York's WNBT was restricted to four hours of programming a week.

NBC continued to demonstrate the potential of television anyway, installing sets in New York's police stations in 1942, and televising training sessions for thousands of air-raid and fire wardens. TVs were also placed in local

military hospitals, broadcasting Gillette-sponsored fights from Madison Square Garden for recovering vets. More than humanitarianism was involved: the work kept the crews in practice, served as an experiment in early television advertising, and helped stimulate future demand.

Meanwhile, the world of network radio was undergoing

radical change. RCA's ownership of both the Red and Blue networks had made the government increasingly uneasy about NBC's dominance of the broadcast airwaves. In 1941, the FCC decreed that no single owner could operate more than one network, and NBC was ordered to divest itself of either the Red or the Blue. Divorcement, as it was

called, was not easy, and the process of unraveling the two networks from each other was not completed until 1943. In that year, the Blue network was sold to Edward J. Noble—a tycoon who had made his fortune in Lifesavers—for $8 million. In 1945, it was renamed ABC, the American Broadcasting Company. (NBC's newest competitor

☆ THE ORTHICON TUBE ☆

Broadcast quality was much improved thanks to the new image-orthicon camera tube developed during the war by RCA engineers under Vladimir Zworykin. Because the image-orthicon had a far greater sensitivity to light, TV cameras could become smaller and more maneuverable; as an added plus, actors no longer had to swelter under the intense heat of TV lighting. This technological innovation remained the foundation for television cameras for decades and was instrumental in making elaborate productions possible.

Strangers kissed, grown men cried, and kids danced as news of the Allied victory in Europe was announced. WNBT was on the air from 8:45 a.m. to 11:00 p.m. with live coverage. For the first time, viewers at home could feel part of a national celebration. A camera on the roof of the Hotel Astor captures the excitement of huge crowds celebrating in Times Square.

broadcast out of 30 Rock for its first couple of years.)

Although network radio was still thriving in 1945, David Sarnoff was certain the medium had passed its prime; network television was the future, and NBC would get there first. WNBT celebrated the end of the war in Europe by broadcasting a marathon fourteen consecutive hours of programming (including remotes from Times Square) to a handful of amazed television viewers in a jubilant city. Three months later, on August 14, 1945, the station aired fifteen hours of V-J Day coverage—this time relaying the coverage to GE's Schenectady station (WRGB) and Philco's Philadelphia outlet (WPTZ). It was an early example of an NBC-TV network and of the kind of programming such a network would be capable of.

Beginning December 10, 1945, New York's WNBT picked up where it had left off—with an ambitious six-day-a-week programming schedule on TV Channel 1. (That particular frequency

soon disappeared. It was discovered that transmissions interfered with police radios.) On February 12, 1946, a permanent Atlantic Coast four-city television network was inaugurated, with Lincoln's birthday ceremonies broadcast live from Washington, D.C.

Later that year, on May 9, NBC's *Hour Glass*—the first network entertainment series—

debuted. It was a grand experiment, the first well-funded and professionally produced TV variety show, with songs, skits, and Chase and Sanborn commercials that sometimes stretched to four-minute lengths. *Hour Glass*, though little remembered today, was the start of something big. Television was on its way.

(Above) A graphic artist at Radio City prepares a collection of title cards and visual effects used in the earliest days of NBC television. *(Below)* In a demonstration at the Westminster Kennel Club show in Madison Square Garden, a Great Dane named Axel responds enthusiastically to his master's face and voice on television.

"We are no longer required to predicate plans for television on the winning of the war. Victory has been won. Peace is here. Television is ready to go."

— NBC President Niles Trammell, addressing the FCC, October 1945

READY, SET, GO!

On September 1, 1945, when Japanese officials signed the terms of surrender on the deck of the USS *Missouri*, NBC Radio correspondent Merrill Mueller was there, reporting the news live via shortwave to an exhausted, grateful nation. TV viewers would have to wait nine days to see film of the event broadcast on WNBT.

Many years would pass before television news could be transmitted instantly by satellite. But in 1945, the lag times were not too important; not many people were watching. Only nine commercial stations were on the air that year, with an estimated 7,500 TV sets tuned in.

David Sarnoff's RCA and NBC had quite a task ahead: to create television programming that would inspire people to buy TV sets (preferably, nice new RCA ten-inch 630-TSs, available for $385—the first mass-produced, reasonably affordable TVs). NBC's earliest attempts at postwar TV broadcasting were generally amateurish, populated with cooking shows, B movies, and watch-the-artist-paint kinds of programming.

What the network needed was a hit show that would make television irresistible.

CBS's William Paley thought the medium was far from ready, and told his radio affiliates there was no need to hurry in pursuit of FCC TV station permits. Sarnoff, on the other hand, in his prescient speech at the 1947 Affiliates Convention in Atlantic City, urged radio

station owners to obtain television licenses without delay. As a result, when the FCC issued a 1948 moratorium on new television permits (one that would last three and a half years), NBC affiliates held the lion's share of licenses. The effects are still being felt today, with NBC continuing to have the strongest performing group of affiliates of any network.

Meanwhile, by 1948, NBC TV had not only found its hit show, it had found a number of them: a vaudeville-esque hour starring a failed radio comedian, a kiddie show with screaming moppets and a marionette, and a variety of sports programs—including World Series games featuring a rookie named Jackie Robinson—that drew people to the TV sets in their neighborhood bars.

By no means was NBC Radio on the skids—yet. Despite the infamous 1948 "Paley Talent Raids" (which lured Jack Benny, Red Skelton, and Burns and Allen to CBS with lucrative financial deals), the network's shows such as *Duffy's Tavern*, *The Life of Reilly*, and *Your Hit Parade* continued to fare very well. As a matter of fact, Bob Hope's 1949 radio shows

did very well, averaging a healthy 23.8 rating.

By 1951, however, Hope's radio show rating had fallen to 12.7. By 1953, his radio rating had sunk to a mere 5.4. Quite the opposite was happening in television. In the same era, Hope's *Colgate Comedy Hour* TV ratings couldn't have been better. By 1954, not too surprisingly, he dropped his radio show.

TAKE ME OUT TO THE BALL GAME

Sports coverage came a long way from its first televised baseball game, the 1939 Princeton/Columbia matchup *(below)*, to the 1947 World Series *(opposite, clockwise)*: The Zoomar telephoto lens helped fans, gathered in bars, to see close-ups of plays; Jackie Robinson slides into second as Phil Rizzuto goes flying; fans stand in a local bar to watch a game; Joe DiMaggio is so happy with pitcher Frank Shea's performance on the mound that he tries to kiss him; Rizzuto tags out Pete Reiser with the umpire in perfect position. *(Below, right)* Boxing hooked the fans on television.

Today's sports fans gather at local bars, bonding over beer and televised baseball. Two generations ago, their grandfathers did exactly the same thing—although the bars weren't called "sports bars" back then.

NBC Radio had been broadcasting sports events since its beginning. W2XBS—the predecessor of New York's local station WNBT (now known as WNBC)—had created many TV sports "firsts" in 1939, including the first televised baseball game (Columbia vs. Princeton, May 17), the first televised boxing match (Baer vs. Nova, June 1), and the first pro football telecast (Brooklyn vs. Philadelphia, October 22). Audiences for these telecasts weren't large, however. There

weren't that many television sets in the New York area.

When Gillette tentatively agreed to sponsor WNBT telecasts of boxing matches from Madison Square Garden in the fall of 1944, it found that the sport and the medium had a natural affinity. With the camera's ability to show two fighters close up in a well-lit, tightly contained space, boxing became television's first high-profile sport. In 1946, a year in which many a local saloon bought its first TV (usually the RCA 630-TS, the workhorse of the era), the Joe Louis–Billy Conn fight generated an estimated audience of 150,000 gathered around 5,000 sets—an average of thirty fans per TV.

The following year, NBC started regularly televising professional baseball, and

introduced the Zoomar, a revolutionary adjustable lens that could capture both close-up and long-distance shots. This advance in technology transported baseball fans off their barstools and into the best seats in the house—right behind home plate. This was something radio could not do, and it took no more than a couple of innings for fans to realize that television offered them an experience that was the next best thing to being in the stands.

In October 1947, NBC presented the first-ever network telecast of the World Series. It was a classic subway series, a matchup between Joltin' Joe DiMaggio's Yankees and "Da Bums"—the Brooklyn Dodgers, with their spectacular rookie Jackie

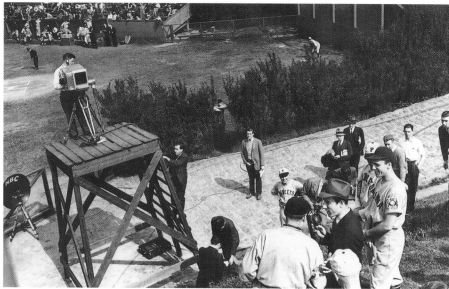

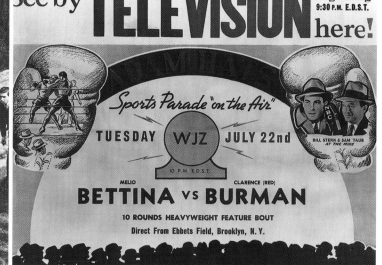

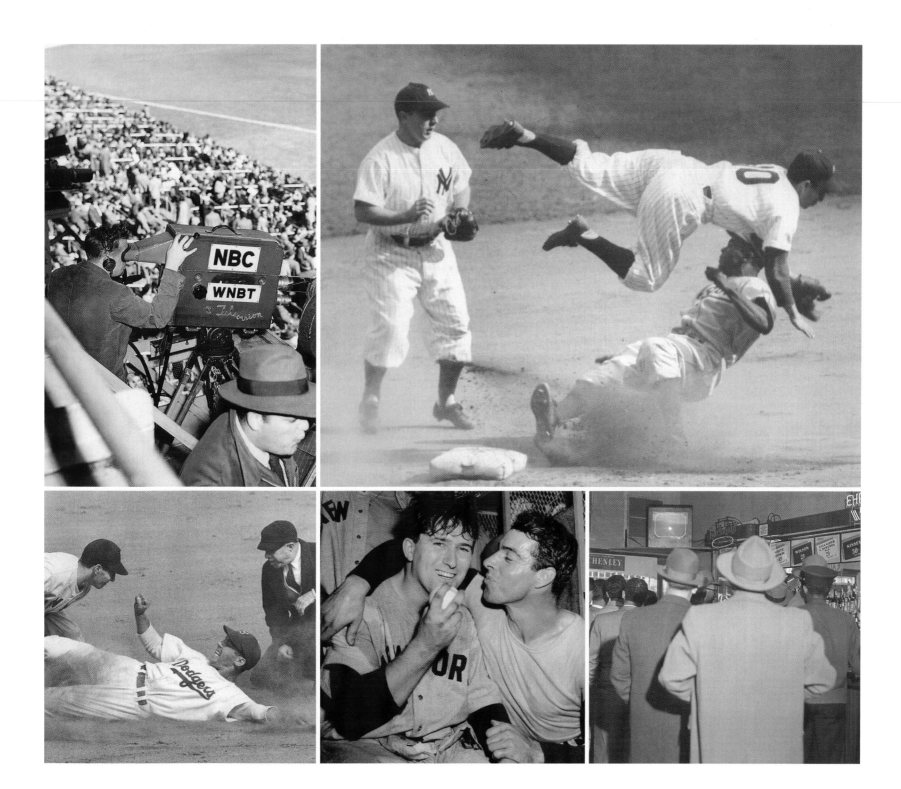

Robinson. The televised games were a phenomenal success for the time, creating far greater impact than anyone had anticipated; nearly four million Americans watched the series on television, over three million of whom saw it in taverns.

In the months following the series, home TV sales took off—a good thing for NBC, as television broadcasting was still a loss leader. The network received just $65,000 from sponsor Gillette to broadcast all seven games of the series. Indeed, NBC's ad revenue for 1947 was barely $100,000, truly meager compared to its overall TV expenditure for the year—a whopping $2,000,000.

Eight months after the 1947 World Series, an estimated six million viewers watched a Joe Louis vs. "Jersey Joe" Walcott prizefight. The enduring love affair between television and sports was well under way.

FROM STAGE TO SCREEN

In 1945, a young man named Fred Coe arrived at 30 Rockefeller Plaza to work as a studio manager at NBC Television. By October 1948, he was producing the *Philco Television Playhouse*, a live, hour-long, Sunday-night anthology series that became one of the quintessential shows of what is now commonly called the Golden Age of Television. To many, Coe was the single most influential, talented force in live New York television drama, and he believed in the power of theater, a writer's medium. "He felt the writer was the center of the universe," said Horton Foote in Jon Krampner's book *The Man in the Shadows*. "Writers like to hear that."

Philco Television Playhouse, *Kraft Television Theatre*, and *Goodyear TV Playhouse* were all writers' dreams: literate, live, and in continual need of new scripts. While every show wasn't

brilliant, more than a few were, even under the stress of live performances. If a mistake happened, millions of viewers would see it. If a line was flubbed, there was nothing to do but move on. The studios were tiny, the lights were brutally hot, and the tension was often unbearable.

Broadway stars and directors scoffed at the thought of working under such difficult conditions—on such a "lowly" medium as television. So Coe and the other anthology show

producers relied on untested new directors such as Delbert Mann, Arthur Penn, and Sidney Lumet, and on hungry young actors such as Grace Kelly, Sidney Poitier, Joanne Woodward, Steve McQueen, Eva Marie Saint, Jason Robards, and Walter Matthau. When James Dean died a week before starting work on Hemingway's "The Battler," Coe replaced him with Paul Newman, and yet another new star was born.

Most of all, Coe cultivated

a brilliant group of writers: Horton Foote ("The Trip to Bountiful"), Tad Mosel ("Other People's Houses"), J. P. Miller ("The Days of Wine and Roses"), and Gore Vidal ("Visit to a Small Planet"). Then there was Paddy Chayevsky, who told Coe one day that he wanted to write about "a middle-aged guy who goes to a lonely hearts' dance." The result was "Marty," produced for the *Goodyear TV Playhouse* on May 24, 1953, starring Rod Steiger and

The Golden Age was not to last. Despite the success of "Marty," Coe came under increasing pressure to produce more upbeat stories. With the introduction of videotape in 1956, the need to do live television disappeared, along with the craft and energy of the live era. More significantly, videotape allowed shows to be rebroadcast and continue to earn money for the networks. The altered financial picture, along with the arrival of the TV western in the latter half of the fifties, would spell the demise of live dramas on television.

Nancy Marchand. Under Delbert Mann's direction, "Marty" transformed what Chayefsky called "the marvelous world of the ordinary" into compelling drama. Critics have long called it a watershed event in the history of televised drama.

In Jeff Kisseloff's oral history of television, *The Box*, scriptwriter Tad Mosel described what it felt like to produce these shows: "I would sit in that control room, and as [the live drama] got closer to air you could feel everything going softer and quieter. In front of me would be the director and his associates and all the earphones, switches, and plugs. Outside that plate-glass window was the studio. You could see the sets for your play. Finally, the lighting people would beam the sets, and the actors would come in and take their places in their costumes, standing quietly, waiting. In that last minute before you went on the air, you would watch the sweep hand going around, and there would be absolute silence, nobody moving. Then, suddenly, the sweep hand would hit the hour, and you would hear a crash of music, and the announcer saying, 'Live from New York,' and you knew that your little play was going out to fifty million people. And nowhere have I ever felt a thrill like that. I love the theater, but it beats opening night in the theater every time."

(Circle) Jose Ferrer in "Cyrano de Bergerac" in 1948, from the first season of *Philco Television Playhouse. (Opposite)* Lauren Bacall and Henry Fonda starred with Humphrey Bogart in Fred Coe's 1955 production of "The Petrified Forest." *(Above)* Rod Steiger and Nancy Marchand in Paddy Chayevsky's "Marty," directed by Delbert Mann—for many, the high-water mark of televised drama. *(Top left)* May 7, 1947: "Double Door," the first *Kraft Television Theatre* telecast, at the beginning of television's Golden Age.

Mr. Television

Uncle Miltie would do anything for a laugh. He jumped onstage in outlandish costumes—sometimes in drag. He would have pies and powder puffs and buckets of water thrown into his face. He would fall over face down—hard—or backward, like a piece of wood. He would tell jokes that ranged from the obvious to the ridiculous, and when a joke died, he would mug, cajole, milk, or beg the audience until they laughed. As an entertainer, he wanted to please, so much so that he gave his all. You had to love him. He insisted on it.

Berle had been one of the guest hosts of the *Texaco Star Theater* when it began in the spring of 1948, and he took over as permanent host beginning with the fall premiere. He was an immediate hit—literally the reason many families decided to buy a television set. He became known as "Mr. Television" because he dominated the small screen in his era, but the moniker stuck because he was an innovator—one of the first comedians to really understand how to use the medium.

Early television audiences had never seen anything like *Texaco Star Theater* before, even if they had seen Berle on Broadway or the vaudeville stage. From the moment the Texaco Service Men launched into the opening jingle ("Oh, we're the men from Texaco") to the end of the show (when he sang his theme song, "Near You"), Uncle Miltie worked tirelessly to entertain, bringing

a frantic and infectious energy to the screen. He was perfect for the earliest days of television: his highly visual, over-the-top, relentlessly loud style was just what people wanted to see and laugh at on the small screens of the era, with a living room full of guests. *Variety* magazine came up with the term "vaudeo"—vaudeville meets video—to describe Berle's style.

No one appreciated Milton Berle's comic genius more than NBC programming chief Pat Weaver. In his memoir, *The Best Seat in the House*, Weaver recalls: "For all Berle's wild costumes and crazy stuff, his main focus was on the comedy lines. No one, not even Henny Youngman or Morey Amsterdam, could top Milton with one-liners." Weaver also knew he would be unable to carry out his innovative programming plans for the network without the revenue Berle was bringing in.

One week in 1949, Berle appeared simultaneously on the covers of *Time* and *Newsweek*. (For *Newsweek*, he dressed up as Carmen Miranda.) To keep the competition from luring Berle away from NBC, Weaver signed him to a thirty-year contract in 1951 at $200,000 a year, whether he worked or not.

Polling data indicated there were Tuesday nights when virtually every TV set in the country was tuned to Uncle Miltie—a ratings phenomenon never to be repeated. Partly due to his immense popularity, TV set ownership exploded: The NBC Research Department estimated there to be only 175,000 sets at the start of 1948, with the number passing one million before the end of the year. David Sarnoff called Milton Berle and Howdy Doody his best salesmen for those early RCA television receivers—and there is little doubt that they were.

Not only did Milton Berle sell TV sets, he sold television itself as a medium. After 1948, there could be no doubt in the minds of sponsors, networks, and Wall Street magnates that this new medium was going to be big. How big remained to be seen.

Berle was a physical comic who cut his teeth on pratfalls and stunts in vaudeville. He appeared as a child actor in *The Perils of Pauline* in 1914 and worked his way up the marquees on the RKO and Loews circuits. By 1943, he was the first star of the *Ziegfeld Follies* to have his name above the title. Despite his ability to deliver a joke with the best of them, he wasn't a big hit on radio, simply because audiences couldn't see him. But by the time television arrived, Berle was fully prepared to make this visual medium his own.

"Do married men live longer than single men, or does it just seem longer?"
— MILTON BERLE

KUKLA, FRAN & OLLIE

Burr Tillstrom's puppets, the Kuklapolitans, made their first TV appearances in the late thirties demonstrating RCA TV sets. In 1948, the Chicago-based *Kukla, Fran & Ollie* first appeared on NBC, featuring bald Kukla (Russian for "doll"), one-toothed Ollie (Oliver J. Dragon), and Fran Allison, who served as the sole human character; Burr Tillstrom did everything else. The proscenium was the only set, and the show was live with no script. (Tillstrom said, "You don't need a script when you're talking to friends.") Produced out of NBC affiliate WMAQ, the program had a quirky, gentle humor that appealed not only to children but to adults as well, who were estimated to make up 60 percent of the show's 7:00 p.m. audience. Appreciative letters came from John Steinbeck, James Thurber, and Orson Welles. Wrote Jack Gould of the *New York Times*, "Without any question whatsoever, it is the most charming and heartwarming excursion into pure make-believe that is to be found in television today."

(Above) "Buffalo Bob" Smith with Clarabell the Clown. The *Howdy Doody* show was such a success that in 1948 Howdy announced he was going to run for "President of All the Boys and Girls," and offered free campaign buttons to kids who wrote in. There were 60,000 requests. A week later, NBC couldn't accommodate all the advertisers who wanted to sponsor the show.

SAY KIDS, WHAT TIME IS IT?

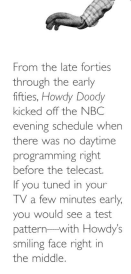

If you were a kid between 1947 and 1960, it is likely you would yell back: "It's Howdy Doody time!"

Howdy Doody was one of the first children's shows on network television and by far the most popular of its time. At 5:30 p.m. every weekday, kids came in from play and sat before the TV, transfixed until dinner. For many moms, this prospect of peace may have been reason enough to buy the family's first TV set—and many did.

Howdy held a special attraction for children because "Buffalo Bob" Smith, the creator and co-star of the show, had a playful sense of humor and a childlike love of nonsense jokes. Howdy Doody was a marionette with big ears, red hair, forty-eight freckles (one for each state in the USA), and a goofy permanent smile. Bob and Howdy were first joined in Doodyville by Clarabell the Clown, who played silly pranks, sprayed seltzer at people, and stayed famously silent—honking his horn twice for "no" and once for "yes." (Clarabell was originally played by Bob Keeshan, who went on to gain fame as Captain Kangaroo.)

Over the years, the list of other puppet characters grew to include Phineas T. Bluster, Dilly Dally, and Howdy's strange pet Flub-a-Dub. The human members of the cast included Judy Tyler as Princess Summerfall

Winterspring, and Bill LeCornec as Chief Thunderthud, who (long before the Ninja turtles) uttered a most remarkable exclamation: "Cowabunga!"

Maybe the most famous feature of *Howdy Doody* was the live studio audience of children, affectionately known as the "Peanut Gallery." From the start, thousands upon thousands of children wrote in for tickets, far more than could ever be accommodated on the forty-seat set.

Howdy Doody was the first kids' TV megahit, and a fond, essential, shared memory of millions of American baby

boomers. It enjoyed an uninterrupted run from 1947 to 1960, eventually airing more than 2,500 episodes. In 1954, it became NBC's first show to be regularly aired in color. One thing, however, never changed: Clarabell's trademark silence. Advertisers constantly asked for the character to mention their products by name, but the request was always turned down. His silence was broken only once: on the last episode of *Howdy Doody*, the show ended with a close-up of a tearful Clarabell, who spoke his first (and last) words: "Goodbye, kids."

From the late forties through the early fifties, *Howdy Doody* kicked off the NBC evening schedule when there was no daytime programming right before the telecast. If you tuned in your TV a few minutes early, you would see a test pattern—with Howdy's smiling face right in the middle.

(Above, left; right) Buffalo Bob and Howdy. A seat in the Peanut Gallery was a major coup for those in the grade school set. Johnny Bench, John Ritter, and Joe Namath were among the lucky ones. In 1951, it was estimated that if all the children on the waiting list had stood in line to get in, those at the tail of the line would have finished college before their turn had come.

GOING THE DISTANCE: *MEET THE PRESS*

It is certainly not the glitziest show on television. Reporters, a moderator, and guests of political import dig into heated questions, answers, and commentary. Simple in design, it is challenging for its panelists and potentially treacherous for guests. In short, it is not the likeliest candidate for the world's longest-running network television program.

Yet *Meet the Press* is still making news, stirring up controversy, and carrying on as the best political talk show on television, an astonishing fifty-five years after its debut. More importantly, the show's pioneering question-and-answer format has become an essential part of the democratic process. The JFK-Nixon presidential

debates and the give-and-take of today's political news conferences would have been unimaginable before the show's arrival. In a post–*Meet the Press* world, we expect to be able to judge our leaders on a firsthand basis.

The show's creators were an odd couple. Martha Rountree, a vivacious radio producer with a South Carolina accent, was host of a lighthearted ladies' radio panel series, *Listen to the Women*. Lawrence E. Spivak, a bespectacled, five-foot-three editor and publisher with a stubborn and serious demeanor, was looking for a way to sell subscriptions to his magazine, *American Mercury*. Rountree suggested that the magazine sponsor a radio press conference, with the biggest names

in politics submitting to a live grilling by a panel of reporters. Spivak quickly agreed, and *Meet the Press*—which began on the Mutual radio network—made its television debut on NBC in 1947, with the pleasant Rountree serving as moderator, and Spivak boring down hard as lead panelist.

Almost immediately, the show began to make headlines, and the world's power brokers sat up and took notice. Washington statesmen and international figures began jockeying for slots on the show, often holding back scoops until it was time for their precious network exposure. Whittaker Chambers accused Alger Hiss of being a communist on the show's radio version. Adlai Stevenson caused a sensation by

not denying he was running for president in 1952.

Pierre Mendès-France, then-premier of France, shocked his country's wine growers by appearing with a glass of milk in front of him. Eleanor Roosevelt denounced McCarthyism, while McCarthy himself made several increasingly weak defenses of himself. Fidel Castro and legendary *MTP* panelist May Craig (known for her flamboyant hats and brilliant questions) engaged in a memorable debate, making the reporter into a Cuban folk hero.

Although Rountree left the show in 1953, Spivak stayed with *Meet the Press* until 1975. "I find Mr. Spivak a thoroughly objectionable, offensive, intrusive, abrasive, tactless, and generally insufferable newsman. He has a monumental impertinence," wrote Jacob Hay, television critic for the *Baltimore News-American*. "In short, Mr. Spivak is the kind of newsman most of us out here would like to be."

(Above) The *Meet the Press* set in the early 1970s. *(Opposite page, top)* On October 15, 1950, New York Governor Thomas Dewey made headlines by endorsing General Dwight D. Eisenhower as a future presidential candidate. From left: Lawrence Spivak, May Craig of the *Portland Press Herald*, Murray Davis of the *New York World-Telegram & Sun*, Dewey, and Martha Rountree. Despite Spivak's misgivings at becoming a TV personality, both he and Rountree became as well known as the newsmakers they interviewed. Rountree was known for her social skills and lavish Washington parties; Spivak enjoyed his tough-guy reputation, refusing to let guests smoke on the air, leading Winston Churchill to call him "a goddamned dictator." *(Opposite page, bottom)* Lawrence Spivak and James Roosevelt, FDR's son and unsuccessful California gubernatorial candidate, August 1950.

CELEBRATING HOLIDAY TRADITIONS

(Above, top; left to right) A float from the Rose Parade; the holiday angels line the walk of Rockefeller Center to the Christmas tree; Lorne Greene and Betty White preside over a Rose Parade for TV; Donald Duck floats along in Macy's Thanksgiving Day Parade. (Circle) Suzanne Wright (wife of NBC Chairman and CEO Bob Wright) gives children and their families a backstage look at Christmas in Rockefeller Center. (Right) A Rose Parade float from 1890. (Opposite, top) The Rockettes at a Macy's Thanksgiving Day Parade. (Opposite, bottom) A more recent Rose Parade float.

Time after time, the medium of television has shown a unique power to bind us together as a nation. It's evident in moments of national triumph, such as the Apollo 11 mission to the moon, and in times of national tragedy, such as the Kennedy and King assassinations and the terrorist attacks of September 11.

Our nation is also bound together by more lighthearted and quintessentially American fare, exemplified by NBC's annual holiday telecasts. These events (TV comfort food, if you will) have become annual classics for the network and are cherished traditions for millions of families.

The Tournament of Roses Parade, in Pasadena, California, is a New Year's event over 110 years old, designed to bring attention to the area's pleasant clime. "In New York, people are buried in snow," announced Professor Charles F. Holder at an 1889 meeting of the Pasadena Valley Hunt Club. "Here our flowers are blooming and our oranges are about to bear. Let's hold a festival to tell the world about our paradise." Initially a modest parade of horse-drawn carriages, today the event is an international festival of equestrian units, marching bands, and dozens of floats, every visible inch of which must be covered in flowers or other vegetation.

NBC, which had been airing the Rose Bowl since 1927, realized that the parade would be ideal for showing off the glorious potential of color TV.

to be televised was in 1951, on *The Kate Smith Show*.

Since those early days, the Rockefeller Center tree-lighting ceremony has blossomed into a full-fledged, nationally televised entertainment event. In recent years, *Christmas in Rockefeller Center* has featured the performances of 'N Sync, Garth Brooks, Tony Bennett, and Destiny's Child. The tree-lighting itself has recently been handled by two first ladies, Hillary Clinton and Laura Bush, and several New York icons, including former mayor Rudy Guiliani and Yankees manager Joe Torre.

So, on January 1, 1954, the network aired its first coast-to-coast colorcast—a showing of the Rose Parade. An estimated 350 million viewers in 80 countries worldwide now watch the event every year.

It wouldn't be a Thanksgiving morning without waving celebrities, the best marching bands in the nation, the Rockettes, and giant helium balloons, perfect for the TV screen. Macy's hosted its first holiday season parade in 1924, with kid-friendly balloons making their debut three years later. (The first was Felix the Cat. Balloons in 2001 included Snoopy, Pikachu, and the Statue of Liberty.)

The parade was first telecast by local New York station W2XBS in 1939. Although the parade and its telecasts were suspended for the duration of World War II, they resumed in 1945. The Macy's Thanksgiving Day Parade has been on NBC every year since 1953. By the time Santa glides past Macy's, officially signaling the beginning of the Christmas season, the turkey is usually in the oven.

The tradition of a lighted Christmas tree looking down on Rockefeller Center is even older than the center itself. In 1931, workers building the complex placed the first tree on their muddy construction site. Two years later, 700 lights were illuminated in the first formal tree-lighting ceremony in front of the brand-new RCA Building. The first tree-lighting

SEEING IS BELIEVING

The beginning of the fifties was marked by a sense of trust—trust that our politicians were honest, our justice system fair, our economic order equitable. We trusted that, for the hard-working and wholesome, failure was impossible. To many, the world, like the images on television, was black and white. America was good; communism was not. Fathers worked steadily at respectable jobs for large corporations; mothers stayed home.

The trust in American values also extended to technology. The television set was a tangible sign of progress; likewise, the relentless optimism of what appeared on the screen was rarely questioned. For the first time, images on the small screen began to shape public consciousness. The sitcom family of the 1950s, for example, was an idealized portrait that reinforced social conformity more than it reflected reality; the neat resolution of all conflict within the twenty-two minutes of a half-hour show suggested a tidiness in life to which viewers could aspire but never achieve.

In 1950, only nine percent of American households owned a television. As the decade progressed, television sets began their migration from the metropolises of the Northeast to cities and towns across the nation, and from public venues

such as bars and auditoriums into private homes. In living rooms from coast to coast, families relegated their radios to the corners and placed a TV set front and center.

You could pull a knob on a box and transport fascinating people right into your home—this was magic far beyond the disembodied voices of radio. You could see facial expressions, gestures, and body language—this fostered a sense of intimacy that reinforced the aura of trust. TV was becoming irresistible.

If you were one of the few on your block to have a set, the glamour of the new medium shone on you as well, as you played host to neighbors who gladly accepted your invitation to watch. Thus the television brought people together— an electronic campfire around which neighbors gathered. You might have to fiddle with the antenna to get rid of the "snow," but you were nonetheless part of something big, sometimes seeming larger than life itself. (How different the experience of television has become fifty years later, when most homes have multiple sets for different rooms and different occupants of the house.)

Even when events such as the Army-McCarthy hearings began to shake our faith in all things American, television was there to ferry us through.

Television was indeed a thing of magic. You just had to believe.

THE MAN WITH THE VISION: PAT WEAVER

Sometimes an entire industry bears the stamp of one individual. This is certainly the case with television and Pat Weaver. An urbane, astute businessman with an eye for talent and a love of comedy, he came to NBC in 1949 from Young & Rubicam, where he had been Fred Allen's producer for his *Town Hall Tonight* show on NBC Radio. Over the next seven years, Weaver created many of the features of network television— both in programming and business—that we take for granted today.

In the late 1940s, most network television programming was created and owned by sponsors or by ad agencies such as Young & Rubicam, which were hired by the sponsors. Sponsors called the shots, dictating content and even where in the weekly lineup a show should be aired. Since an advertiser had to bankroll an entire show, only the largest companies could afford to advertise on network television. When Weaver came to NBC, he embarked on a mission to

make television advertising more affordable—and, incidentally, to give networks more control of programming. He did this by instituting the now standard "magazine" style of advertising: networks produced the shows themselves and sold blocks of sixty- and thirty-second commercial time to individual sponsors, just as publishers in the print world sold

advertisers pages in magazines. This represented a gradual yet radical shift in power to the networks, while at the same time opening the door for many new advertisers, who could now buy a minute or two here and there, rather than an entire show.

Weaver's first official act upon walking into 30 Rock as the new vice president for television

programming was to save *Meet the Press* from cancellation. He then solidified NBC's relationship with Milton Berle by offering him a lifetime contract (Weaver rightly suspected that CBS would try to steal Berle).

He was a prodigious memo writer: his memoranda would

(Right) Left to right: NBC executive Robert Sarnoff (David's son), *Your Show of Shows'* Max Leibman, Bob Hope, and Sid Caesar chat with Pat Weaver.

(Above) Pat Weaver with his family: wife, Elizabeth, daughter Sigourney (the actress), and son Trajan. (Left) Weaver mugs with J. Fred Muggs, the chimp who saved the *Today* show. (Below) Weaver clowns with *All Star Revue* host Jack Carson.

eventually fill forty bound volumes, now at the Library of Congress. One of Weaver's most legendary memos, his 1949 missive "The Course to Be Followed," laid out his plan for NBC's success of the next several years, emphasizing that sponsors should sponsor, programmers should program, creators should create, and everybody should stay out of everybody else's way. "You wouldn't tell Milton Berle what jokes to use," wrote Weaver in his book, *The Best Seat in the House*. "You wouldn't tell a producer like Fred Coe how to climax a dramatic story for *Television Playhouse*. Once you've chosen the creative people and put them to work,

you leave them alone."

Within his first couple of years at NBC, the relentlessly creative Weaver proposed the basic concepts for an astonishing number of innovative programs: *Today*, *The Tonight Show*, *Home*, *Your Show of Shows*, *The Colgate Comedy Hour*, *Producers' Showcase*, *Project XX*, *Wide Wide World*, and *The Huntley-Brinkley Report*. He devised NBC Radio's *Monitor*, a weekend service with a format of news, talk, sports, comedy, interviews, music, and remotes from around the world, similar to today's National Public Radio. Not only was it a critical and popular success, it kept NBC Radio profitable and

viable for decades.

Even though David Sarnoff appreciated Weaver's ability to create programming that could sell television sets and make money for the network at the same time, the General never liked Weaver. They were simply different kinds of men. (Behind his

back, Weaver gave Sarnoff the nickname "General Fangs.") In 1956, Sarnoff installed his son, Robert, as president, and attempted to move Weaver upstairs as chairman of the NBC board, with no real decision-making power. Weaver quit. But his legacy is seen every time a television set is turned on.

COMEDY COAST TO COAST

(Circle) Jimmy Durante, aka the Great Schnozzola (a reference to his oversized nose), had an unquenchable need to entertain and an uncanny ability to make guest stars look good (including unlikely comedic talents such as John Wayne, Bette Davis, and Ethel Barrymore). A fine ragtime pianist, he once joked that he had written a symphony; instead of calling it "Rhapsody in Blue," he called it "Inka Dinka Do." That hit from the thirties became his lifetime signature song. Durante always ended his shows with seven poignant and mysterious words: "Good night, Mrs. Calabash, wherever you are." Many believe there never was a real Mrs. Calabash and that his sign-off was probably a gentle salute to the lonely hearts of the world.

Upon his arrival at NBC in 1949, Pat Weaver had an idea he wanted to try as soon as possible. "I had decided on a strategy of comedy every night at eight o'clock, right after the news, and drama at nine," he wrote in his book, *The Best Seat in the House*. "At eight, the kids were still up, and they controlled the sets."

The theory was a smart one and is still in use today. The problem was to attract top-name talent for such a program. Stars had been accustomed to the ease of weekly radio, which allowed them to perform while reading scripts. They were wary about the rigors of TV production, which required memorizing lines, worrisome camera angles, and a lot of physical situations. Weaver's solution was to ask stars to commit to only one show a month—thereby introducing the innovative feature of rotating hosts.

By the fall of 1950, two 8:00 p.m. comedy-variety shows had debuted: the Wednesday night *All Star Revue*, with Jimmy Durante, Danny Thomas, Jack Carson, and Ed Wynn; and the Sunday night *Colgate Comedy Hour*, with Eddie Cantor, Abbott and Costello, and Dean Martin and Jerry Lewis. Both shows were designed to be big-name events, and both shows succeeded—especially *Colgate*, which bested the competing *Ed Sullivan Show* in the ratings.

Soon after, NBC's new coast-to-coast coaxial cable made these two shows even more star-studded. "This is the first time that a television show is going commercial from Hollywood across the nation!" announced Eddie Cantor on the September 30, 1951, *Colgate Comedy Hour*. The technical innovation allowed the network to use Los Angeles as an origination point, enticing

more celebrities to host—names such as Bob Hope, Talullah Bankhead, Donald O'Connor, Martha Raye, and even Charlton Heston. Some, like Hope, took on the once-a-month slot. Others stayed for only a show or two. (One memorable evening, Ethel Merman, Frank Sinatra, and Bert Lahr starred in a *Colgate* version of the musical "Anything Goes.")

Perhaps the perfect hosts were Dean Martin and Jerry Lewis, the nightclub sensations who went far beyond their scripted lines, written for them by TV newcomer Norman Lear. They giddily let their shows descend into pure anarchy, frequently mugging their sets, crew, and guest stars, such as Burt Lancaster and Mary McCarty (below).

By mid-1955, both shows were off the air. As television became more competitive, these celebrity-driven vehicles became too expensive to produce.

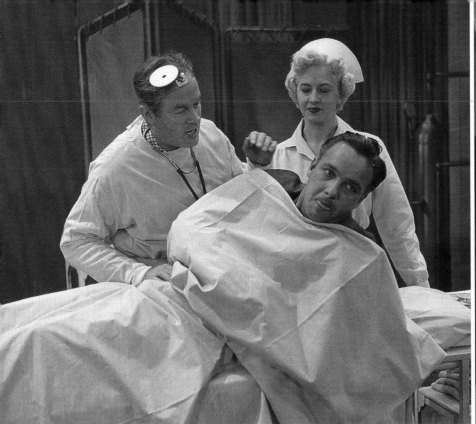

(Top left) Bob Hope plays doctor with the help of Marilyn Maxwell on a most unwilling Bob Crosby. *(Top right)* Perry Como is mellow no matter what the winter weather brings. *(Above, left to right)* Bud Abbott and Lou Costello are masterful comedic foils; the Marx brothers (Harpo and Chico) cavort with Tony Martin; and Dorothy Lamour and Danny Thomas are doing who knows what..

YOUR SHOW OF SHOWS

On *Your Show of Shows*, Sid Caesar and company performed ninety minutes of live television every week, thirty-nine weeks a year. It was a startling achievement that involved large casts, elaborate costuming, huge production numbers, and sixteen-hour rehearsal days, with no teleprompter, no cue cards, and no videotaped retakes. The show was brilliantly funny, and its pressure-cooker atmosphere produced some of the most engaging and vividly memorable moments of the Golden Age. It was tightrope television—a wild mix of comic invention, high energy, and on-the-spot improvisation—and it dominated Saturday night from 1949 through 1954.

It all started with an imaginative producer named Max Liebman, who was staging a theatrical review at a Catskills resort called Tamiment with a cast featuring two then-unknown comedic talents—Sid Caesar and Imogene Coca. When Pat Weaver caught the show, he asked Liebman if he thought the review could be produced before a televised audience…weekly. Liebman and company quickly said "Yes," and by October 1949, the hour-long *Admiral Broadway Review* was on the air. By the fall of 1950, the show was such a hit that it was expanded to ninety minutes, and retitled *Your Show of Shows*.

Caesar was supported by a now-legendary group of comedy writers and a brilliant cast that included Coca, Carl Reiner, and Howard Morris. (The diminutive Morris was cast once it was realized Sid needed someone he could lift by the lapels.)

Your Show of Shows usually featured a parody of some recent movie, such as "From Here to Obscurity," with Sid and Imogene soggily re-creating the Lancaster/Kerr beach love scene. Caesar was especially good at takeoffs of foreign films, delivering double-talk dialogue in hilarious mock German, French, Italian, or Japanese. (John Belushi's *Saturday Night Live* samurai was a direct descendant of a Caesar character.)

In addition to some large production numbers staged by Bob Fosse and Marge and Gower Champion, Caesar performed as many as ten

The comic chemistry between Sid Caesar and Imogene Coca was pure genius. Coca had a face almost as flexible as Caesar's rubbery countenance, and she would respond to his wild comic tantrums with equally forceful and hilarious retorts. They improvised so well together that the specific bits of dialogue in a skit were often invented as they were performing live on television. *(Opposite page)* Frequently, the entire cast would be soaked with mud or water, just as Howard Morris, Sid Caesar, Imogene Coca, and Carl Reiner are pictured here. *(Top, right)* Caesar confers with writers Mel Tolkin, Lucille Kallen, and Mel Brooks.

CAESAR'S WRITERS

"Writing for Sid Caesar was my college education," recalls Mel Brooks. "It was my Harvard University of comedy." And what a classroom! They screamed, they improvised, they stood on tables, and together they wrote some of the most brilliant comedy material ever seen on television. Along with Brooks, Tony Webster, and Joe Stein, the team writing *Your Show of Shows* was headed by Lucille Kallen, one of the first women to write comedy for television, and Mel Tolkin, who later became senior writer on *All in the Family*. At one point, Neil Simon and his brother Danny briefly stepped in when Kallen went on maternity leave. Later, Woody Allen, Larry Gelbart (*M*A*S*H*), Sheldon Keller (*The Dick Van Dyke Show*), Aaron Ruben (*Sanford and Son*), and Gary Belkin (*The Carol Burnett Show*) would write for Sid. Collectively, this group created an extraordinary number of the comedy hits of the past fifty years, both on television and on film, including Brooks's *Young Frankenstein* and *The Producers* to Gelbart's *M*A*S*H*, Allen's Oscar-winning *Annie Hall*, Reiner's *Enter Laughing*, and Simon's Pulitzer Prize-winning *Lost in Yonkers*.

comedy sketches each show, often playing recurring characters such as Progress Hornsby, a spaced-out jazz musician; or the Professor, a confused German expert on all matters. Sid and Imogene's Charlie and Doris Hickenlooper were a bickering couple, arguably an antecedent of *The Honeymooners'* Ralph and Alice. Some of the duo's most memorable scenes were done entirely in pantomime, such as

miming the percussion section of an orchestra during the "1812 Overture."

Regrettably, this perfect team broke up in the fall of 1954. Liebman went on to produce Pat Weaver's "spectaculars," while Sid hosted his own *Caesar's Hour* with co-star Nanette Fabray. Imogene Coca starred in her own show, written by Lucille Kallen, but it wasn't a success. The Sid-Imogene magic was gone.

Say the Secret Word and...

In the 1950s, millions in America knew what came next: The duck came down and a happy contestant won a hundred dollars. The money to be won on *You Bet Your Life* wasn't a very big deal, even for its time. But watching contestants win big bucks on this show really wasn't the point, anyway. The best part of this quiz show was what happened before the quiz.

Groucho Marx—the pivotal Marx Brother, a master of American stage and film comedy, and a failure in the radio business—had finally found a broadcasting niche that worked for him. *You Bet Your Life*, initially on ABC radio, allowed Groucho to do what he did best: ad-lib. The host teased and bantered with his contestants, turning average folk into straight men or comedians as the moment dictated. (Groucho to a used car salesman: "How many times have you been indicted?")

Marx looked for, and usually found, the risqué and ridiculous in his chats with guests. When *You Bet Your Life* came to NBC television on October 5, 1950, viewers had the added bonus of watching Groucho puff his cigar and roll his eyes as the smoke and double entendres filled the air. The off-color humor was so worrisome for the network's censors that the half-hour show (shot on film) was edited down from an hour's performance; some of Groucho's funniest lines ended up on the cutting room floor. (Typical Groucho banter: Once, he asked a young woman why she wasn't married. "I'm waiting for Mr. Right," she said. "Wilbur or Orville?" he replied. Another contestant, a man with a thick accent, claimed he spoke eight languages. Marx responded, "Which have you been speaking so far?")

(Right) A pretty girl, the duck, and Groucho promote the show's move from 8:00 p.m. to 10:00 p.m. Thursdays for the fall 1958 season. The duck—a nod to the classic Marx Brothers movie *Duck Soup*—was replaced in the final season by attractive women descending on a swing. Once, Harpo Marx came down on the swing. (Opposite, top) Sidekick George Fenneman, with Groucho, was also the announcer for *Dragnet*. (Opposite) Surprise! The host caught chatting with yet another pretty girl.

2 HOURS LATER

Quiz shows would become a television phenomenon in the fifties. The thought that anyone, even briefly, could become a TV star—maybe even win some cash in the process—proved irresistible for millions of Americans. Networks and sponsors also loved quiz shows because, at least initially, they were inexpensive and virtually trouble-free to produce.

Groucho stepped down from the hosting job in 1961, making only occasional public appearances after that, most memorably on *The Tonight Show*. He had loved *You Bet Your Life* because the role of host was so well suited for his particular brand of genius. Ironically, the world's perception of Groucho Marx as one of the century's funniest and most brilliant men had come in the twilight of his performing years.

THIS IS YOUR LIFE

Ralph Edwards created and hosted a popular radio show called *Truth or Consequences* beginning in 1940. One time, a few years into the show's run, he told the story of a World War II veteran's life. The audience feedback from that segment was so positive that Edwards created a new show called *This Is Your Life*, which debuted on radio in 1948 and came to television in 1952. The format of the show was straightforward: Edwards would surprise an unsuspecting guest by announcing, "This is your life!" Then, in front of a studio audience, he would narrate the person's life story with the help of family, friends, and colleagues whose voices were sometimes first heard from off-stage.

As the show progressed through its nine-year run, more and more of the surprised honorees turned out to be celebrities. Legendary newscaster Lowell Thomas refused to crack a smile during his show, continually hissing "This is a conspiracy."

This Is Your Life would also prove to be the final American public sighting of the great comedic team of Laurel and Hardy (*below*), who appeared on December 1, 1954. Both comedians smiled pleasantly, if awkwardly, for the cameras, despite the fact Stan Laurel was reportedly miffed that they had been tricked into doing the show—it offended his professionalism.

53

THE KATE SMITH HOUR

was the first significant network daytime television program, debuting September 25, 1950, on NBC. Back then, most TV stations aired nothing in the middle of the day. This pioneering show brought to television the portly woman who had made "God Bless America" her signature anthem. Smith's daily one-hour afternoon variety program continued her reign as one of the era's most popular and beloved performers. (An evening program also ran on NBC television during the 1951–52 season.)

Smith proved to be as popular on television as she was on radio; her homey show was filled with pleasant interviews, uplifting songs, and recurring dramatic segments. Appearing with Kate was Ted Collins, her ever-present announcer/host/producer/manager. His career was so closely identified with hers that most people assumed they were married; they weren't. When NBC cancelled the show in June 1954, the network received 400,000 letters of protest.

☆ HUGH DOWNS ☆

Hugh Downs has the notable distinction of appearing on all three of NBC's classic talk shows. He was a regular on *Home* and was Jack Paar's sidekick on *Tonight* before hosting the *Today* show.

NETWORK TV FINDS A HOME

While Pat Weaver was still at the advertising agency Young & Rubicam, he noticed that a stereotype of American women didn't quite ring true. Conventional thinking was that the typical post–World War II, stay-at-home mom was watching her baby, doing the ironing, and washing the dishes while listening to daytime dramas and quiz shows. Actually, research showed that at least half of all women at home during the day weren't turning on their radios or TVs at all.

After coming to NBC, Weaver devised a show precisely aimed at that audience: *Home*. Neither a melodramatic soap nor an overhyped game show, *Home* was a literate and innovative "women's magazine of the air," with Arlene Francis as its "editor-in-chief."

Much like *Today*, *Home* had its own ultramodern set, a large houselike studio with sections for cooking, fashion, furniture, beauty care, and other topics. Francis and a large cast of contributing "editors" informed, demonstrated, interviewed,

and presented useful tips and "news with a woman's touch." It was a breakthrough show for its time, taking seriously women's needs for intelligent talk and information.

Like Weaver's other triumphs, *Today* and *Tonight*, *Home* not only pioneered a new time of day for network television, but appealed to advertisers as a prestigious way to communicate with new audiences outside of prime time. Weaver not only invented and defined new "dayparts," he found ways to finance them.

(Opposite, below) NBC President Pat Weaver talks with Arlene Francis on the set of *Home*. In *Arlene Francis: A Memoir*, she wrote: "We were an educational program, and the one it educated most of all was me." (*Left, both top images*) Announcer Hugh Downs, a veteran of the WMAQ "Chicago School" of television, got his first national exposure on the show, appearing in segments on topics ranging from finance to fashion. In addition to conversations on the set (*lower far left, with Arlene Francis*) *Home* took viewers out to locations around America. (*Lower left*) A weather reporter in front of Los Angeles City Hall tells southern California residents what to expect for the day.

QUEEN FOR A DAY (*right*) wasn't quite a game show and wasn't quite tasteful, but it certainly was a success. It quickly became the top-rated daytime show after coming to NBC in 1956. Hosted by Jack Bailey, the show featured four women who would come up from the audience to describe why they should be named the day's queen, usually telling sad stories, each more maudlin than the next. The most deserving contestant, as determined by an audience applause meter, inevitably cried as a sable-trimmed cloak was draped over her shoulders and a tiara perched on her head. The Queen for a Day was showered with presents and sympathy, before (presumably) returning to her hard-luck life the next day.

SPECTACULAR TELEVISION

Television specials have been around for a long time. When done well, they bring out the very best in those who create them and present the very best the art of television can offer. From 1958's brilliant "An Evening with Fred Astaire" (which eventually won ten Emmys) to 1983's "Motown 25" (featuring Michael Jackson's stunning "Billie Jean" moonwalk) to 2001's "America: A Tribute to Heroes" (which ran on dozens of different broadcast and cable networks, raising millions for the victims of the terrorist attacks of September 11), specials can unite, entertain, and enlighten.

One of the earliest and greatest of all television specials was an opera commissioned by NBC and written by Gian Carlo Menotti, "Amahl and the Night Visitors," which first aired live on Christmas Eve, 1951. NBC had convinced a somewhat doubtful Joyce C. Hall, the founder and CEO of Hallmark Cards, to sponsor the special—even though it was barely finished in time for broadcast. The hauntingly beautiful parable about the three wise men and a crippled young boy making their way to Bethlehem was so well received that the network rebroadcast it every Christmas season for the next sixteen years.

Pleased with his first television experience, Joyce Hall soon began to regularly sponsor culturally uplifting NBC specials, which eventually became known as the *Hallmark Hall of Fame*. The series, which ran exclusively on NBC until 1979, has garnered more than seventy Emmy Awards.

In the years to follow, Pat Weaver was eager to create more specials, as was RCA's David Sarnoff—but for quite different reasons. Weaver wanted to "uplift humanity" with what he called "spectaculars," the biggest, brightest, and most brilliant specials the medium could offer.

(*Hallmark Hall of Fame*). Yet the first of these broadcasts was anything but spectacular. On September 12, 1954, Betty Hutton made her television debut in the lavishly produced and extensively hyped musical "Satins and Spurs." It bombed. The critics hated it and the ratings were awful, leading one of the disappointed sponsors to dub the show "Nails and Coffins."

Despite this inauspicious beginning, many of NBC's spectaculars would live up to the name. Thirty million viewers watched Margot Fonteyn dance with the Royal Ballet in "Sleeping Beauty"; Humphrey Bogart, Lauren Bacall, and Henry Fonda appeared in "The Petrified Forest"; Dave Garroway starred as Santa Claus in a production of "Babes in Toyland"; and Laurence Olivier directed and starred in a three-hour "Richard III."

Sarnoff needed a high-profile way to show off RCA's brand-new color televisions.

So for the 1954 fall season, NBC announced it would preempt regular entertainment programming on Mondays, Saturdays, and Sundays once a month to show "color spectaculars." (The fact that almost no one had a color set at the time didn't seem to matter.) The decision was a gamble because the specials had to deliver ratings and revenue high enough to underwrite their tremendous costs.

The three producers assigned to this project were the best in the business: Fred Coe (*Philco / Goodyear Playhouse*), Max Liebman (*Your Show of Shows*), and Albert McCleery

JUST THE FACTS, MA'AM

Jack Webb *(above)* successfully brought *Dragnet* back to NBC in 1967, after the original series was cancelled in 1959. *(Opposite, top)* This time, Harry Morgan (right) played Friday's partner, Officer Bill Gannon. (Morgan would later go on to fame as Colonel Sherman Potter on *M*A*S*H*.) The late sixties' version of *Dragnet* reflected the worries of what President Nixon called the silent majority: An increasingly shrill Sergeant Friday frequently lectured those around him on the dangers of drugs, hippies, and a godless society.

In the history of television, *Dragnet* arguably has done more to shape the public's perception of law enforcement than any other program. After beginning as an NBC radio show in 1949, *Dragnet* moved to television in December 1951. An immediate hit, it ranked among the nation's top-rated shows through 1956. As critic Steven Stark argues (in his book *Glued to the Set*), *Dragnet* not only established many of the conventions of the cop show, but taught the American public how to think about cops and crime. It also launched television's most ubiquitous genre: nearly one-third of all prime-time shows since have been about crime

and law enforcement. And virtually every one of them is indebted to *Dragnet*—either honoring its conventions, or consciously rejecting them.

Before *Dragnet*, the heroes of popular culture were often romantic lawbreakers. *Dragnet*, however, reversed this: its hero was not only emphatically unromantic, but operated within—not outside—the establishment, winning our trust through his relentless pursuit of justice. The show presented crime-solving in a more realistic, unglamorous light. Getting bad guys meant doing a lot of interviews, staring at files, and praying for small breaks.

A monotone voiceover

began each episode: "This is the city. Los Angeles, California. I work here. I carry a badge. My name's Friday." This, of course, was the stoic Sergeant Joe Friday of the Los Angeles Police Department, badge 714. He was played by Jack Webb, who was also a producer of the show, and the actor Webb's deadpan delivery was in part due to the producer Webb's efforts to cut costs: to keep rehearsal time down, the cast read its lines off a teleprompter, either well or badly—each episode was shot in three days. Intentionally or not, the wooden and stark style of the acting, writing, and sets gave the original *Dragnet* an unforgettable noir feel.

Webb offset his dispassionate on-screen performance with a passion for authenticity concerning police jargon and procedure. LAPD case files were used as source materials, and each episode had an officer from the appropriate department standing by to make sure Friday was going by the book. His detailed narration—"Tuesday, April sixteenth, nine thirty-six a.m., we were working the day watch out of homicide when the call came in"—put the viewer right into the scene.

The series introduced catchphrases that still resonate: "Just the facts, ma'am," "The story you are about to see is true." It taught the public police lingo such as "Book him on a 390." But most

significantly, as *Time* magazine reported in 1954, *Dragnet* made the nation forget "that it is a nation of incipient cop-haters."

Dragnet delivered an unambiguous moral message: Crime does not pay. Each episode concluded with George Fenneman's epilogue reassuring the audience that the perp was doing hard time in the Big House. Last of all, that powerful, glistening hand swinging the hammer to chisel "Mark VII," the name of Webb's production company, into stone left no doubt that justice had been served. The show was a weekly testimonial to our faith in authority and the belief that right always triumphs—if backed by enough dogged persistence.

PAULINE FREDERICK

Pauline Frederick was NBC's Voice of the United Nations from 1953 to 1974. She began her career with the network in 1938 as a radio interviewer and later covered the Nuremberg trials for a news syndicate. After returning to NBC in 1953, she covered the Korean War, the Cuban Missile Crisis, and the Vietnam War, in addition to reporting from the United Nations. Among many honors, Frederick was the first woman to receive the Peabody Award for excellence in broadcasting.

Frederick once stated, "When a man gets up to speak, people listen, then look. When a woman gets up, people look; then, if they like what they see, they listen."

About the first generation of women in television news, Jane Pauley once said, "They were the ones who had to be tough as nails, and smarter than everybody else."

By the early 1950s, a revolution in the broadcast news business was under way. For the first time, news images from around the world were becoming commonplace in TV viewers' homes, allowing Americans to actually *see* the realities of war and the impact of world politics. It was a shock similar in impact to the political conventions and speeches of the 1920s and 1930s, when radio listeners first were able to hear the voices of the politicians who affected their daily lives.

NBC's television news department got off to a modest start in 1946 with the twice-weekly *Esso Newsreel*, narrated, edited, and produced by Paul Alley. There was a brief 1947 Washington-based news commentary show called *Current Opinion*, and of course there was *Meet the Press*. But NBC's first real nightly news show didn't get off the ground until 1948, with the ten-minute *Camel Newsreel Theater*, hosted by John Cameron Swayze. For several years, the network had no real news cameramen of its own and was largely reliant on footage shot by the Fox Movietone newsreel studio.

In 1949, the ten-minute newscast was expanded to fifteen minutes and was renamed *Camel News Caravan*. The network grappled with the implications of having a cigarette sponsor attempt to control news content. For instance, Camel demanded that no one be shown smoking a cigar—Winston Churchill excepted—and that the newscast would always end on a shot of Swayze's lit cigarette in an ashtray.

When President Truman ordered U.S. servicemen into South Korea in June of 1950, Fox Movietone cameramen, most of whom had covered World War II, grabbed their

(Circle and left) John Cameron Swayze was NBC's first national TV newscaster. He had a talent for memorizing large chunks of news copy and repeating them into the camera without benefit of a teleprompter. Toward the end of his fifteen-minute news program, Swayze "hopscotched the headlines," meaning that he read one-sentence summaries of important news events that had no accompanying film footage. For eight years at the *Camel News Caravan* desk, he always closed with his signature sign-off: "Glad we could get together." *(Opposite)* Soldiers proudly plant a flag on a hill in Korea.

gear and accompanied the troops overseas. They were soon sending back gritty images of Americans in combat. All news film from Korea was days—if not weeks—old by the time it aired, since it had to be flown stateside from the Far East. Despite the delay from film to broadcast, and the additional reliance on official (i.e., censored) footage, the reality of war was brought into living rooms in a way it

had never been before. Korea was our first "television war," and the very concept of a televised war would affect all conflicts to come.

On September 8, 1951, NBC broadcast an important news first: the signing of the final peace accord with Japan. Diplomats from forty-nine nations signed the document in San Francisco as NBC's cameras broadcast the event live, thanks to the

just-completed transcontinental coaxial cable. With the new cable, NBC could now go anywhere in the nation to televise news remotes.

The presidential inaugural on January 20, 1953, was yet another milestone in live television newscasting. From coast to coast, sixty million Americans gathered around twenty-one million TV sets as Eisenhower solemnly took the oath of office as our

thirty-fourth president—the first truly major national moment we shared as a people via television. Just four years earlier, ten million had watched the Truman inaugural. Burgeoning television ownership, coupled with the completion of the transcontinental cable, furthered the democratic ideal of an informed electorate in ways that earlier generations never could have imagined.

THE *TODAY* SHOW —
THE DAVE GARROWAY ERA

The debut of the *Today* show, on January 14, 1952, was an inauspicious one. The very idea of a live two-hour, early-morning news and entertainment program was strange back then: Who would want to watch TV that early? On the first telecast, Dave Garroway, the bemused and easygoing host, gamely pointed at news photos, played pop records, peered out

at startled onlookers on 49th Street, and introduced pointless remotes. For example, a reporter stationed at the Pentagon cornered Chief of Naval Operations William Fechteler: "How's the Navy going these days, Admiral?" the reporter asked. "Guess it's all right," replied the Admiral. "It was there last night when I left it."

Yet another brainchild of Pat Weaver, *Today* was referred to as

"Weaver's folly" in its first, uneven year. "Do yourself a favor, NBC," wrote one critic, "roll over and go back to sleep." Yet the show slowly began to find its footing as 1952 progressed, even though audiences—and advertisers—initially stayed away.

Today was designed to be a television alternative to the morning papers and chatty wake-up radio shows of the era.

Weaver thought that a hard-news approach would be too unappealing for American viewers trying to ease into their day. "We cannot and should not try to build a show that will make people sit down in front of their sets and divert their attention to the screen," he wrote. "We want America to shave, to eat, to dress, to get to work on time. But we also want America to be well-informed, to be amused, to be lightened in spirit and in heart, and to be reinforced in inner resolution through knowledge."

Although pretentiously articulated, Weaver's vision was on the mark, and a major reason *Today* is still thriving a half-century after its debut. The show has long been America's favorite way to wake up, with hosts carefully striking a balance between serious news, useful information, light entertainment, and pleasant conversation.

With his chatty, winsome presentation style, Dave Garroway was the perfect first host. He was a veteran of the low-key and intelligent WMAQ "Chicago School" of television, and his mellow presence and oddball humor struck the right tone for morning TV. Jack Lescoulie, the show's sportscaster and Garroway's sidekick, could

(Above) Dave Garroway points to the day's top stories on January 14, 1952, the first day of broadcasting for the *Today* show. *(Opposite, clockwise)* Estelle Parsons chalks in the weather forecasts; Garroway and Jackie Gleason; *Today* show sidewalk fans look on and show off their signs for friends and family members back home.

always be counted on for energizing dull interviews. And then there was the audience—always the audience. Visitors from around the country happily stood outside the show's windows, waving at the folks back home; one woman memorably showed off the progress of her pregnancy to her parents out west, profiling herself to the camera.

By early 1953, *Today* was on the verge of cancellation—when a baby chimpanzee bounded into the office of Dick Pinkham, one of the show's producers. Quickly made a regular on the show, the chimp, named J. Fred Muggs, was *Today*'s salvation. Kids across America began to insist that their parents turn on their TVs to see the cute ape. Adults, between sips of coffee, began to notice a morning show coming into its own, inventing a new genre of programming and influencing television itself.

Fifty years later, *Today* still eases people into their day and dominates morning television. Yet the fact remains: If it weren't for a chimpanzee, the *Today* show would never have made it.

"Peace." This was Dave Garroway's famous sign-off from every show.

EVERY PICTURE TELLS A STORY

What do you do with sixty million feet of war footage? NBC's answer was to create twenty-six episodes of *Victory at Sea*, a groundbreaking documentary series that set the standard for the genre and influenced the way we think about war.

While working on his fifteen-volume *History of United States Naval Operations in World War II*, historian Samuel Eliot Morison had gained access to the Navy's extensive archive of combat film. Morison's research assistant, a young war vet named Henry Salomon, recognized the film's potential for television and brought the idea of a World War II documentary to the attention of his former Harvard classmate, Robert Sarnoff (son of the General), head of NBC's new film division.

Encouraged by the younger Sarnoff, Salomon pitched the concept to programming chief Pat Weaver, who in 1951 greenlighted a special production unit with Salomon at the helm. By stressing the human drama in the footage he chose, Salomon pioneered an approach that still prevails in documentaries today. Each half-hour segment followed a well-defined story arc—from anticipation to battle and finally to victory—tinged with mourning for those who perished. The result was at least as much drama as documentary, and nothing highlighted this as forcefully as the series' music, scored by famous Broadway composer Richard Rodgers.

While our forces were still doing battle in Korea, *Victory at Sea* was a powerful, emotionally charged look back at "the good war." The show debuted to both critical and popular acclaim. NBC, which originally aired the program without a sponsor, eventually recouped much more than its $500,000 investment. Because it was on film, *Victory at Sea* went on to a remunerative afterlife in syndication, playing on 206 local stations in the U.S. and in forty foreign countries over the next decade. Rodgers's dramatic score was also turned into gold as a series of successful LPs

Using 60,000 index cards, Henry Salomon catalogued 60 million feet of footage and eventually edited out 99 percent of it. *(Above)* He kept this shot of downcast Japanese POWs on Guam as they listened to Emperor Hirohito announcing Japan's unconditional surrender; and *(right)* a German shell exploding on the beach at Anzio as a group of amphibious crafts known as "Ducks" approached the shore.

released by parent company RCA on its Victor label.

After the critical and commercial success of *Victory at Sea*, NBC launched *Project 20* (or *Project XX*). The mission of this documentary unit was to deliver intellectually challenging programming designed to give Americans a perspective on history and social movements. The documentaries were innovative in their use of still photos to bring history to life—a now predominant method of television news and documentary production, as exemplified by Ken Burns's *The Civil War*.

One of the most notable *Project 20* documentaries was March 1961's "The Real West." Gary Cooper had just been diagnosed with cancer and knew his career was ending. After making many movies that perpetuated cowboy-and-Indian myths, he felt an obligation to set the record straight about the real history of the American West. Deeply moved by the pictures Salomon and director Donald Hyatt wanted to use, Cooper waived his usual fee and narrated the special. With the aid of Cooper's drawing power, "The Real West" aired in prime time to a massive audience and was an important turning point in American society's opinion of the plight of Native Americans.

PETER PAN

Do you believe in fairies?" asked Mary Martin in "Peter Pan," and millions of us answered with a resounding "Yes!" Broadcast on March 7, 1955, with the original Broadway cast, "Peter Pan" was a musical about not wanting to grow up and about the power of imagination. This enchanting show embodied everything Pat Weaver wanted in a spectacular and was a dazzling demonstration of NBC's new color television technology.

"Peter Pan" had enjoyed a successful run of 152 performances at the Winter Garden Theater beginning in 1954, after Martin revised the role that Jean Arthur had first played in 1950. The show was completely revamped with new songs from Betty Comden, Adolph Green, and Jule Styne, and, at the age of 47, Martin was flying high with rave reviews and a Tony Award.

Since the first stage production of "Peter Pan" in London's West End in 1904, the role of Peter has always been played by a woman. Mary Martin soared into the role on Broadway, and the televised productions made her beloved by the American public. By 1960, she may not have been as enthralled as her audience was with her character. Reportedly, she flew through a wall during the taping of the special, breaking her leg in the process.

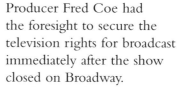

Producer Fred Coe had the foresight to secure the television rights for broadcast immediately after the show closed on Broadway.

The musical translated brilliantly to television, retaining all the warm emotional appeal the Broadway production had developed so well. It was directed by the original Broadway director, Jerome Robbins, with the original cast, including Cyril Ritchard as Captain Hook

and Kathleen Nolan as Wendy. Lynn Fontanne added cachet as the program's narrator. The two-hour television version was broadcast live from NBC's new Brooklyn Studios, which at one time were Warner Brothers film studios, now adapted for big color productions.

The televised "Peter Pan" was a huge hit, drawing some sixty-five million viewers—the largest audience in the history of television for many years to

"We won't grow up! We don't want to wear a tie, or a serious expression in the middle of July!"

— THE LOST BOYS IN THE 1955 NBC TELEVISION PRODUCTION OF "PETER PAN"

come. It won an Emmy for Best Single Program of the Year, along with Martin's Emmy as Best Actress in a Single Performance. "Peter Pan" was broadcast again live with much of the same cast in January of 1956, and was restaged one last time in 1960, this time on videotape. This is the version seen today; the 1955 and 1956 versions were recorded only on infrequently screened black-and-white kinescopes.

Mary Martin continued her Broadway career, starring in such hits as *The Sound of Music* and *I Do, I Do.* Coe went on to produce other extraordinary shows for *Producers' Showcase*, such as "The Lord Don't Play Favorites," with Louis Armstrong, "Mayerling" with Audrey Hepburn, and "The Great Sebastians," starring Alfred Lunt and Lynn Fontanne.

In 1956, Coe almost convinced Marilyn Monroe to make her television dramatic debut in "Lysistrata." It would have been a stunning coup, but Monroe got cold feet and turned down the opportunity. Failure on a film set is one thing; failure live in front of millions is quite another.

THIS COULD BE THE START OF SOMETHING BIG

With hoots and whistles and salutations of "Hi ho, Steverino!" *The Tonight Show* roared into television history in 1954 and changed the sleeping habits of a nation.

Steve Allen brought what was called in those days a "hip" edge to this late-night "funfest." His wacky sense of humor went with a keen intelligence, and he was an accomplished musician ready to improvise at both the piano and the microphone. More than anyone on television ever before, Steve interacted with the audience, and this participation became a much-anticipated part of the show. Later in life, Allen recalled, "It was tremendous fun to sit there night after night reading questions from the audience and trying to think up funny answers to them; reading angry letters to the editor; introducing the greats of comedy, jazz, Broadway, and Hollywood; welcoming new comedians like Shelley Berman, Jonathan Winters, Mort Sahl, and Don Adams."

The conventional wisdom among TV executives in the early 1950s was that no one would watch television after 11:00 p.m. In fact, most TV stations signed off before midnight with the "Star-Spangled Banner." Nonetheless, Pat Weaver developed the outline of a late-night show that would engage a youthful demographic and bring stars to television inexpensively. Although Weaver came up with the idea for this new kind of late-night network TV, he credited Allen with bringing his concept to life. (Weaver had originally wanted Fred Allen as host before he saw Steve.)

Allen had already established some of his signature elements on his 1953 local late-night talk show on NBC's New York affiliate, WNBT. With the larger budget of network TV, he brought aboard conductor Skitch Henderson and The Tonight Show Band, which featured some of the finest jazz musicians in New York. Then he wrote the prophetic theme song, "This Could Be the Start of Something Big," which continued to be used during the Johnny Carson era. The conversational interview was a staple of radio that transferred to TV, and Allen interjected ad-lib sarcasm and silliness that enlivened the chats with famous folk.

Under the guidance of Allen and producer William "Billy" Harbach, the show became an important spotlight for new

talent and for people who did not normally show up on television. Jack Kerouac, Lenny Bruce, Elvis Presley, and Jim Henson's Muppets all made appearances on *The Tonight Show* (or on his prime-time *Steve Allen* variety show) early in their careers.

Allen had a talent for spontaneity that made *The Tonight Show* a showplace for the unexpected. Someone in the audience would yell out a phrase and Allen would run to the piano and improvise a song based on those words. Within seconds, the entire

band would join in behind him and, eventually, Allen would have the entire audience singing along. It was marvelous madness. On a whim, he also began to create questions in response to answers submitted by the audience, presaging Carson's Carnac and *Jeopardy*. He assembled a repertory company featuring singers Steve Lawrence and Eydie Gorme, Don Knotts, Tom Poston, and Louis Nye. Allen established late night as a time to hang loose, have fun, and raise hell— a description Jay Leno would certainly recognize.

Never, ever afraid of looking ridiculous, Steve Allen brought a literate looniness to late-night television. He crashed through the barriers between the stage and the street, and between the stage and the audience, taking microphones and cameras with him as he went, and making everyone feel they were part of the party. He was television's innovator of "found comedy," a style David Letterman in particular uses to great effect.

TELEVISION GOES WEST

On October 4, 1952, Rosalind Russell, Milton Berle, Phil Harris, George Jessel, Harpo Marx, Dinah Shore, Red Skelton, and Jimmy Durante performed on a live episode of NBC's *All Star Revue*, the inaugural broadcast from NBC's studios in Burbank, California. The studios had been built to give NBC Television a serious presence in Los Angeles.

This broadcast, certainly a happy affair, was a harbinger of things to come. Television was going Hollywood.

Although the television industry had been born in New York, Hollywood steadily became the central home of prime-time television. The movie studios, initially contemptuous of the new medium, soon realized that going into business with the

TV networks would be good for business because the networks would need programming, preferably with feature-film production values and Hollywood stars.

Slowly at first, the television business moved West. With the support of film studios, the vast new popularity of filmed westerns, and the advent of videotape, live New York production didn't make financial

sense. With the move came profound changes in the television landscape. Even though viewers remained in their same seats at home, their viewing experiences shifted from New York–centered settings—mostly indoor studio, predominantly urban—to images with multiple locations and exterior shots that were predominantly Californian.

The juxtaposition of film,

color, videotape, and West Coast locations—including studio back lots conveniently filled with western scenery—ushered in an era of western serials that perfectly reflected the postwar spirit of America. As an idealized self-portrait of America itself, the western invariably presented images of hard work overcoming tremendous odds, and good overcoming evil. It revolved around themes of pioneering and exploration, daring and danger, competition and confrontation.

After the huge ratings for the Eisenhower inaugural speech, no one doubted that television would remain an important part of the political process. That was proved again with the Nixon-Kennedy debates and in President Kennedy's almost daily television appearances and speeches that inspired and reassured the nation.

As the 1950s drew to a close, the signs of an end to American innocence were clear, and again, television played a central role. Found by many inexcusable was the abuse of trust exhibited by the quiz show scandals. At the time, however, these were still only imperfections in a portrait of national harmony more typified by *Sing Along with Mitch*.

A long period of general tranquility, unity, and trust in America—the entire postwar era, through Eisenhower and Kennedy—ended when shots rang out in Dealey Plaza on November 22, 1963. For much of that day and for several days to follow, the nation was riveted to the television. It was a sad and terrible communal event, televised in every gruesome and touching detail. From that day onward, America was never the same.

THE QUIZ SHOW SCANDALS

(Above and below) Scenes from *Twenty-One*, where contestants were isolated in soundproof booths where they answered questions. Geritol sponsored the show—and no one seemed to mind that the contestant would fill the small booth with smoke from his pipe. (*Opposite*) Charles Van Doren (on the right) awaits entry to the stage at the start of a show.

During the 1956–57 season, NBC was desperate to get a toehold in the Nielsen ratings, as nine of the ten top shows were on CBS. (Only Perry Como broke the stranglehold, coming in at No. 9.) At the same time, under Robert Sarnoff, the network was experiencing serious cost cutting and was searching for less expensive programming. The solution to both problems was the quiz show. The format had proven to be a surefire audience pleaser since the early days of radio, and the concept of average people sharing some of the exciting, new television spotlight was an idea whose time had come. The quiz show

Twenty-One was NBC's first big-money response to the runaway prime-time success of *The $64,000 Question*, which aired on CBS. *Dotto* soon followed.

Loosely based on the concept of blackjack, *Twenty-One* featured two contestants enclosed in individual isolation booths who were awarded points based on their answers to questions worth from one to eleven points. The quickest way to score twenty-one, and thus be assured of at least a tie, was to answer two questions, worth ten and eleven points each. The questions were difficult, and many of those who scored well had ties to academia.

Hosted by Jack Barry, this was

the show that made telegenic Columbia University English professor Charles Van Doren an overnight celebrity, and for a brief shining season, eggheads were cool on television.

Dotto aired on CBS during the day and on NBC at night, beginning in July 1958. Contestants were confronted by a collection of dots on a screen and answered questions to win line segments connecting them. As the image became clearer, the first contestant to identify the person represented on the screen was the winner.

Both shows were produced by Jack Barry and Dan Enright, and it was *Dotto* that began what has become known as the quiz show scandal. (Barry and Enright also produced the prime-time *Tic Tac Dough*, a *Hollywood Squares*-like show that avoided getting caught up in the madness to come.) Edward Hilgemeier, Jr., a *Dotto* contestant waiting in the wings for his turn onstage, happened upon a notebook belonging to a victorious woman contestant. The notebook contained a crib sheet with answers to questions she had been asked on the program. Hilgemeier talked to the contestant she had defeated, and the two together confronted the producers.

Both were paid to keep silent; and it might have ended there, but for the fact that Hilgemeier

learned that he had been paid far less than the on-camera loser. Miffed, he got in touch with the New York State Attorney General's Office. It didn't take long for the rigged house of cards to collapse. Hilgemeier's complaint flushed out disgruntled *Twenty-One* contestant Herb Stempel, who spilled the beans about how he took a dive on national television. In those days, contestants kept returning to the program until they lost, and over time, many built up a fan base of sorts. Stempel, who was deemed less attractive than challenger Charles Van Doren, revealed that Van Doren had been given some of the answers.

Van Doren, who had parlayed his fame into a gig on the *Today* show as a substitute host for Dave Garroway, went from famous to infamous in a heartbeat. By the fall of 1958, it was all over, and big-money quiz shows disappeared from the networks. Only the hearings and lawsuits lingered on.

"I would give almost anything I have to reverse the course of my life in the last three years.... I have deceived my friends, and I had millions of them." – Charles Van Doren, testifying about the quiz show scandals before the House of Representatives

WESTWARD HO!

Perhaps because the Cold War encouraged us to see the world in terms of good guys and bad guys, the late 1950s saw an unprecedented interest in the western genre. Action was "in," as American viewers found solace in seeing villains get their just deserts. As NBC began to replace live shows with filmed productions, the already-built western scenery sitting in Hollywood back lots provided further impetus. This particular piece of American mythology had been a favorite overseas since the days of Buffalo Bill's Wild West Show, and the syndication made possible by film would enable the Old West to travel to foreign television markets. At home, the western was ubiquitous: During the 1958–59 season, there were thirty-one prime-time westerns on television, and seven of the Top 10 programs belonged to the genre.

One of the first, *Wagon Train*, debuted in 1957, and starred veteran character actor Ward Bond as wagonmaster Major Seth Adams, who shepherded his string of Conestogas out of St. Joseph, Missouri, and across the West to California. Bond's character was a reprise of sorts—he had starred in the 1950 John Ford classic,

(Far right) In *Tales of Wells Fargo*, Dale Robertson played troubleshooting agent Jim Hardie. *(Left)* When Hardie bought a ranch just outside San Francisco, the series surrounded him with Barbary Coast saloon girls. *(Above)* In *The Virginian*, ranch hands Trampas (Doug McClure) and Steve (Gary Clarke) flanked Judge Garth's daughter Betsy (Roberta Shore) as they surveyed the Shiloh Ranch from a split rail fence. *(Right)* Robert Horton and Ward Bond were the original scout and wagonmaster who guided settlers across the prairie on *Wagon Train*. Rifles were part of the mystique of TV's Old West, as *Laramie*'s Robert Fuller *(right, middle)* and many others demonstrated.

Wagon Master. He and other show regulars, including Frank McGrath as cook Charlie Wooster and Robert Horton as scout Flint McCullough, provided sympathetic characters and much-needed continuity. A significant part of the show's popularity, however, derived from its convoy of notable guest stars, among them Hollywood legends Bette Davis, Barbara Stanwyck, Mickey Rooney, and even John Wayne. These marquee names, coupled with quality scripts and deluxe production

Tales of Wells Fargo was another Top 10 show of the 1958–59 season. For most of its tenure on NBC, it was a good example of the classic western, with Dale Robertson as Fargo troubleshooter Jim Hardie. Premiering in spring of 1957, the program was a half-hour show until its final year, and Robertson was *Fargo*'s only regular cast member during that time. As the western craze lost steam, the program expanded to an hour, took on added supporting cast members, and had Hardie settle down on

Sherman, who with his younger brother Andy (Bobby Crawford, Jr.) struggled to maintain the family cattle ranch in Wyoming. They were aided by newly arrived drifter Jess Harper (Robert Fuller), and for the first season, by Hoagy Carmichael as Jonesy, a friend of the Shermans' late father. The family supplemented its ranch income by maintaining a stagecoach way station, which afforded an ongoing flow of good guys and bad guys passing through town.

Loosely based on the 1902

relied on an ensemble cast featuring Doug McClure as the wild-and-wooly cowhand Trampas; veteran character actor Lee J. Cobb as Judge Henry Garth, owner of the Shiloh Ranch in Wyoming Territory; and James Drury in the title role. (His given name was never revealed.) Airing until 1971 (in its last year rechristened *The Men from Shiloh*), *The Virginian* remains TV's third-longest-running western, following *Gunsmoke* and *Bonanza*.

values made possible by a then-lavish $100,000 per week budget, made *Wagon Train* more like a weekly made-for-television movie than a conventional TV series. The show held down the No. 2 spot in the Top 10 for three seasons and was the highest-rated show of the 1961–62 season.

a ranch just outside San Francisco. These *Bonanza*-like changes were not well received by the audience, and *Wells Fargo* ended its run in 1962.

Laramie debuted at the height of the national passion for westerns and aired from 1959 to 1963. The show featured John Smith as Slim

Owen Wister novel, *The Virginian* took *Wagon Train*'s solid scripts, name guest stars, and rich production values a step further by adding a half-hour to the show, thus breaking new ground as the first ninety-minute series. Premiering in 1962, well after the western craze had peaked, *The Virginian*

FAMILY LIFE ON THE PONDEROSA

Never just a western, by the end of its fourteen-year run, *Bonanza* had earned a permanent place in American popular culture. Its beginnings in 1959 were not auspicious, but after two years of mediocre ratings in a Saturday time slot, the show finally caught fire, much like the burning map in the opening credits. After it moved to Sunday night at 9:00 p.m., *Bonanza* consistently placed in the Top 10 and anchored NBC's Sunday-night lineup for over a decade. Americans of all ages were caught up in the saga of patriarch Ben Cartwright (Lorne Greene) and his sons Adam (Pernell Roberts), Hoss (Dan Blocker), and Little Joe (Michael Landon). We cared as if they were relatives of ours—and in a way, they were.

The series was one of the first westerns to play up family relationships. Ben Cartwright had married—and buried—three wives, and each of them had borne him a son. There was a touch of the old man in

Virginia City, Nevada. The "Bonanza" of the title referred to the riches Americans hoped they would find as they moved west to make their fortunes—specifically to the Comstock lode of gold and silver found near Virginia City in 1859.

The Cartwrights had standing in the community; unlike the footloose heroes or itinerant gunslingers of earlier TV westerns, they were landed gentry. The huge family fiefdom, the Ponderosa, was more than just a backdrop. Lavishly filmed, it functioned almost as another character in the series. This was no accident. *Bonanza* was the first western televised in color, and the sweeping vistas of the ranch provided weekly proof to viewers that they couldn't fully appreciate the program unless they were seeing the gorgeous landscape on a color TV—

made by RCA, of course. (Producer David Dortort had insisted on shooting the show in color, which made the production far more expensive. Dortort then saved money by casting then-unknown actors.)

Bonanza's run spanned an era of great change in television. Color programming became the norm, not the exception. Shows, including *Bonanza*, displayed an increasing willingness to tackle significant issues, including alcoholism and racial equality. The series weathered the departure of Pernell Roberts in 1965 but was unable to survive a real-life tragedy: Dan Blocker died suddenly before the beginning of the 1972–73 season. After 440 episodes, *Bonanza* rode off the airwaves in January 1973. There has not been a western to equal it since.

all of the boys, but the personality of each of the three half-siblings was distinct and fully developed. Adam was serious and cerebral; Hoss was beefy and jovial; Little Joe was romantic and impetuous.

Sometimes the boys played tricks on each other. Sometimes they got along and sometimes

they didn't. The one thing you could depend on, however, was that the civic-minded Cartwrights would put aside their disagreements and their horseplay to deal with an outside threat—if possible, with a minimum of violence.

Bonanza was set in picturesque

(Opposite, top) Each of the Cartwrights—*(left to right)* Hoss (Dan Blocker), Ben (Lorne Greene), Adam (Pernell Roberts), and Little Joe (Michael Landon)—was proficient with a six-shooter *(see Pernell Roberts, top, and Michael Landon, bottom, second from left)* but the family strove to settle problems and disputes without gunplay. Father and sons had relationships with women *(bottom left and second from right)*, but *Bonanza* continued to be popular with female viewers in part because all of the Cartwrights remained eligible. Because of his size, Hoss (whose given name, Eric, was almost never used) ended up with much of the physical humor on the program *(far right, bottom)*.

THE GREATEST GAME EVER PLAYED: FOOTBALL HITS THE BIG TIME

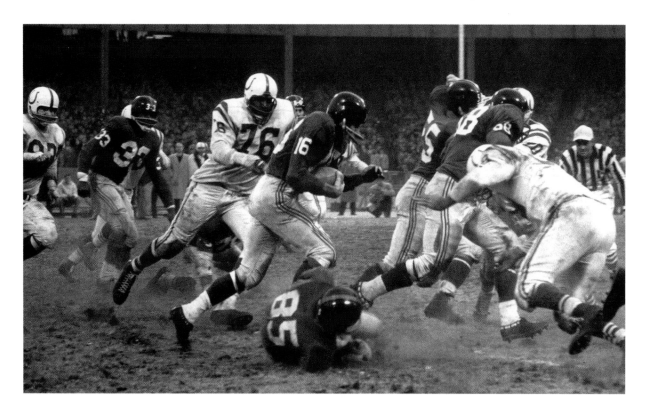

(Below) The Giants' Frank Gifford runs through the line. Some say that the official misplaced the ball at the end of a Gifford run, causing the Giants to miss a first down that would have all but sealed the game. *(Right)* Alan Ameche gets a perfect block from halfback Lenny Moore as he heads for the first winning score in overtime history.

When the New York Giants lined up against the Baltimore Colts in Yankee Stadium on December 28, 1958, they were playing for the NFL Championship and, as it turned out, much more. In the course of one winter afternoon, the communal fortunes of football, fans, and television were galvanized forever, forged in the fire of a barn-burner game—the first to be decided in overtime. We can trace the lineage of our national mania for professional football

back to this one contest, televised on NBC. More than forty years later, to the football faithful, it remains "The Greatest Game Ever Played."

The playoff was truly a clash of the titans, a game that pitted the Colts, with the league's best offense, against the Giants, with the league's premier defense. Even the brawny, bare-knuckled names of the players tell you a lot of what you need to know— Dick Modzelewski, Sam Huff, Andy Robustelli, and Jim Katcavage from the Giants faced off against Gino Marchetti, Alex

Sandusky, Gene "Big Daddy" Lipscomb, and "Buzz" Nutter from the Colts. The players on the field that day became part of football lore—in all, fifteen participants were inducted into the Pro Football Hall of Fame. Both teams boasted superstars on their rosters, men who are still legends of the game—including quarterback Johnny Unitas and receiver Raymond Berry from the Colts, and halfback Frank Gifford, lineman Roosevelt Grier (in his pre-needlepoint days), and placekicker Pat Summerall from the Giants. There were legends on the sidelines as well—Giants' assistant coaches Vince Lombardi and Tom Landry went on to greater glory in Green Bay and Dallas, respectively.

After a seesaw battle through fifty-eight minutes, Unitas led a last-ditch Colts drive in the waning moments of the fourth quarter, capped by a Steve Myhra field goal that tied the contest at 17–17. Time ran out, and the nation, watching on television, held its breath as the officials tried to figure out what to do.

"Everybody was confused," Unitas recalled. "I remember standing on the sideline next to Alan Ameche and asking him what happened next. Nobody really had any idea whether or not the game was over."

Enter sudden-death overtime.

The Giants went nowhere on their first possession but the Colts were driving when NBC lost its video feed—apparently someone had knocked loose a power cable—blacking out millions of viewers. With the climactic moments at hand, a man suddenly ran onto the field and play stopped. While he was being shuttled away, NBC had the time it needed to fix the problem. Soon after, fullback Ameche plunged over the goal line for the winning score.

"I've joked for years," said Chuck Thompson, who did the overtime play-by-play, "that it must have been some highly paid NBC executive, but I still have no idea who it was."

This was the blue-collar era in football, when the men who played the game needed jobs in the off-season, and when playoff money, paltry as it was, mattered. There were no agents and no lucrative endorsements.

The Colts were the NFL champs, and each team member received $4,718.77 for his day's work. Each Giant took home $3,111.33. But in the dying light of that December day, our national passion for football was born.

FEEL-GOOD AMERICA

NAT "KING" COLE

Although others had preceded him on television, Nat "King" Cole was the first black entertainer with major crossover appeal to host a network variety show. *The Nat "King" Cole Show* debuted as a fifteen-minute program in November of 1956 and became a half-hour show seven months later. Even with a stunning array of musical guests (Count Basie, Peggy Lee, Mel Torme, Mahalia Jackson, Ella Fitzgerald, and Tony Bennett), Cole's charm was not enough to overcome entrenched racism at a few affiliate stations and on Madison Avenue. From the start, sponsorship was a problem. National advertisers refused to underwrite the program, fearing repercussions from affiliates who refused to air a show starring a black man. In December of 1957, *The Nat "King" Cole Show* was cancelled.

The sound of the Eisenhower era was neither the earlier jitterbug jazz of Benny Goodman nor the later rock 'n' roll of the Beatles. On mainstream American television—with rare exceptions—it was Mitch Miller's "Yellow Rose of Texas," Dean Martin's "Memories Are Made of This," and Perry Como's "Round and Round." Several hit NBC shows urged viewers to feel good, sing along with their favorite singers, and let the world roll by. A younger generation was beginning to disturb this blissful fifties idyll with the twang of guitars from Bill Haley, Elvis Presley, and Dick Clark's *American Bandstand*. But if you turned up Tennessee Ernie Ford's "Sixteen Tons" loud enough, you wouldn't have to listen to that kid stuff for a few more years.

Ford's folksy country-and-western-flavored *Tennessee Ernie Ford Show* first appeared in 1955 as a daytime half-hour series. Ford moved to Thursday nights in the fall of 1956 and won the cornpone hearts of viewers with his guitar and baritone voice. Ironically, his producer, Bud Yorkin, would later bring to the world the decidedly un-cornpone *Sanford and Son*.

Your Hit Parade was a bridge from the swing era into the fifties. A successful radio show from 1935 until 1953, it was part of the national switch to television in the early fifties. Each Saturday night, a group of singers—which at various times included Snooky Lanson, Russell Arms, Dorothy Collins, and Giselle MacKenzie—sang the top hits, with different costumes, scenery, and dancers. Whether or not you could call these musical vignettes early music videos is debatable, but it was fascinating to see how many settings they could give a particularly hardy hit such as "How Much Is That Doggie in the Window?" or "Mr. Sandman."

The popularity of *The Dinah Shore Chevy Show*, sponsored by General Motors, gave Chevrolet sales a measurable bounce. Her sign-off theme song, "See the U-S-A, in your Chev-ro-let…" always concluded with her trademark giant-size hand-to-mouth smooch—"mwah!" Shore was already a popular vocalist before she became one of the few women to headline a hit musical variety show on television. With her warm, down-home presence, she had the knack of looking completely at ease on television. Attractive without being overtly sexy, her girl-next-door appeal registered with men without threatening women. She could put others at ease as well—picture Frank Sinatra sharing the stage with her and baseball great Dizzy Dean. The show was a Sunday-night 9:00 p.m. standard starting in October 1957 until *Bonanza* took its slot four years later.

If Dinah was universally appealing, Perry Como was universally inoffensive. Like Dinah, he was already a popular

singer before the one-hour *Perry Como Show* came to NBC in 1955. Como, however, had been on NBC Television as early as December 1948 and had been featured on NBC Radio before that. His first TV show, *The Chesterfield Supper Club*, was actually a simulcast of his radio program.

The format of his Saturday one-hour show, which aired through 1963, never wavered. Como opened with his theme song, "Dream along with me, I'm on my way to a star…" Invariably, there was a request segment: "Letters, we get letters. We get stacks and stacks of letters," sang the cutesy female

chorus. "Dear Perry, would you be so kind…" Como epitomized easy listening, and his relaxed onstage demeanor became a running gag on the show. His easy persona was spiced up by the presence of the Ray Charles Singers and the Louis DaPron Dancers, as well as a parade of guest stars, including Burl Ives and Nat "King" Cole.

Sing Along with Mitch may have been the "squarest" show of all. The goateed, ever-smiling Mitch Miller encouraged all of us at home to "follow the bouncing ball," as he guided us through the lyrics of old-time favorites such as "By the Light of the Silvery Moon." Miller

was a composer-arranger ("The Yellow Rose of Texas" was his big hit) who had been head of A&R at Columbia Records. He had guided the careers of Patti Page and Frankie Laine, but his reactionary opinion of rock 'n' roll (a passing fad that he referred to as "pimple music") hastened his departure from the record company. In January 1961, he found a home on NBC, actually saying little, just waving his baton for the orchestra, the Sing Along Gang, and popular soloists Leslie Uggams, Diana Trask, and Sandy Stewart, each of whom went on to individual success as recording artists.

(Above, left) Clad in his golf sweater, Perry Como always looked relaxed. His casual style was borrowed by other popular male vocalists of the time, including Andy Williams. *(Above, right)* There was never any bad news on *Sing Along with Mitch*, especially during the holidays, as Mitch joined the smiling women of his Sing Along Gang for yuletide favorites. *(Opposite)* Dinah's trademark "Mwah!" kiss said goodnight on Sundays and got us ready to face Monday mornings in a good mood.

SMALL VIEWERS, BIG IDEAS

(Circle) Miss Frances rang the bell at the beginning of the educational fun on *Ding Dong School. (Above)* Don Herbert captured young scientists' imaginations on *Mr. Wizard. (Opposite, top)* Bullwinkle Moose sometimes failed to pull a rabbit out of a hat, much to Rocky's dismay. *(Opposite, bottom)* One of the most famous equine stars in Hollywood, *Fury,* poses with Pete (William Fawcett), Joey (Bobby Diamond), and Jim (Peter Graves)

The birth of television coincided with a powerful American commitment to the family. After World War II, our soldiers returned home to a nation of seemingly limitless abundance, energy, and newly built tract housing in the suburbs. The baby boom was one result. The postwar culture centered on family values and children was to become, in the 1960s, a culture centered on teenagers. But before we shifted to drugs, sex, and rock 'n' roll, the Eisenhower era of good public schools, safe streets, and Dr. Spock demanded wholesome television programming for children.

America wanted an electronic tutor, and the networks responded. Parents and educators had already observed early television's powerful influence on children's learning habits, knowledge about the world, and general behavior, and many embraced the optimistic promise of children's programming to uplift and educate. In the first decade of TV, that promise was fulfilled by shows such as *Mr. Wizard* and *Ding Dong School. Quiz Kids* gave every "C" student across the land something to aim for and something to worry about—in terms of parental expectations. Although it was only a puppet show, *Kukla, Fran & Ollie* discussed current events and opened children's minds to the larger world.

The networks were quick to notice the popularity of *Howdy Doody* and the boost to television sales that one show was providing. By 1951, there were up to twenty-seven hours of children's programs every week. Soon, children began to spend almost as many hours in front of the television set as they spent in the classroom. Some children's shows continued the tradition of live television, with programs such as *The Paul Winchell and Jerry Mahoney Show* (which was switched to Saturday morning from prime time), *Smilin' Ed McConnell and his Buster Brown Gang* (remember "Twang your magic twanger, Froggie"?), *The Gabby Hayes Show*, and *The Pinky Lee Show* ("Yoo hoo, it's me, Pinky Lee!"). As the decade wore on, many

shows were junior versions of the filmed adult serials, particularly in western settings, such as *The Lone Ranger*, *Fury*, *Hopalong Cassidy*, and *Sky King*.

In 1961, one show changed the course of children's television forever. The delightfully witty *Bullwinkle Show* was an NBC prime-time cartoon spin-off of ABC's *Rocky and His Friends*.

The colorful characters dazzled children, and the clever writing even amused Mom and Dad. But what network executives saw most of all was the answer to a financial prayer. Jay Ward, who created *Bullwinkle* and its predecessor, *Crusader Rabbit*, pioneered something called "limited animation." What Disney and Warner did for theatrical cartoons at forty cels (cartoon images) per foot of film, Ward was able to do for television cartoons at four cels per foot of film. The nineteen-and-a-half minutes of animation needed for each show cost only $2,500—one-tenth the cost of traditional cartoons and much less than shows with live actors. Rapidly, Kiddie Gulch, as the lucrative Saturday-morning children's slot became known, was filled with relatively inexpensive half-hour cartoons.

GOODNIGHT, DAVID... GOODNIGHT, CHET

NBC made sure that its news team went into the 1960 presidential season fully equipped. To cover the Democrats in Los Angeles and the Republicans in Chicago, the network brought in the heavy artillery—Huntley and Brinkley anchored the coverage, and the supporting cast numbered some 300 news staffers, thirty-two cameras, and for the first time, on-site electronic editing. The all-out approach paid off as NBC's ratings beat those of CBS and ABC combined. *(Below)* On election night, NBC utilized split-screen technology to broadcast reports from *(clockwise)* David Brinkley, John Chancellor, Sander Vanocur, and Chet Huntley.

Every news program on the air looks essentially as we started it with The Huntley-Brinkley Report. *We more or less set the form for broadcasting news on television which is still used. No one has been able to think of a better way to do it.*

— DAVID BRINKLEY

Chet Huntley and David Brinkley were the first superstars to emerge from television news. Huntley, a newscaster in the Jack Webb just-the-facts-ma'am tradition, found his perfect partner in the droll, wry, and at times puckishly witty Brinkley. They first teamed up to anchor NBC's coverage of the 1956 national political conventions, and their synergy as a reporting duo changed the face of news broadcasting.

The Huntley-Brinkley Report was America's top-rated news program for most of its fourteen-year life span. It began in October 1956 after the duo's convention coverage and was expanded from fifteen minutes to a half-hour in 1963. This fast-paced newscast was a startling change from the days of *Camel News Caravan*. It brought personality and a new kind of intimacy to news reporting. Its success brought NBC News—and the entire TV news industry—a new level of authority. More people were getting their news from TV at dinnertime, specifically from the trustworthy Chet and David. In 1965, a consumer survey organization found that Chet and David were more recognizable in the U.S. than Cary Grant or Jimmy Stewart—or even John, Paul, George, and Ringo.

One of the hallmarks of the show was its crisp writing. Brinkley in particular was noted for penning short, straightforward sentences that registered with the viewer. Both men also understood—in a way that many others on the air before them had not—when to keep quiet and let the footage do the talking.

The appeal of the team was based not just on the rapport and repartee between the two anchors, but also on the novelty of their geographic separation—Huntley was in New York and Brinkley reported from Washington. Having newscasters in two different cities converse with one another was a new concept—at least at that time. Their signature closing exchange—"Goodnight, David...Goodnight, Chet"—was initially suggested by producer Reuven Frank, who had been seeking a way to bridge the geographic gap and introduce a stronger personal connection into the telecast. Huntley retired in August 1970. On the last broadcast, his final "Goodnight, David" was answered by Brinkley's "Goodbye, Chet."

THE TONIGHT SHOW — THE JACK PAAR ERA

The tone of the Jack Paar *Tonight Show* was urbane and thoughtful—perfectly suited for middle-class Americans looking to television for clues about how to behave in a newly affluent society. Steve Allen had been about high energy and music. He was a talented comedian who frequently took *The Tonight Show* into the audience or into the streets, and his youthful viewers loved it. Jack Paar, in contrast, loved sophisticated conversation with a lot of opinions. Beginning in 1957, he brought a new emphasis to the guest couch (no small piece of symbolism in an age fascinated by psychoanalysis), and he established a sedate atmosphere with José Melis and his orchestra. In short, Paar made the show like a witty, entertaining adult cocktail party, and grown-ups embraced this enjoyable short course in mature behavior— even if many of them saw it through their toes on the TV at the foot of the bed.

Paar was far from staid, however. He loved to argue and picked fights with Walter Winchell, Dorothy Kilgallen, Ed Sullivan, and even William Paley. He nurtured a regular group of eccentric and opinionated talkers, including Alexander King, Oscar Levant, Elsa Maxwell, Peter Ustinov, and Bea Lillie—with whom he fought and laughed and cried. A sensitive and compassionate man, Paar wore his heart on his sleeve and was openly emotional and intimate with his audience. He also courted controversy. He debated religion with Billy Graham, talked about the Mafia influence in the Teamsters with Robert Kennedy (which brought a lawsuit from Jimmy Hoffa), chatted about politics with Richard Nixon, and visited Albert Schweitzer in Africa to discuss apartheid. One of his most controversial segments was a visit to Cuba, where he offered his wholehearted

Sophisticated and stimulating folk such as Peggy Cass and then-Senator John F. Kennedy *(above)* in Paar's cocktail party atmosphere. The cocktail party analogy was punctuated by the way both Paar and announcer Hugh Downs *(opposite page, top, far left)* regularly dressed. Visitors to the show followed suit—note Peggy Cass's little black dress *(above)*—and the chic attire of the guests arrayed on Jack's couch *(opposite page, top)*. Paar's fighting with TV icon Ed Sullivan made the cover of *Life* magazine.

endorsement of Fidel Castro, which was a courageous and provocative position to take in Cold War America.

Paar provided the best description of himself: "I'm complicated, sentimental, lovable, honest, loyal, decent, generous, likable, and lonely. My personality is not split; it's shredded."

On February 11, 1960, Paar astonished viewers by walking off the program after he learned that NBC censors had edited a water-closet joke. Minutes into the opening of the show, he tearfully announced, "I am leaving *The Tonight Show*. There must be a better way of making a living than this"— leaving a stunned Hugh Downs to host the rest of the ninety-minute show. A month later, after lengthy negotiations with NBC executives, he returned, and his first words as he looked into the camera were: "As I was saying…" The actual end of his tenure at *The Tonight Show* came two years later on March 30, 1962.

THE FIRST TELEVISION PRESIDENT

John F. Kennedy's rise to prominence in national politics mirrored the growth of television. Throughout his life he used the medium more effectively than any public figure before him. JFK had charm, intelligence, and charisma that radiated from him in every situation, whether in one-on-one conversations or huge convention halls, and he knew how to bring those qualities to life on television. The effectiveness of radio for one of his idols, Franklin Delano Roosevelt, was not lost on Kennedy, but by the early 1950s, he saw television emerging as the dominant medium.

Many politicians after JFK have tried to emulate his mastery of television. For former TV actor Ronald Reagan, it came easily; and Bill Clinton took a lesson from JFK, enhancing his stature through televised appearances until his credibility was tainted by scandal.

JFK's education in television began in 1952, when, for the first time, seventy million viewers watched the Democratic and Republican conventions on TV.

As a young congressman, Kennedy closely observed national coverage of the six-day struggle that was the Democrats' first open convention since 1932. Americans were entranced by the dramas of delegate manipulations, backroom deals, and fights on the floor that resulted in the nomination of Adlai Stevenson. When JFK was sworn in as a senator on January 3, 1953, his personal secretary, Evelyn Lincoln, rushed around

the office searching for his blue shirt. Kennedy knew that this color would make him look best on TV. His father, Joseph Kennedy, was an expert at handling media and had arranged for JFK to be coached by a television executive in New England. Joe boasted, "We're going to sell Jack like soap flakes!" And they did.

By the time JFK was campaigning for the presidential nomination in 1958–59, studies showed that 78 percent of voters used television as their primary source of information to decide how they would vote in the 1960 election. In that campaign, Kennedy used television to establish a national visibility, prove his capability as a leader despite his youth, and overcome widespread prejudice against his Catholicism. A turning point in

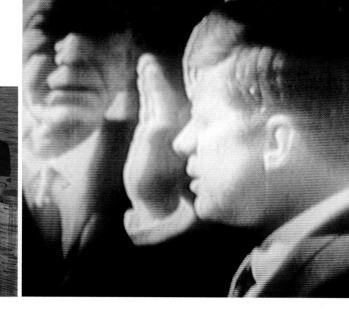

"And so, my fellow Americans: ask not what your country can do for you—ask what you can do for your country. My fellow citizens of the world: ask not what America will do for you, but what together we can do for the freedom of man."

– JFK INAUGURAL SPEECH, 1960

the primaries came in West Virginia, where the religious issue was a sticking point for the 95 percent Protestant population. By spending $34,000 on TV spots that emphasized JFK's strong stand on the separation of church and state, he was able to soundly defeat Hubert Humphrey, 61 to 39 percent.

Without a doubt, the decisive events in the 1960 elections were the first nationally televised debates between JFK and Richard Nixon. Visually, Kennedy had the advantage of a youthful, vigorous appearance, reinforced by a California tan and a dark blue suit that contrasted well with the set. Nixon, who had

strong statements on the issues—in fact, a poll of radio listeners showed Nixon had a slight edge. But seventy million viewers were focusing on what they saw, not what they heard. JFK looked presidential, erased any argument that his youth and relative inexperience would be a detriment, and was judged the winner.

Elected by a thin margin, Kennedy used television throughout his presidency to build consensus and political power. Before his inaugural speech on January 20, 1961, he insisted on not wearing his overcoat in the biting cold because he wanted to present a strong, youthful image of the

rights struggles, the Berlin Wall, the Nuclear Test Ban Treaty—all of the history-making events of the Kennedy administration—played like episodes in a hit TV show called *Camelot*. The president and his staff or family dominated TV news during the era, and as though that were not enough coverage, Jackie Kennedy hosted a one-hour *Tour of the White House* on February 14, 1962, that was broadcast simultaneously on NBC and CBS prime time and rebroadcast four nights later on ABC. Syndicated to fifty countries, it was the most widely seen documentary of the decade.

On November 22, 1963, JFK

ASSASSINATION

Almost immediately after President Kennedy was assassinated, regular programming was preempted on all three networks. From the first announcements of the shooting to the burial at Arlington National Cemetery, the country shared a period of shock and mourning through television. One of the saddest moments in our nation's history was also one of the proudest moments for television broadcasting, as the news, the emotions, the memories, and the images poured out of sets all over America in an extraordinary manifestation of grief. Frank McGee was right when he said, "This afternoon, wherever you were and whatever you might have been doing when you received the word of the death of President Kennedy, that is a moment that will be emblazoned in your memory and you will never forget it… as long as you live."

As preparations were being made on Sunday, November 24, to take the president's body to the Capitol Rotunda, NBC cut away from the coverage in Washington, D.C., to show accused

just spent two weeks in a hospital for a knee injury, had decided to hide his heavy beard with Max Factor's Lazy Shave, which melted under the hot TV lights and streaked down his face giving him the appearance of being sweaty. His gray suit blended into the monotone colors of the set behind him. Both men made

presidency to the TV cameras. Five days later, he held the first televised presidential press conference and dazzled viewers with his spontaneous answers to reporters' questions. The Cuban Missile Crisis, the Space Race, the Peace Corps, the antiracketeering legislation, Hyannis Port, the White House concerts, civil

arranged to make a thirteen-minute flight from Carswell Air Force Base in Fort Worth to Love Field in Dallas, rather than drive by car because the airport arrival provided a more dramatic scene for television cameras. In one of our greatest national tragedies, he was assassinated later that day in Dallas.

assassin Lee Harvey Oswald being transferred from the Dallas city jail to the county jail. It was the only network to be on the air live at 11:21 a.m. CST when club owner Jack Ruby slipped past the police lines and fired a fatal shot into Oswald. NBC reporter Tom Pettit's narration expressed the sense of disbelief at the scene as he repeated, "He's been shot! He's been shot!" CBS's Walter Cronkite, along with the rest of the country, heard the news by watching NBC.

TUNED IN, TURNED ON

Viewers tuning in to catch *Your Hit Parade* on Saturday night, September 7, 1957, may not have realized they were watching NBC history unfold before their eyes. But unfold it did. Right before the show began, an animated peacock—composed of six colors: maroon, orange, yellow, green, blue, and violet—opened its feathers grandly, as announcer Ben Grauer intoned: "The following program is brought to you in living color, on NBC!" Most viewers watched this soon-to-be-ubiquitous introduction on a black-and-white TV; color sets were still novelties at the time, not really catching on until the *Disney/Bonanza* era of the mid-sixties. But the National Broadcasting Company was announcing something big. As the world around us grew closer, faster, and more accessible; as television news of an increasingly turbulent world became ever more important; and as the space age was about to become a reality, NBC was going to lead us all into the future, with the best and most technologically advanced broadcasting, brought right into your home. That peacock wasn't just a network logo— it was a promise of American ingenuity and splendor: Life…in Living Color.

With the loss of innocence marked by the assassination of President Kennedy and the end of "Camelot," television struggled to reflect both the social turmoil of the time and wholesome prime-time fantasies. The hit shows of the era tell us much about

how America saw itself. We explored new frontiers with *Star Trek* and the triumphs of NASA (above, a crowd gathers around a TV in an auto dealership to witness the moon landing), yet we stayed earthbound with old-fashioned ideals of home and hearth (*Hazel*, *Bonanza*, *Father Knows Best*, and *Walt Disney's Wonderful World of Color*). We were fascinated with the high-tech espionage of *The Man from U.N.C.L.E.*, *I Spy*, and the delightfully witty *Get Smart*, while we watched Huntley and Brinkley closely for troubling details of the Cold War, the battle for civil rights, and the increasingly unwinnable war in Vietnam.

We watched *Julia* to see a woman stand up for her rights as a single, black, breadwinning Mom, yet we also watched *Jeannie* to see a genie disappear and reappear whenever it was most convenient for her "master." Some of us giggled at Dean's Golddiggers and loved his mellow melodies. Others lived for the rock 'n' roll messages of freedom in *The Monkees* and *Hullabaloo*. And then there was *Rowan & Martin's Laugh-In*, a show that showcased the counterculture through a comedic filter safe enough for even Republican presidential nominee Richard Nixon to be willing to ask "Sock it to Me?" on national television.

The world seemed to be rotating faster in the 1960s, and NBC—more often than not—expressed both the exhilaration and fears of a changing world more vividly, in full color, than ever before.

THE TIMES THEY ARE A-CHANGIN'

Few decades in history have been as turbulent as the 1960s. Until then, none had been played out before bewildered, shocked, and angry citizens in their living rooms. As the civil rights movement, the Cuban Missile Crisis, the Cold War, Vietnam, student unrest, and political assassinations rocked the country, audiences looked to television news, not just to bring them coverage of major stories but to help them sort it all out.

NBC News dealt with the explosive issues of the day through both reportage and in-depth analysis, and behind much of that coverage was a man named Reuven Frank. Frank, the original producer of *The Huntley-Brinkley Report*, became executive vice president and then president of NBC News during these tumultuous times. Despite tremendous pressure, Frank did not shrink from politically sensitive issues. In 1962, in the face of concerted opposition from the State Department, he produced and fought to air "The Tunnel," a documentary that chronicled the dangerous and laborious task of digging an escape tunnel from East Berlin—and its eventual use by fifty-nine refugees. The following year he produced "The Trouble with Water...Is People," a probing look at the politics of the Colorado River Project, in particular the environmental problems associated with the use of the river for irrigation.

That same year, NBC preempted an entire prime-time lineup to broadcast "The American Revolution '63," a three-hour documentary on the civil rights movement, airing it without commercial interruption. The Emmy-winning program placed NBC at the forefront of coverage on this issue. As the civil rights struggle grew more heated and at times violent, how television covered the movement became controversial. Amid suggestions that TV coverage of demonstrations was actually inciting black activism (and anti-Vietnam activism), Frank held steadfast in his belief that television had an obligation to present the news—however disquieting.

Most disquieting of all was Vietnam. The Korean conflict may have been glimpsed on our TV screens, but the Vietnam War received unprecedented coverage. Although the networks had initially dealt with Vietnam as an "us versus them" conflict, that attitude changed as the war dragged on. As reporters and cameramen went into combat side-by-side with U.S. troops, Americans received nightly battle updates, just like they got the weather or the baseball scores.

> "The highest power of television journalism is not in the transmission of information but in the transmission of experience."
>
> — REUVEN FRANK, PRESIDENT, NBC NEWS

Television didn't just cover the war; it played a crucial role in turning the tide of public opinion against the conflict, especially as Vietnam moved rapidly to center stage as a hot issue in 1968, an election year. Night after night, the footage, especially during February's Tet Offensive, made it clear that we were not really winning. Moreover, there was a great deal of debate about whether "winning" in the traditional military sense was even possible. Faced with censorship and outright misinformation from the government, reporters found it increasingly difficult to reconcile optimistic military press briefings with the images that were coming back from the field. As the inflated body counts reported by the Pentagon departed ever further from reality, many journalists were unable to mask their skepticism, and the "credibility gap" was born. In January, NBC reporter Frank McGee declared during a broadcast that the United States was losing the war. Anchor David Brinkley refrained from speaking about his opposition to the war on the air but did so in print in *TV Guide*. CBS anchor Walter Cronkite expressed skepticism about the war at about the same time.

These "no confidence" votes by prominent and respected on-air journalists shocked the White House. Lyndon Johnson was losing the battle to control the image of the war that was put before the American people. In February, when South Vietnamese Brigadier General Nguyen Ngoc Loan executed a Vietcong officer on a Saigon street in front of an NBC cameraman, Reuven Frank didn't hesitate to air the graphic footage, and viewers were universally appalled by the barbarism of the act. The scene became one of the enduring images of the war and contributed to the plummeting popularity of our involvement in a struggle where it was hard to tell the good guys from the bad guys, and where there was no clear-cut victory in sight.

Not only did TV coverage

humanize "the enemy," it also humanized opposition to the war. From the outset, the administration had tried to portray those who were antiwar as being anti-American—a collection of draft-dodging, pro-communist, hippie ingrates out to undermine the country. But protesters of the baby boom generation had been raised on television and knew how to generate media coverage. TV cameras captured not just the rock throwing and flag burning, but young women putting flowers down the gun barrels of riot police and students going limp as they were hauled off to jail. On March 31, 1968, Lyndon Johnson's surprise announcement that he would not run for reelection was met by unrestrained jubilation on college campuses, and the TV cameras transmitted those images as well.

Suddenly all of the nation's problems seemed to merge. Less than a week after Johnson's announcement, Martin Luther King was murdered and black neighborhoods were set ablaze

from coast to coast. In June, viewers watching California primary election returns were again shocked by a political homicide, this time the assassination of Robert Kennedy.

That August, the 1968 Democratic National Convention was held in Chicago. Although Mayor Richard Daley tried to confine TV coverage to the convention center itself and to isolate demonstrators from the TV cameras, he failed. What the country saw broadcast was later termed a "police riot," especially as TV-savvy demonstrators chanted, "The whole world is watching! The whole world is watching!" NBC was roundly criticized for devoting so much attention to the actions of the protestors. Mayor Daley asked for "equal time" to respond to what he considered NBC's biased coverage. In response, Reuven Frank said, "I set down the rule that if we could not cover live, we would cover with television tape as soon as it became available; if tape was

ruled out, we should do it with film; and if film was out of the question, we might try the sound signal from walkie-talkies and show still pictures on the television screen. But we would do what we could, as we could, to discharge our responsibility to the television audience to cover the entire story in the manner it had

come to expect....The managers of the convention have not yet learned well enough to realize what it means that television is there. The politician tends to see this as giving him access to the public. Now the public has access to him. The fact that television is there makes the difference."

EDWIN E. ALDRIN, JR

WE'RE ON THE MOON

NEIL ARMSTRONG

SPLASHDOWN!

THE NEW FRONTIER

(Circle) Frank McGee, NBC's main anchor for space coverage, was also noted for his reporting on the battle for civil rights. The success of our first manned space flights by Alan Shepard *(opposite, top)* and John Glenn *(right,* shown with wife Annie and then–Vice President Lyndon Johnson), made heroes of the *Mercury 7* astronauts. *(Top, left to right)* Television sets displayed the images and words of Buzz Aldrin *(top, left)* and Neil Armstrong *(top, mid-dle-right)* and the *Eagle* lunar landing module on the moon's surface *(top, middle-left).* TV coverage also followed the mission through to splashdown and recovery *(top, far right).*

In October of 1957, Americans were shaken to hear the "beep…beep" of *Sputnik* broadcast on radio and TV news reports. The Soviet launch of the first orbital satellite was a complete success, the Space Age had begun, and the United States—with its embarrassing spate of early "missile fizzles"—looked like it had been left behind at the starting gate. By the time of Yuri Gagarin's orbital flight in 1961, the "race for space" had become a must-win part of the Cold War, and President Kennedy had boldly announced that the United States would land on the moon before the end of the decade. Television news, eager to report uplifting American successes in a turbu-lent era, was ready to cover the race in unprecedented depth.

For Americans fresh from an infatuation with the TV western, NASA's telegenic astronauts—clean-cut, polite, and brave—were the Space Age equivalent of the good guys in the white hats. Beginning with the suborbital launch of Alan Shepard in 1961 and the orbital mission of John Glenn the following year, what unfolded live on television was a classic hero saga played large on the stage JFK had christened the New Frontier.

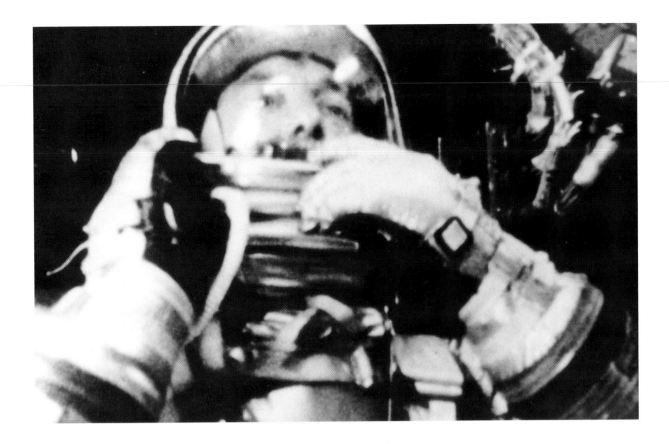

NBC News took on the challenge of space coverage as the story of the decade, even as a patriotic necessity. It commandeered Studio 8H as its "mission control" for NASA reporting, equipping the large studio with tracking maps and up-to-date simulations of the events in space. Veteran news-caster Frank McGee became NBC's resident expert on the space program, along with on-location reporter Jay Barbree.

The launches from Cape Canaveral (Cape Kennedy, for some of these years) became moments of national bonding via the medium of television, and the culmination of TV's love affair with the space pro-gram was surely the *Apollo 11* mission. In July 1969, Neil Armstrong and Buzz Aldrin left Michael Collins in the

Columbia, boarded the lunar expeditionary module (LEM) known as the *Eagle,* and went to the moon.

Understanding the power of television, NASA had designed the live broadcast of the moonwalk into the *Apollo 11* mission. TV signals were transmitted from the craggy surface to three stations 120 degrees apart on the Earth's surface (one in the Mojave Desert, another in Spain, and the third in Australia) then to the Kennedy Space Center in Houston.

The mission itself was astonishing enough, but more amazing was that 600 million people—one-fifth of the world's population—watched it live on television. The nation held its breath as the two Americans maneuvered toward

the lunar surface with Armstrong taking over manual control of the module when the original designated landing site proved to be too rough: "Looking good, down a half... thirty feet, down two and a half...kicking up some dust... drifting to the right...okay. Engine stop. Houston, Tranquility base here. The *Eagle* has landed." A few hours later, Armstrong took those historic first steps, transmitted to TV sets on Earth in fuzzy, glorious, astonishing black-and-white.

The network devoted sixty hours of coverage to the lunar mission, including thirty-one hours nonstop from the 20th through the 21st of July. McGee was at the anchor desk for twenty-four of those thirty-one hours. That year, NBC won an Emmy for its space coverage.

SPACE WITNESS

Like Frank McGee, NBC journalist Jay Barbree fell into covering the space program because Florida was part of his assigned territory from the days of the civil rights movement. Barbree, though, has a distinction no other person in the world will ever be able to claim: He is the only journalist to have witnessed every American space mission of the twentieth century.

In 1986, Barbree, with Tom Brokaw, broke the news of the reason behind the shuttle *Challenger* explosion live on the *NBC Nightly News. The New York Times, Newsweek,* and others credited him with uncovering the facts behind the year's top story, and Jay won his second Emmy. (He shared his first for space coverage in the year of the first moon landing.)

Larry King once wrote, "Jay Barbree of NBC News is arguably the best correspondent to ever cover the space program."

Today, Barbree is still reporting for MSNBC, CNBC, *NBC Nightly News with Tom Brokaw,* and the *Today* show, and has also witnessed every mission of the twenty-first century. He is a finalist to be the first journalist in space.

BEAM ME UP, SCOTTY!

The excitement of the real NASA space program inevitably spilled over into television entertainment, where Gene Roddenberry envisioned a "*Wagon Train* to the stars" set in the twenty-third century. *Star Trek* was filled with science-fiction adventures in space, as well as familiar human struggles.

Quickly dubbed "space opera," the show developed a passionate youthful following that sustained the original series through three years (1966–69), despite network threats of cancellation. NBC was not unreasonable to consider dumping a show that placed a dismal fifty-second in its initial season.

Happily, executives were swayed by more than a million letters of support from Trekkies.

The spaceship *Enterprise*, with its sturdy tritanium hull, zoomed around the galaxy—often at "warp speed"—finding new civilizations everywhere and spreading the gospel of peace and

democracy. Embracing space as "the final frontier," the show intentionally echoed the romantic era of television westerns. Roddenberry called upon the themes and tropes he had mastered as a writer for *Have Gun, Will Travel* and *Bat Masterson*: frontier justice, the gunfight, posse loyalty, and love at the edge of nowhere.

(*Circle*) The Vulcan salute.
(*Above, left to right*) Frank Gorshin as a half-black, half-white man; the starship *Enterprise*; Kirk explores his feminine side in "Trouble with Tribbles."
(*Right*) On the Transporter.

The crew was multiethnic and multispecies. The cast (*opposite*) included (back row, left to right) James Doohan (Chief Engineer Montgomery "Scotty" Scott), Walter Koenig (Security Chief/Navigator Ensign Pavel Chekov), Nichelle Nichols (Communications Officer Lt. Nyota Uhura), and George Takei (Flight Control Officer Lt. Hikaru Sulu); and (front row, left to right) DeForest Kelley (Chief Medical Officer Leonard "Bones" McCoy), Majel Barrett (Nurse Christine Chapel), William Shatner (Capt. James Kirk), and Leonard Nimoy (Vulcan First Officer/Science Officer Lt. Cmdr. Spock).

He was supported by some of science fiction's literary giants, including Harlan Ellison, Robert Bloch, Norman Spinrad, and Theodore Sturgeon, who wrote for the show. Fans loved the inventiveness of teleportation, space warps, photon torpedoes, Klingons, Romulans, ion storms, androids, space hippies, giant amoebas, and tribbles. However, even as the *Enterprise* crew confronted new forms of life on other planets, they often explored various facets of the serious question: What does it mean to be human?

The original series ("TOS" in Trekland) was cancelled in September 1969, apparently because sponsors were not interested in the youthful demographic drawn to the show. But it was an idea that refused to die. Four more series followed over the next thirty years: *Star Trek: The Next Generation*, *Star Trek: Deep Space Nine*, *Star Trek: Voyager*, and *Enterprise*. Nine motion pictures, 150 novels, and countless reruns later, *Star Trek*

has become deeply woven into the fabric of American culture. NASA named its prototype space shuttle the *Enterprise*, and Roddenberry was the first television writer to be honored with a star on

Hollywood Boulevard. *Star Trek* truly went boldly where no TV show had gone before and honored the Vulcan salute—come on, get those split fingers up there— "Live long and prosper."

Spies Like Us

Espionage programs such as *The Man from U.N.C.L.E.*, *I Spy*, and *Get Smart* played off both the make-believe cloak-and-dagger glamour of James Bond and real-life fears of Soviet expansion and nuclear annihilation. *I Spy* (above) was driven by the chemistry between its two stars, Robert Culp and Bill Cosby. In *The Man from U.N.C.L.E.* (below), Robert Vaughn and David McCallum used both devastating puns and deadly force against the enemy. In *Get Smart* (opposite), cartoon gadgetry, such as the famous shoe phone, and Barbara Feldon (Agent 99) often saved Don Adams as Agent 86—most often from himself.

Television never met a fad it didn't like, and the spy genre was no exception. After the first James Bond movie, *Dr. No*, hit big in theaters, TV rushed to cash in. First out of the box was *The Man from U.N.C.L.E.*, starring Robert Vaughn as the suave, shaken-not-stirred agent Napoleon Solo and David McCallum as his broodingly handsome Soviet partner, Illya Kuryakin—the first on-air détente duo of the Cold War. Leo G. Carroll (familiar to older viewers as Cosmo Topper) portrayed their spy-master-in-chief, Alexander Waverly, who directed U.N.C.L.E.'s activities from

its world headquarters, cleverly accessed through Del Floria's tailor shop in Manhattan.

The men from U.N.C.L.E. (United Network Command for Law Enforcement) were in constant battle with the nefarious agents of THRUSH—the evildoers behind every wickedness on Earth. In each episode (all named "The —— Affair") the men from U.N.C.L.E. battled cartoonishly grotesque foes, mass hypnosis, killer bees, even hiccup gas. They ultimately saved the day, thanks to their wits and witticisms—wordplay was as important as swordplay and gunfire in the series. Invariably, Solo and Kuryakin were aided

by the heroics of an ordinary citizen who had unwittingly become caught up in international intrigue.

At a deeper level, the spy genre was a response to the anxieties of the Cold War and the real threat of nuclear war underlying the shadowy battles of the CIA and the KGB. From its debut in 1964, *U.N.C.L.E.* was wildly popular with college students, who responded to its tongue-in-cheek spoofery and in-joke references to contemporary political figures. Pinups of Vaughn and especially McCallum adorned the rooms of coeds across the country. Even though *U.N.C.L.E.* was a pop culture phenomenon with this

the beautiful and clever Agent 99, portrayed by Barbara Feldon. Although she was bright, 99 was no feminist icon. As many times as she saved Smart, she made sure he got all the credit for their success.

After five seasons on the air, *Get Smart* has lived on as a cult favorite, in part because of enduring catchphrases such as Smart's apologetic "Sorry about that, Chief," but more because of Smart's hysterically off-the-wall spy gadgetry. Seemingly invented by MI-5's Q under orders from Monty Python, the gizmos were silly both in form and function, and viewers never tired of them, especially the shoe-phone, which was clearly an early cell phone.

"Would you believe...?"

desirable demographic, ratings were feeble at first—which may say more about the Nielsens than about the show. Because college kids were considered an "institutional population" (like prisoners and mental patients), their viewing habits were not surveyed. Eventually, the rest of the country caught on.

I Spy premiered the year after *U.N.C.L.E.* Robert Culp played tennis pro Kelly Robinson, and Bill Cosby was Alexander Scott, his trainer and pal. The two used the tennis circuit as a cover for their espionage activities. Although having a black actor

in a lead dramatic role was a novelty, it was an even bigger accomplishment that no big deal was made of it. *I Spy* was the first color-blind program on network TV.

One of the hallmarks of the show was the good-natured bantering between Kelly and Scotty. Unlike the campy, over-the-top humor of *U.N.C.L.E.*, however, the jokes on *I Spy* were more down-to-earth. In fact, everything about *I Spy* was more realistic. Kelly and Scotty were no cardboard heroes; they were fully developed characters who were allowed to explore the human aspect of espionage,

warts and all. They got injured, second-guessed their orders, and found shades of gray in dealings with adversaries who were no longer the epitome of evil.

Get Smart, which also debuted in 1965, was espionage on a banana peel. Don Adams played bumbling Agent 86, whose real name was Maxwell Smart. Created by veteran comedy writers Buck Henry and Mel Brooks, Smart's cinematic lineage stemmed more from Inspector Clouseau than from James Bond. Whatever triumphs he had were due to the efforts of his partner,

The Wonderful World of Color

(Right) Mickey Mouse and two old friends, former Mickey Mouse Club stars Darlene Gillespie and Annette Funicello, get in the spirit for the Christmas season, together again in "Mickey's 40th Anniversary" on NBC's *Walt Disney's Wonderful World of Color.* *(Above)* Dean Jones was a frequent star of Disney movies on both the small and large screens. *(Opposite)* Professor Ludwig von Drake plucks a peacock feather as Uncle Walt looks on.

On the suburban prestige meter of the early 1960s, getting a color TV ranked just below getting a swimming pool. As was the case with the advent of both radio and black-and-white television, pioneering families with the first color set on the block experienced a sudden surge in popularity, and wide-eyed kids gathered around the new tube to check out what their favorite shows "really" looked like in "living color." The program that showed off best those breathtaking hues was *Walt Disney's Wonderful World of Color.* The weekly series had started on ABC in 1954, but in 1961, Disney jumped ship for NBC, which had the color broadcasting capability that ABC then lacked.

With the move came the introduction of Professor Ludwig von Drake—Donald Duck's uncle. The German-accented Professor, the first Disney cartoon character created for television, starred in the show's first broadcast—the appropriately named cartoon "An Adventure in Color," which aired on September 24, 1961.

Despite a couple of name revisions for the program and even the death of Walt Disney in 1966, the show remained a durable fixture on NBC's Sunday-evening lineup for twenty years. The program was originally hosted by Uncle Walt himself, who was comfortable conversing with both children and cartoon characters. Disney's presence helped put the "family values" stamp of approval not just on the program, but on TV as an entertainment medium.

Although NBC had been broadcasting some shows in color since late 1953, early sets were expensive and erratic. Despite being well publicized, the shows were not seen in color by many. The combined lures, however, of *Wonderful World of Color* and *Bonanza* made color sets irresistible. From the show's opening, with Tinkerbell sprinkling a rainbow of fairy dust over Cinderella's castle as the chorus crooned "Color…," everything about the show sold the desirability of color television. *Bonanza* followed, also in color, and older kids looked forward to the special privilege of staying up to watch it. Much as the popularity of *Howdy Doody* had kids clamoring for a black-and-white set a decade earlier, the magic of color set off a new round of badgering, and parents across the country caved in.

Disney's preeminence in children's entertainment today owes a debt to twenty years of NBC Sunday nights and the promotional value of *Walt Disney's Wonderful World of Color.* In the two decades since, the Disney empire has grown dramatically under the guidance of longtime CEO Michael Eisner.

With *Wonderful World of Color* and *Bonanza*, NBC finally had a programming block that was more than a match for Ed Sullivan on CBS. Probably more than any others, these two shows together form the warm and fuzzy core of television history for baby boomers.

(Above) The *Laugh-In* company of regulars, with guest stars John Wayne and Tiny Tim. *(Back row, left to right)* Johnny Brown, Larry Hovis, Tiny Tim, Lily Tomlin, Barbara Sharma, Alan Sues. *(Middle row, left to right)* Joanne Worley, Anne Elder, Ruth Buzzi, Gary Owens, Dennis Allen, Judy Carne, Theresa Graves, Richard Dawson. *(Front row, left to right)* Dan Rowan, John Wayne, Dick Martin.

"Sock It to Me!"

With its wire-to-wire shtick, one-liners, and non sequiturs, *Rowan & Martin's Laugh-In* wrote a new chapter on television comedy. Never had so many gags been delivered so rapidly, and never had a show produced so many memorable characters. In its use of recurring characters and catchphrases, *Laugh-In* influenced later comedy shows such as *Saturday Night Live*, and with its quick cuts, presaged the kind of camera work commonly associated with music videos.

Arriving in 1968 to a television schedule dominated by unthreatening fare such as *Gomer Pyle, U.S.M.C.* and *Bonanza*, *Rowan & Martin's Laugh-In* brought an anarchic energy to the screen that perfectly captured the times. If America could have "sit-ins" and "teach-ins," why not a "laugh-in"? The show managed to appeal not just to the irreverent jeans-clad younger generation but resonated with audiences across the demographic gamut, earning the No. 1 ratings spot in each of its first two full seasons.

Laugh-In started as a one-time special in the fall of 1967, but it proved such a hit that a weekly series was ordered to debut the following January. Airing during one of our nation's more turbulent eras, the show both embodied

and lampooned the cultural upheavals of the times, from its debut through its final broadcast in May 1973. Stylistically, the show was clearly in tune with the pop sensibilities of the time. Politically speaking, however, antiestablishment messages were safely wrapped in silliness. Lampooning everything in sight, *Laugh-In* made irreverence more about aesthetics than politics, and the show quickly had scores of celebrities and politicians clamoring for a guest appearance. Even Richard Nixon couldn't resist.

Produced by George Schlatter, *Laugh-In* was hosted by the urbane Dan Rowan and off-the-wall Dick Martin. Many of its large ensemble cast of unknown actors—and many of their signature phrases—became household

words. Arte Johnson's comically menacing German soldier murmuring "Verrrrry innnterestingggg" in exaggerated imitation of stock characters from World War II movies; Judy Carne's "Sock it to me," invariably followed by a cold shower, the camera zooming in on her dripping face; Dick Martin's challenging "Look that up in your *Funk & Wagnalls*"—a reference to a popular encyclopedia of the 1960s.

Few television shows have captured the spirit of their times so completely and few have wielded as much influence. For this, and for its many technical and aesthetic innovations, *Rowan & Martin's Laugh-In* remains one of the most significant series in television history.

Many *Laugh-In* performers became indelibly linked with the recurring characters they portrayed. The show brought fame to Lily Tomlin, who gave audiences precocious tot Edith Ann *(above, left)* and Ernestine the Telephone Operator—and her famous line, "Is this the party to whom I am speaking? (snort snort)"

(Above, right) Buzzi's frumpy Gladys and Johnson's old-man-on-the-make Tyrone, seen here on their park bench with guest Ringo Starr. Tyrone pursued Gladys relentlessly on the show, and week after week he would be rewarded with a predictable smack from her pocketbook that would topple him over like a stiff board.

GOLDIE HAWN is perhaps best known for her starring roles in movies such as *Cactus Flower*, *Shampoo*, and *Private Benjamin*. But she got her major break in show business as America's favorite ding-a-ling on *Laugh-In*. "There was an NBC executive who was watching rehearsals and complained to me about this blonde girl who couldn't keep anything straight," recalls Schlatter. "He just didn't get it." She was notorious for her outrageous ad-libs and for her infectious giggle, which often claimed fellow cast members as helpless victims. One of the most memorable recurring skits on *Laugh-In* was Goldie-as-op-art, bikini-clad, and adorned with gags and humorous graffiti.

The much-feared Flying Fickle Finger of Fate Award, delivered with deadpan solemnity by ROWAN AND MARTIN, was the precursor of humorous takes on the news that eventually became a staple of later comedy programs. "I had worked with Dan and Dick in saloons and they were the funniest nightclub act ever, but at that time there was no place for them on television," says Schlatter. "They were ready to break up when I persuaded them to host *Laugh-In*, and they were perfect for that show."

"You Bet Your Bippy!"

Appearing as a guest on *Laugh-In* was considered a coup, and Schlatter sought out a diverse mix of guests, who willingly participated in the spoofs and sight gags of the show. (Imagine John Wayne in a feather boa.) Shown here, TINY TIM, clad à la Liberace, singing his hit, "Tiptoe through the Tulips," accompanying himself on the ukulele. "Tiny Tim was just so weird nobody could figure him out," recalls Schlatter. "Dick Martin's reactions to seeing him were priceless. Tiny Tim became a star because he was so weird and vulnerable and very intelligent."

THE LAUGH-IN COCKTAIL PARTY was a brilliant innovation. As cast members danced onstage, periodically the music would stop and the action would freeze, allowing members of the company to wisecrack and ridicule current news events or the affairs of the day.

THE JOKE WALL was the traditional closer of the show. Like a clock with so many crazy cuckoos, the doors would pop open and one-liners would burst forth from members of the cast. "The Joke Wall was created because the set designers brought in a fabric for the script book and the fabric was great," remembers Schlatter. "I said, wouldn't it be great if you could open windows in those panels? And they did." (The version of the wall shown here is from the short-lived revival of the show in the late seventies.)

GEORGE SCHLATTER

"*Laugh-In* was an accident. I had tried to sell it for four years but nobody understood it. Finally, NBC literally had nothing to put on after the 1967 *Miss America Pageant* and decided to take a chance on me. There was a strong feeling that this show would be a disaster, but it only cost them $125,000 to fill the air time. When I ran the first rough cut for the execs, they all laughed hysterically, and then they said: 'You can't do this. This isn't a television show. There's no opening, no closing, no middle, no production numbers.' I said: 'OK, this is a different kind of show than the variety shows I produced for you before. But you laughed. You got it. Give it a chance.' NBC President Herb Schlosser had the courage and confidence to put *Laugh-In* on the air, and, the rest, as they say, is history.

"The show was always a great playpen for me. It came out of burlesque, radio, Fred Allen, and vaudeville. It came out of all of the great comedy things that preceded it: Milton Berle, Steve Allen, Sid Caesar, Jackie Gleason, knock-knock jokes, *That Was the Week That Was, The Goon Show, Carry On, Nurse*, all of the British comedies. I often credited Ernie Kovacs because I learned so much about television comedy from him. We even did Henny Youngman jokes. We stole, lifted, copied, appropriated, or revised every known form of comedy. Then we put it into an electronic bag and shook it up.

"*Laugh-In* was a total blast of outrageous, irreverent, machine-gun comedy, a combination of silly and meaningful or sexy and political. But there was a balance among those elements. If you took out one of the political pieces, suddenly the show became too silly. If you took out the silly, it suddenly became angry. So it was a question of balance."

THE GAME WITHIN THE SUPER GAME

(Above) Kyle Rote interviews Joe Namath in the locker room after the Jets' historic upset over the Colts. *(Below)* Legendary coach Vince Lombardi, surrounded by the media, proudly displays the game ball after his Packers win the Super Bowl. *(Opposite, top)* Green Bay Packers quarterback Bart Starr steps up to loft a pass against the AFL's Oakland Raiders in the second AFL-NFL World Championship Game. *(Opposite, below)* Namath gets a hug in celebration of the huge win.

On October 22, 1939, NBC aired the first televised National Football League game. The Brooklyn Dodgers defeated the Philadelphia Eagles, 23-14. Few took notice—literally. Only about 1,000 homes in New York City were able to pick up the fuzzy signal. It wasn't until the 1958 NFL Championship Game that the league and television really hit it off.

Then came the Super Bowl, and things have never been the same since.

The first AFL-NFL World Championship Game, as the original event was officially called (the name change occurred two seasons later), was played at the Los Angeles Coliseum on January 15, 1967, pitting the American Football League champion Kansas City Chiefs against the National Football League champion Green Bay Packers. The one-game playoff figured prominently in the grand plan of then-AFL Commissioner Al Davis and NFL Commissioner Pete Rozelle to merge the competing leagues, even though regular-season games weren't scheduled until 1970.

Perhaps in the spirit of first-time competition, both NBC and CBS—already the weekly broadcasters of the AFL and NFL, respectively— were granted rights to televise the inaugural Super Bowl. NBC matched its booth-mates, Curt Gowdy and Paul Christman, against CBS's four-man crew of Ray Scott, Jack Whitaker, Frank Gifford, and Pat Summerall. While they shared a common feed from CBS for the game itself, the networks vied for pregame coverage—at one point Gifford and Christman scrambled onto the field to simultaneously interview Packers head coach Vince Lombardi.

The off-the-field game featured other odd plays. As sportscasting lore has it, NBC producer Ted Nathanson arranged to have as big a TV set as could be found mounted in the mobile production truck. He trained a camera on the screen, occasionally zooming in and beaming that tighter shot over the air. A confused CBS crew apparently couldn't figure out how NBC managed to get its "exclusives." In the end, a combined national audience of eighty-five million witnessed a close first half, before Green Bay turned it on and routed the Chiefs, 35-10.

Super Bowl II, seen only on CBS, marked another victory for

the Pack—33-14 over Davis's Oakland Raiders. It was also Lombardi's final game with Green Bay, with whom he had won six Western Conference championships, five NFL championships, and two Super Bowls. Appropriately, the Tiffany-designed statuette presented to today's Super Bowl winner is named the Vince Lombardi Trophy.

The NFL alternated broadcast rights between CBS and NBC until Super Bowl XIX in 1985, and while eventually ABC and Fox got in on the Super Bowl act, the four most-watched Super Bowls all aired on NBC. A record audience of 138.5 million watched Dallas defeat Pittsburgh 27-17

in Super Bowl XXX in 1996.

The most memorable Super Bowl was also on NBC. On paper, Super Bowl III appeared to be a cakewalk for the NFL's mighty Baltimore Colts, who lost only one of their fourteen games during the 1968 season and stampeded the Cleveland Browns, 34-0, for their league title. Yet the AFL champion New York Jets and their brash quarterback, Joe Namath, would have none of that. The Thursday before the big game, "Broadway Joe" went so far as to pronounce to reporters, "We're going to win the game. I guarantee it."

Naturally, the pledge only turned up the heat of anticipation. "They could have

sold 150,000 tickets to the game," said Curt Gowdy, who called the game. In fact, more than 75,000 fans packed Miami's Orange Bowl on January 12, 1969, while another fifty-five million viewers witnessed one of the greatest upsets in sports history. Namath backed up his words, completing 17 of 28 passes for 206 yards, Matt Snell rushed for 121 yards and a touchdown, Jim Turner kicked three field goals, and the dominating defense of the Jets notched four turnovers, including four interceptions. "That game," the well-traveled Gowdy stated thirty years later, "will always stand out as the most memorable event in my broadcasting career."

The *Today* Show — The Walters and Downs Era

Shortly after the *Today* show got started in the early fifties, a young woman right out of college was trying to get a job on the program. Buck Prince, one of the show's producers, told her there was nothing available. As she got up to leave, the woman defiantly told Prince she'd be back. "One day everyone is going to know about me at NBC," said Barbara Walters, "and I hope you're going to be around to remember this visit."

She was right.

In the fifties and early sixties, a series of attractive and pleasant women (including Estelle Parsons, Lee Meriwether, Florence Henderson, and Anita Colby) came and went, known as "*Today* Girls." They chatted about the weather, opined about fashion, and smiled a lot. Meanwhile, the male hosts—from Garroway (who retired in 1961) to John Chancellor (a serious newsman, uncomfortable with the show-biz aspects of his job) to Hugh Downs (Jack Paar's famously erudite announcer)—presided over a show steadily losing focus, momentum, and ratings.

By 1964, the latest "*Today* Girl," Maureen O'Sullivan, was let go after a rocky six-month stint with co-host Downs. Barbara Walters, who—true to her word—was back at NBC as a *Today* show writer and reporter, campaigned heavily for the job. Despite producer Al Morgan's concerns that Walters was too "Jewish" for mainstream American audiences, and that her now-famous voice inflection would grate on viewers, Walters was finally given her long-awaited shot.

Immediately, the chemistry was apparent. Hugh was an excellent host: comfortable, low-key, quick on his feet, and very knowledgeable about a wide variety of subjects. In Barbara, he finally found an acerbic complement to his mellower journalistic instincts.

(Above) *Today*'s "Salute to Duke Ellington," November 5, 1964. (Opposite, top) Barbara Walters, Joe Garagiola, Hugh Downs, and Frank Blair. (Opposite, bottom) The *Today* set looked quite different forty years ago when Downs sat anchor-style with Jack Lescoulie and Maureen O'Sullivan.

one omnipresent today. The hosts, especially Walters, went easily from hard news to entertainment news, subtly and steadily blurring the lines between the two. Barbara would ask a Hollywood star's opinion of the political landscape, and ask a Beltway veteran if he ever felt lonely.

She was—and still is—highly skilled at mixing the personal with the political, the seemingly trivial with the profound. Barbara Walters understands a principle that has deeply influenced news coverage at NBC News and elsewhere: The essential aspect of a news story is not the bare facts…but how it touches our shared humanity.

And so the second golden age of *Today* was born. Unlike the "Girls" who had preceded her, Barbara would go in for the kill. She would pull up the slack on a dull interview by asking the kind of obvious questions that viewers would have on their minds but that more "experienced" journalists tended to avoid. (*Newsweek* magazine once characterized her questions as "dum-dum bullets swaddled in angora.")

By 1967, when sportscaster Joe Garagiola joined the crew—which still included personable newsreader Frank Blair, a *Today* veteran since 1953—the show was getting higher ratings than ever. Barbara's rise coincided with the women's movement and with a growing seriousness on the show championed by producer Al Morgan. Under Morgan's tenure, Downs, Walters, and Garagiola concentrated on the troubling issues of a fast-moving era: the Vietnam War, the political assassinations, and the struggle for civil rights.

Although the show was a major political force of the era (LBJ was a daily viewer), *Today* was beginning to pioneer a new form of television journalism—

You've Got a Long Way to Go, Baby

If Betty Friedan, Germaine Greer, Gloria Steinem, and other pioneers of the Women's Movement in the 1960s needed reminders of what they were up against, all they had to do was turn on the television. The Golddiggers *(right, surrounding Dean Martin)* were the embodiments of antifeminist stereotypes. Barbara Eden in her diaphanous harem outfit *(above and opposite page)* would go up in smoke when she crossed her arms, nodded her head, and disappeared.

Despite having contributed greatly to the war effort in factories and offices during World War II, many American women resumed their traditional roles in the postwar era. In 1963, Betty Friedan's plea for recognition of women in a male-dominated world, *The Feminine Mystique*, had little immediate impact, and on television, for the most part, female stereotyping was visible everywhere. There were exceptions, such as Dinah Shore, Arlene Francis, and Loretta Young, but the stars of most shows were men, and the views expressed in both variety shows and serials on all networks were often sexist by today's standards.

The chorus line of pretty women was a staple of television from its earliest days, an accepted part of variety shows inherited from Broadway and vaudeville. Dean Martin took the concept to extremes. On the *Dean Martin Show*, he was practically decorated with beautiful young women. When the show debuted in September 1965, they were known simply as "Dean's girls," and their role on the show, in addition to providing sex appeal, appeared to be the adoration of Dino. Later, Dean's ladies' auxiliary was dubbed the Golddiggers, twelve young women who sang, danced, and performed occasionally in skits. Eventually, the Golddiggers were so popular that they hosted their own syndicated show without Dean. Meanwhile, Martin formed yet another collection of women, the Ding-a-Ling Sisters, who provided the show with one of its weekly highlights as they sang

JULIA

Reaching back to Eddie "Rochester" Anderson on *The Jack Benny Show* or Ethel Waters in *Beulah*, NBC had presented a number of African-American characters. The network stood by Nat "King" Cole's variety show when most of the advertising agencies would not. Still, more than a decade passed between Nat's show in 1957 and *Julia* in 1968. Julia Baker, played by Diahann Carroll, was a refreshing black image on television. She was a nurse, a respected professional, and, if not exactly a feminist, a strong, contemporary woman. A single mother after her husband died in Vietnam, Julia was devoted to her son, Corey, played by Marc Copage, but pursued several love interests. Carroll had a quiet elegance—not to mention a dry wit—that attracted viewers. The show was an immediate hit and continued to do well in the ratings for its four-year run. Although some critics at the time complained that Julia was not an accurate portrayal of the real hardships most black Americans endured, in retrospect, the show was a positive presentation of an African-American woman and her son living with dignity and in harmony with her white neighbors.

"C'mon Down, Dean" while they giggled and wiggled.

One of the most innovative ways to bring sex to the sitcom was seen in *I Dream of Jeannie*. The premise that creator/producer Sidney Sheldon sold to NBC was that astronaut Tony Nelson (Larry Hagman) finds a mysterious bottle on a deserted island during an aborted space mission. In the bottle is Jeannie, a 2,000-year-old genie, played by gorgeous Barbara Eden, who becomes Tony's every-man's-wish-come-true.

"NBC was very upset when they realized that an unmarried young woman would be running around the home of an unmarried young man in this show—even if she was a genie," recalled Sheldon. "The censors complained about her navel and about the flirtatious way she winked. But the audience winked at the premise along with us and kept the show popular for five years."

Perhaps the last straw for sexism and silliness was

My Mother the Car—a 1965 show that still shows up on lists of the Ten Worst Television Shows of All Time. Poor Jerry Van Dyke, as lawyer Dave Crabtree, discovers that his mother, Gladys, has been reincarnated as a 1928 Porter sedan. Only Dave can hear his mom, and Ann Sothern, as Mom's voice, never appears.

SANDS THROUGH THE HOURGLASS

(Above) The cast of *Sunset Beach*. (Opposite, right, from left to right) *Another World*'s Ryan (Paul Michael Valley), Jake (Tom Eplin), Paulina (Judy Evan-Lucciano), Amanda (Christine Tucci), and Kathleen (Julie Osborn). (Opposite, left) *Days of our Lives*'s Alice and Tom Horton (Frances Reid and MacDonald Carey). (Opposite, bottom) *Passions*'s Sheridan and Luis (McKenzie Westmore and Galen Gering). (Opposite, sidebar) *Passions*'s Tabitha (Juliet Mills) and her doll Timmy (Josh Ryan Evans). (Below) Two scenes from *Days*: (left) Peter Reckell dances with Kristian Alfonso; (right) Drake Hogestyn lights a candle with Deidre Hall.

Like sands through the hourglass, so are the days of our lives.
– INTRODUCTION BY MACDONALD CAREY TO *DAYS OF OUR LIVES*, HEARD SINCE 1965

There's something both relentlessly modern and reassuringly old-fashioned about soap operas—as they've been called since detergent companies realized that daytime dramas were a great way to sell suds to housewives. Soap operas constantly introduce new characters and plotlines, yet they weave their endlessly intricate stories across years, decades, and generations. Every day is new, yet the shows themselves are among the oldest in broadcasting history. The stories always revolve around love and treachery, hope and doom, yet there is new ground to be broken in this classic genre— a healthy and fascinating part of NBC's past, present, and future.

It all goes back to Irna Phillips. A little-known name outside the world of soaps, Irna was a Chicago spinster who wrote, at her peak of productivity, approximately two million words a year for the several radio programs she supervised, including *Today's Children, The Guiding Light*, and *Young Doctor Malone*. Almost single-handedly inventing the genre, Irna—along with the married couple Ted and Betty Corday—also created *Days of our Lives*, which first aired as a half-hour show on November 8, 1965 (the first daytime serial produced in color).

Days of our Lives is now an hour long and still a family affair: It is produced by Ted's and Betty's son, Ken Corday. "When my father created *Days of our Lives* in partnership with Irna, he never imagined the family legacy he was establishing," says Corday, who is grateful to be bringing his parents' show, healthier than ever, into the twenty-first century. "*Days* has managed to maintain its popularity by not reinventing the wheel. We tell the same heart-warming love stories that have been told since the inception, especially with regard to the all-important first love."

A show that *is* reinventing

INTERVIEW

JAMES E. REILLY

James E. Reilly is the creator and head writer of *Passions*. "In creating *Passions*, I wanted a show people would talk about. When I pitched the show, I didn't think NBC would go for it, but they loved it. From the start, the goal was to develop something unique that would appeal to a younger and more diverse audience than the traditional soap, while not abandoning our roots in the genre. *Passions* is classic soap storytelling with a supernatural twist, an hour of pure entertainment every day. We have our traditional super-couples, vixens, and villains. In addition, we have a witch, a talking doll, and the occasional demon and warlock.

"I think *Passions* represents a new era in daytime television. Not only have we found a way to connect with younger viewers—which is essential to the future of soaps—but we've also accomplished many things that didn't seem possible for daytime television. The success of our tie-in novel, *Hidden Passions,* is unprecedented, as is the level of special effects that we use on the show."

the wheel is *Passions*—which uses classic soap opera elements then adds on a sometimes bizarre yet always fun layer of supernatural occurrences. Two characters even non-soap fans seem to be aware of are witch Tabitha (Juliet Mills) and her talking doll Timmy (Josh Ryan Evans). This zany pair weaves evil schemes over the people of the seaside New England town of Harmony who frequently suffer ship sinkings, trips to the gates of hell, and the occasional beheading. "This is definitely not your grandmother's soap opera," wrote *Entertainment Weekly* in June 2001. "Heck, it's not even your mother's."

Other well-loved and well-remembered NBC soaps include *Another World* (also created by Irna Phillips, and running from 1964 to 1999), *The Doctors* (shot in New York from 1963 to 1982, giving Kathleen Turner and Alec Baldwin their first national exposure),

the cult hit *Santa Barbara*, and *Sunset Beach* (a relatively short-lived nineties serial, produced by the prolific prime-time soaps producer Aaron Spelling, that pioneered the use of Los Angeles outdoor locations).

When soap operas are thriving, they maintain a living relationship with the most loyal and caring audience in all of broadcasting. "Soap operas are a defining form of broadcast network programming," says

Sheraton Kalouria, NBC's senior vice president of daytime programming. "Soaps not only endured but thrived in the evolution from radio to TV because they told great stories that delighted the audience. When we give audiences a great story, they make the time to watch. This was true when broadcasting was invented, and it will continue to be true for the foreseeable future."

AND THE BEAT GOES ON...

Television had always been a dicey medium for rock 'n' roll, until the debut of MTV in 1981. Since the mid-fifties, networks fretted about presenting music connected with youthful freedom, sex, and (especially in the sixties) drugs. Many old-school celebrities were threatened by the music, or just didn't get it. Typical of the era was Dean Martin's eye-rolling, almost-contemptuous introduction of the Rolling Stones on a 1965 *Hollywood Palace*.

But the teen market became increasingly hard to ignore, no matter how strenuously Mitch Miller waved his baton. At least some at NBC realized the network was ignoring the "rock revolution" at its own peril. When *Hullabaloo*, a music performance show, premiered on January 12, 1965, American teens were able to see an impressive lineup of acts (sometimes lip-syncing): the Animals, Mitch Ryder, Herman's Hermits, the Shangri-Las, the Kinks, Junior Walker and the All-Stars, Peter

and Gordon, the Outsiders, and Petula Clark—even Soupy Sales doing "The Mouse." Beatles manager Brian Epstein did regular segments from London, introducing British acts to America. (The Beatles themselves only appeared after Brian had stopped doing the show.) *Hullabaloo* resembled a swinging disco—or a least a "G-rated" version of one.

"G-rated" was certainly one of the prerequisites for the Monkees, a prefab boy band that was cast from auditions held expressly for the sitcom.

(The casting call in *Daily Variety* went out for "four insane boys, aged 17–21.") Unapologetically adapted from the Richard Lester Beatles movies *A Hard Day's Night* and *Help!*, *The Monkees* as a TV series debuted in September 1966 and featured not only a madcap quartet of mop-headed young men, but fast and slow motion, blurred and distorted focus, and other "psychedelic" camera techniques.

Cast at least as much for looks and personality as for musical talent, the Monkees

"Hey, hey, we're the Monkees...and people say we monkey around, but we're too busy singing, to put anybody down."

were not quite Milli Vanilli—they sang but didn't play their own instruments, at least not at first. But a funny thing happened after they were manufactured: like Pinocchio, they became real, mostly because people loved them. Thanks to the impish personas of the foursome and the great songwriters, sidemen, and aggressive marketing campaign that backed them, the Monkees were a hit on radio as well as on TV. Their string of Top 40 successes led off with "I'm a Believer," "Last Train to Clarksville," "Steppin' Stone," and "Daydream Believer." Other hit singles followed, as did a popular concert tour replete with the requisite screaming girls at every stop.

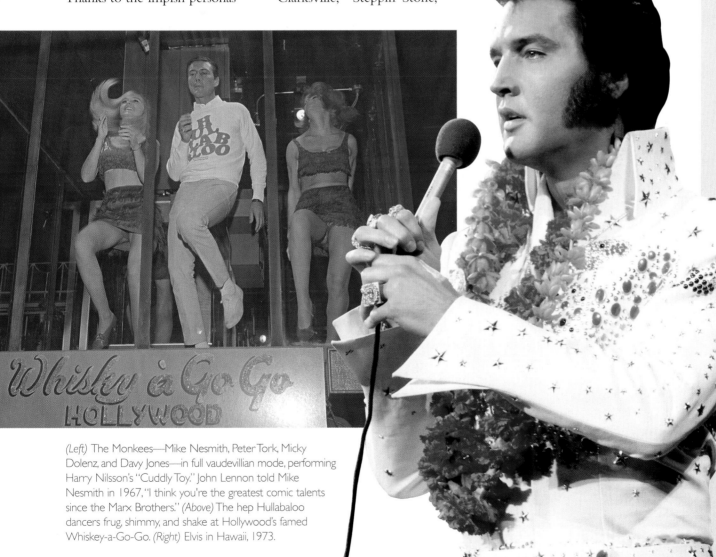

(Left) The Monkees—Mike Nesmith, Peter Tork, Micky Dolenz, and Davy Jones—in full vaudevillian mode, performing Harry Nilsson's "Cuddly Toy." John Lennon told Mike Nesmith in 1967, "I think you're the greatest comic talents since the Marx Brothers." (Above) The hep Hullabaloo dancers frug, shimmy, and shake at Hollywood's famed Whiskey-a-Go-Go. (Right) Elvis in Hawaii, 1973.

ELVIS PRESLEY ON TV

By the mid-sixties, Elvis Presley had gone from hip-grinding rebel to main-stream vocalist. His popularity with young people had ebbed accordingly, especially in the face of the British invasion of the Beatles and the Rolling Stones. Even though he'd never really left, on December 3, 1968, he appeared on an NBC "comeback" special. Elvis defied his mentor, Colonel Tom Parker (who wanted a conventional Christmas program), and gave an edgy performance, looking trim and tan. The huge ratings resuscitated his career.

Presley's greatest television victory came on April 4, 1973, with the U.S. broadcast of his "Aloha from Hawaii" special, the biggest music event of the era and the first concert ever televised worldwide. Broadcast via Intelsat IV satellite to forty countries, the show was seen by an estimated 1.5 billion people. In the U.S., more viewers tuned in to Elvis than had watched Neil Armstrong's walk on the moon: 51 percent of the viewing audience.

At age 38, Presley presented a glamorous figure as he performed for a live audience at the Honolulu International Center Arena. The $2.5 million cost made this the most expensive and extravagant television special ever produced, with its dramatic costumes in a patriotic American theme by Bill Belew. The show opened with Elvis arriving in a helicopter as the theme of his 1965 movie, *Paradise, Hawaiian Style*, played in the background. He sang many of his hits and some Hawaiian-themed songs. He closed with "I Can't Help Falling in Love" and threw his specially designed gem-laden eagle cape into the audience at the end of the show. The King of Rock 'n' Roll died four years later.

HE-E-E-E-E-RRRE'S JOHNNY!

Carson's easy, joking relationships with Doc Severinsen and Ed McMahon *(right)* were part of the enduring familiarities of *The Tonight Show*. Whether it was Tiny Tim's marriage to Miss Vicky in December 1969 *(opposite, top)*, one of Johnny's frequent animal visitors *(opposite, bottom left)*, or the appearance of Johnny in one of his famous alter egos *(opposite, bottom right)*, viewers took comfort in knowing that no matter how wiggy things got onstage, Johnny, Doc, and Ed were forever.

O n October 1, 1962, Johnny Carson took over *The Tonight Show* and began a thirty-year reign unlikely to be replicated in television history.

The Nebraska-raised comic was hardly an overnight sensation. Cancellation of his CBS prime-time show in 1956 sent him back to doing stand-up in small nightclubs. He then worked his way to New York and landed a successful stint as host of the ABC game show, *Who Do You Trust?*, which led to a guest host spot on NBC's *The Tonight Show*, then hosted by Jack Paar. Carson's smooth manner and quick wit won him the full-time job when Paar decided to leave.

Critics questioned whether Carson could replace the beloved Paar—but not for long. Staying true to his roots as a comedian, Carson turned *The Tonight Show* into a performance show with a cocktail party atmosphere. While Paar was a storyteller who thrived on controversial issues, Carson pro-

vided viewers with a comforting escape, and *The Tonight Show* became more popular than ever.

With his effortless delivery, Carson was a master of the double entendre ("We've got a real humdinger of a show tonight—and if you think it was easy for our producer to find a dinger that could hum…"). And his boyish, midwestern demeanor kept him from ever

seeming offensive. Carson was often at his funniest when reacting silently with a Jack Benny–like stare.

In an age before MTV, Johnny was television's most influential trendsetter. "Carson actually set a tone for male behavior in the sixties," said director Hal Gurnee. "People dressed the way he did. They used his little catchphrases. There

❝I wanted the show to make the most of being the last area of television that the medium originally was supposed to be—live, immediate entertainment. I decided the best thing I could do was forget trying to do a lot of preplanning. It all boiled down to just going out there and being my natural self and seeing what would happen.❞

– JOHNNY CARSON

was a kind of cool nonchalance that he had that I saw in a lot of people." Necktie manufacturers had a few tough years after Carson started wearing a turtleneck sweater under his sports jacket. He even had his own successful clothing line.

Over time, Carson's opening monologue on *The Tonight Show* became a barometer of public opinion. Politicians who were the subjects of his jokes often had reason to worry. As Carson's stature as a cultural icon grew, an appearance on *The Tonight Show* became a rite of passage for young stand-up comics. Making Carson laugh and getting waved in to sit on the couch next to him was a career-maker.

Even though he was in millions of homes every night for decades, viewers knew little about the private Carson, who rarely spoke to the press. They learned about his marriages and divorces through the gossip

columns and occasional cracks in his monologue ("I heard from my cat's lawyer....My cat wants $12,000 a week for Tender Vittles"). When not in front of an audience, he considered himself shy, which only added to his mystique.

Carson's enduring popularity made *The Tonight Show* a consistent profit engine for NBC even in years when its prime-time lineup was under pressure. With each new contract, Carson was able to extract more money and fewer workdays—earning a reported $25 million annually in his final deal.

In 1992, at the age of 66, Carson called it quits while he was still on top. Despite an open invitation to return to NBC, he's chosen to make only a handful of TV appearances since. Like all great comedians, he understood the importance of timing. "It's been said that even

some great performers stayed a little longer than they should have," says NBC executive Rick Ludwin. "He never wanted that to happen to him." And it certainly did not. As NBC Chairman and CEO Bob Wright puts it, "For the better part of thirty years, Johnny was the signature of NBC."

The popularity of *The Tonight Show* lured Hollywood's top personalities, including Elizabeth Taylor and Michael Douglas, to the program to spend some time chatting with Johnny.

Never reluctant to look ridiculous in order to get a laugh, Johnny donned a dark wig and strapped on the biceps and the six-pack abs to become John Rambo when the Sylvester Stallone films were popular in the mid-1980s.

Big-name artists such as Madonna appeared on *The Tonight Show* to sing a number or two and plug their current album.

" I admire a man who can do what John has done to his network as many times, as many ways, and in as many positions." – BOB HOPE

When Tom Selleck was TV's No. 1
heartthrob as Thomas Magnum on
Magnum, P.I., Johnny attempted
to copy his look, but it lost a
little in translation.

Carnac the Magnificent
was one of Johnny's most
popular characters. Carnac was a
mindreader who divined humorous
questions based on one-word answers
supplied by the studio audience.

Carson was a good mimic,
and did a very credible—
not to mention funny—
takeoff on Ronald
Reagan holding a
presidential press
conference.

Carson spoofs Columbo
in a 1975 sketch with
Peter Leeds and Sandra
de Bruin.

CHAPTER SEVEN

1971
1979

TV GETS REAL

The baby boomers, who dominated the sixties as teenagers, drove the culture of the seventies toward a more realistic, sometimes cynical, view of life. This was the "Me Decade," according to author Tom Wolfe, and the self-absorption suggested by that phrase was reflected in television entertainment filled with irony, such as *All in the Family*, *Real People*, and *Saturday Night Live*. The decade began with a series of sobering blows for American society: the fall of Saigon, Watergate, and President Richard Nixon's resignation. Viewers were in no mood to dwell on problems, however. Indeed, the painful social issues of the sixties were fodder for the seventies' laugh track.

Three pieces of news from Washington, D.C., in 1970 required a shift in network strategy: the Congressional ban on cigarette advertising, the Prime Time Access Rule, and the "Fin-Syn," or Financial and Syndication Rules. In that year, an estimated $220 million in advertising was abruptly yanked from television as cigarette manufacturers were ordered to go elsewhere. At the same time, the FCC's Prime Time Access Rule effectively removed an hour of programming from network hands in order to provide affiliates a greater opportunity to present local programming. "Fin-Syn" was a set of FCC rules restricting the amount of prime-time programming networks could produce themselves, and limiting network participation in the increasingly lucrative area of syndication. The net effects were to discourage network production and give incentives to independent producers.

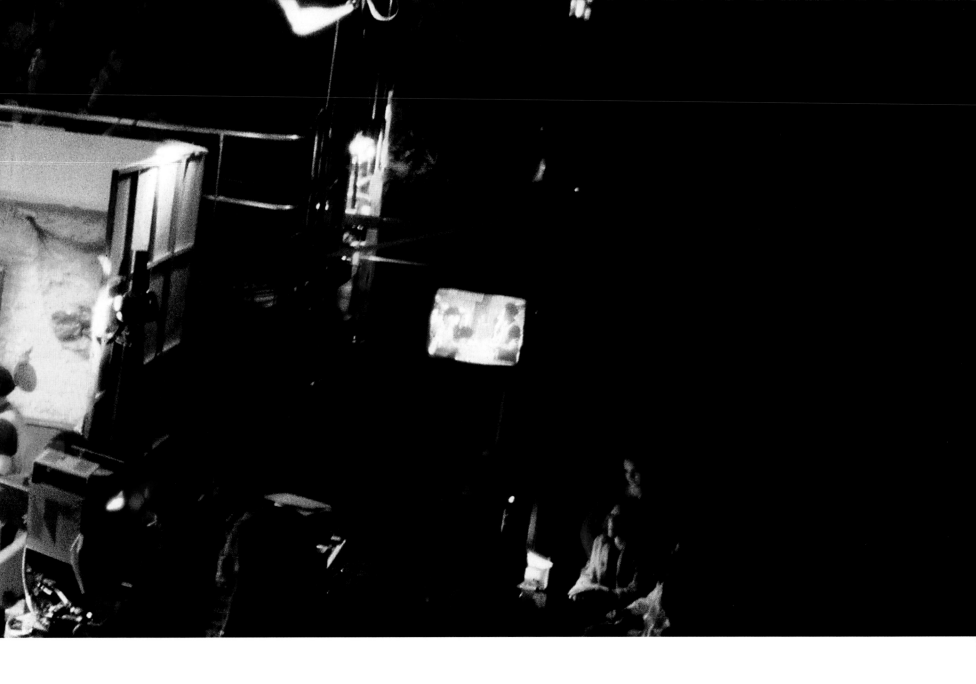

Whether stimulated by the government regulations or not, the seventies offered a remarkable variety of programs. The Norman Lear/Bud Yorkin team that created *All in the Family* brought their brand of social commentary humor to NBC in *Sanford and Son*. A major diversity breakthrough came with the success of *The Flip Wilson Show*. The first successful Hispanic sitcom, *Chico and the Man* with

Freddie Prinze, reached out to a new, large American demographic. Crime shows such as *Columbo*, *Police Woman*, and *The Rockford Files* presented new views of law enforcement. Building on the success of *The Tonight Show*, late-night programs such as *The Midnight Special* and *Tomorrow* with Tom Snyder were popular with younger audiences. And for that big group of viewers still clinging to traditional

values, *Little House on the Prairie* kept the faith for nine seasons.

All of those efforts were not enough, however. With NBC mired in a distant third place, RCA CEO Thornton Bradshaw hired Fred Silverman as NBC president in 1978. Silverman had exhibited a Midas touch as a programmer at both CBS and ABC, but his magical powers failed at NBC. The ratings dive continued

with disastrous notions such as *Supertrain*. Silverman did bring his imaginative young assistant, Brandon Tartikoff, with him, and to his credit, presided over NBC's growing success with miniseries, the first taste of "reality TV" with George Schlatter's *Real People*, and the innovative, high-energy antics of *Saturday Night Live*. But NBC would not see the top of the ratings mountain again until the eighties.

The Fall of Saigon and a President

seven-day-a-week schedule for almost two years, but Watergate was one of the most compelling stories in the history of broadcast journalism. Brokaw remembers, "I was very proud of NBC News for its aggressive but fair coverage of the biggest political story of the twentieth century. Watergate was a true constitutional crisis and the country was bitterly divided, so it was an emotional time for us all."

As the 1960s segued into the 1970s, and as the Age of Aquarius seemed to get lost in the haze, Americans came to terms with increasingly grim national and international headlines. The unwinnable Vietnam War and the unstoppable Watergate scandal—two stories carried in unprecedented depth by television news—gripped the nation's attention. NBC News covered it all, with a new evening anchor and a young reporter making a name for himself on the White House lawn.

The trustworthy *Huntley-Brinkley Report* was on its way out as the new decade began. Chet Huntley had retired in 1970, and David Brinkley was interested in doing longer, more thoughtful news pieces. So, in 1971, John Chancellor, a refined news reporter with an unmatched record covering politics and civil rights issues, became sole anchor of the newly named *NBC Nightly News*. "With clarity and restraint, Chancellor guided viewers through a difficult decade," Tom Brokaw recalled in a 1996 *Dateline* piece about the legendary anchor.

Brokaw, like Chancellor, grew up in the NBC News tradition, working first for NBC affiliates in Omaha and Atlanta before joining the network in Los Angeles in 1966. During his California years, Brokaw worked a dual assignment: anchoring the local news and reporting on national political campaigns for the various network news broadcasts. In 1973, he was summoned East to become NBC's chief White House correspondent during the Watergate scandal. The assignment kept him on a

resigned in disgrace) granted Nixon an unconditional pardon for whatever crimes he might have committed while in office.

Meanwhile, NBC continued to cover the painful last days of the war in Vietnam. When Vietcong forces closed in on Saigon, helicopters airlifted the remaining American personnel from the embassy roof. The last helicopter lifted off on April 30, 1975, but intrepid NBC reporter/cameraman Neil Davis stayed behind, capturing legendary footage of a North Vietnamese tank crashing through the presidential gates.

Brokaw made a name for himself with his coverage of the unfolding scandal. The Watergate hearings, carried throughout the day and recapped by the evening news, were as compelling as any nighttime drama or daytime soap, turning millions of Americans into hearings junkies. The nation followed every tragic, ironic, and nefarious twist in the evolving story. Committee Chairman Sam Ervin, Jr., who confessed to being a "pretty fair country lawyer," became revered as a folk hero.

By 1974, Nixon's approval rating had taken a nosedive, Congress was debating a bill of impeachment, and even Republican stalwart Barry Goldwater was calling for a presidential departure. Richard Nixon resigned on August 8 of that year, on television, steadfast in his refusal to acknowledge any wrongdoing. A month later, new President Gerald Ford (who had been appointed vice president when Spiro Agnew

(Above) Created on February 7, 1973, the Watergate Committee was officially known as the Senate Select Committee on Presidential Campaign Activities. *(Left)* Watergate was headline news virtually every day. *(Opposite)* On April 30, 1975, U.S. Marines coordinated the final evacuation of embassy personnel from Saigon.

REALITY COMES TO THE MEAN STREETS

The life-and-death excitement of crime stories and medical series has been a staple of broadcasting since the early days of radio. In TV series such as *Dragnet* and *Dr. Kildare*, police officers and doctors were more often symbols of justice and medicine than fully realized characters.

In the 1970s, those genres became more realistic in two ways: first, they were more violent; second, they portrayed cops and docs as people. *Police Story*, created by former Los Angeles policeman Joseph Wambaugh, focused on the psychological toll on the men who faced death and violence every day. Shows such as *McMillan and Wife* and *The Rockford Files* were as much about the personal lives of the detectives as they were about the crimes. And through the powerful acting of Raymond Burr, audiences entered the very active life of a handicapped cop in *Ironside*.

Not all of NBC's hit dramas reflected a "real" view of crime-enforcement and life-saving: *Police Woman*, *Emergency!* and *CHiPs* were fun to watch but now seem excessively campy in our post–*Hill Street Blues* world. Yet each of these shows spoke to a nation increasingly concerned with rising crime and tarnished ideals.

COLUMBO (1971–77) *(Above)* "Oh, listen, there's just one more thing…" Columbo's offhand comment, spoken as he draped his perpetually rumpled raincoat over his arm, disarmed the killer into thinking he was dealing with a bumbler. *Columbo* was not so much a whodunit as it was a "howcatchem"—the fun was in watching Columbo corner the murderer, and we never tired of the game. He poked and probed and prodded until he inevitably uncovered the one tiny loose end that the killer had forgotten to tie. Memorably portrayed by Peter Falk, Lieutenant Columbo was a costumer's vacation. The clothes all belonged to Falk, and he wore the same suit, shoes, and raincoat each time he played the disheveled detective.

EMERGENCY! (1972–77) *(Opposite)* was a Jack Webb creation that followed the efforts of Squad 51 of the Los Angeles County Fire Department's Paramedic Rescue Service. The regular cast included the two paramedics of Squad 51 (ladies' man Johnny Gage, played by Randolph Mantooth, in blue shirt, and family man Roy DeSoto, played by Kevin Tighe, not pictured), four members from Engine 51 (including a real fireman), and the staff of Rampart Hospital (including Julie London, Webb's ex-wife, as the head nurse). For much of its run, *Emergency!* was ranked the most popular show among 2- to 11-year-olds. (Jack Webb produced many other shows for NBC in the 1970s, including *Adam-12* and *Hec Ramsey*.)

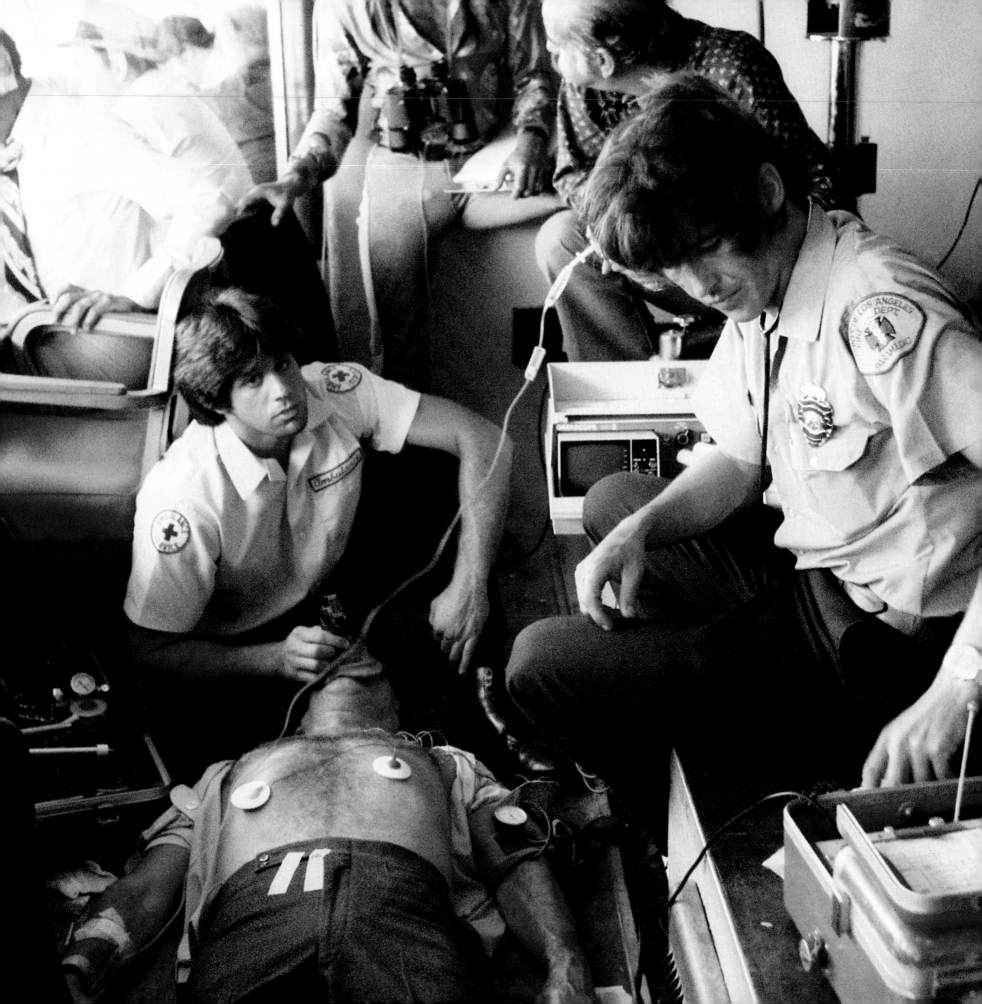

POLICE STORY (1973–77) *(Right)* This anthology series was based on the stories of former police officer Joseph Wambaugh. They differed from other TV cop fare by taking a gritty and realistic look at the challenges and dangers of police life. Corruption, racism, and pressures at home—even mundane tasks—were not overlooked. Vic Morrow is seen here with Chuck Connors.

IRONSIDE (1967–1975) *(Left)* Former Chief of Detectives Robert Ironside (Raymond Burr, seen here with Barbara Anderson), was paralyzed by a would-be assassin's bullet. Chief Ironside continued his war on crime as a department consultant.

POLICE WOMAN
(1974–78) *(Right)* Although it was a spin-off from *Police Story*, this show took a decidedly less realistic (and much more glamorous) view of police work. Angie Dickinson, who starred with Earl Holliman, often wore tight clothes and unbuttoned tops as she fought crime.

McCLOUD (1970–77) *(Above)* Along with *Columbo* and *McMillan and Wife*, this was one of the rotating Sunday-night shows on the innovative *NBC Mystery Movie* series. Dennis Weaver played U.S. Marshal Sam McCloud, who was on loan from Taos, New Mexico, to the New York Police Department. McCloud fought crime on the streets using the same techniques that worked for him back home.

CHiPS (1977–83) *(Left)* Larry Wilcox (left) and Erik Estrada (right) played motorcycle cops with the California Highway Patrol. Estrada's Officer Poncherello ("Ponch") became a major sex symbol of the era.

McMILLAN AND WIFE
(1971–77) *(Below)* San Francisco Police Commissioner Stewart McMillan (Rock Hudson) and his wife Sally (Susan Saint James) kept stumbling upon unsolved crimes, and solved them with panache.

THE ROCKFORD FILES
(1974–80) *(Left)* James Garner played an ex-con/private investigator who lived in a trailer on the beach and took the unlikely cases that proved the cops wrong. He didn't shoot guns ("I just point it") and considered quitting cases if they got too rough.

129

SANFORD AND CHICO

Sanford and Son was the second hit produced by Norman Lear and his partner Bud Yorkin. They had previously bought the rights to a British domestic sitcom called *Till Death Us Do Part*, transplanted it to Queens, N.Y., and morphed it into the top show in the United States, *All in the Family*. When a British contact introduced them to another English comedy called *Steptoe & Son*, they relocated it to South-Central Los Angeles and transformed it into *Sanford and Son*, starring the inimitable Redd Foxx as widowed junk dealer Fred Sanford. (Foxx had been born John Elroy Sanford.)

The show ended up on NBC because Fred Silverman, head of programming at CBS, was too slow to drop by and see Foxx and his costar, Demond Wilson, in rehearsal. Exasperated with Silverman, Lear and Yorkin invited NBC executive Herb Schlosser to take a look; he picked it up right away. *Sanford* premiered in January of 1972 and shot immediately into the No. 2 spot behind *All in the Family*.

Sanford and Son remained NBC's top-rated show for four years. It broke new ground with its unabashedly ethnic humor,

which had people of all races laughing from coast to coast. At the heart of it all was the comedic genius of Redd Foxx, especially his running gags, such as Sanford's any-minute-now heart attack, which threatened at least once each episode to propel him heavenward to be reunited with his departed spouse:

"I'm coming, Elizabeth! It's the big one!"

The show bridged America's painfully tense racial divide via the universally recognizable humor created by the generational tension between Sanford and his son Lamont. Older but not necessarily wiser, Fred Sanford was relatively content with his life and feared Lamont's upwardly mobile aspirations, mostly because his son's departure from the junk business would greatly inconvenience him.

The success of *Sanford* emboldened NBC to venture further into ethnic comedy; *Chico and the Man* premiered in September 1974. With veteran actor Jack Albertson as crabby garage owner Ed Brown (the Man), and up-and-coming heartthrob comedian Freddie Prinze as Mexican-American Chico Rodriguez, the show turned on the cross-cultural understandings and misunderstandings between the two protagonists. Despite his sour disposition, the Man allowed Chico to insinuate himself into the life of the garage. In fact, he was inwardly pleased to have someone who cared about him, and the two established a quirky but symbiotic relationship.

An instant hit, the program vaulted into third place in its first season, right behind *Sanford and Son*. In fact, *Sanford* and *Chico* were the only NBC shows in the Top 10 that year—CBS, powered by the Norman Lear juggernaut (*All in the Family*, *The Jeffersons*, *Good Times*, *Maude*) held down the other eight spots. *Chico's* success was short-circuited by tragedy. Prinze, unable to cope with the pressures of his meteoric rise to stardom, took his own life in 1977.

By making us laugh with them but not at them, *Sanford and Son* and *Chico and the Man* helped us extract the humor from the uneasy relationships among races and cultures in America. Whether it was Fred Sanford's recurring phony heart attack *(opposite, bottom)*, his ongoing near-fisticuffs feud with Aunt Esther (LaWanda Page; *opposite, top*), or Ed and Chico in funny hats *(above)*, these shows leveled the playing field because everyone—black, white, Latino—was fair game for a poke in the ribs.

THE DEVIL MADE HIM DO IT

Flip Wilson was welcomed into American living rooms, not as a character on a drama or comedy series, but as himself—or rather, as himself and an entourage of hilarious characters. In the tradition of Jackie Gleason, Red Skelton, and even Jonathan Winters, Clerow "Flip" Wilson kept a closetful of alter egos, both male and female, and used them to lampoon both the ordinary and extraordinary goings-on of everyday life.

After gaining a following from multiple stints sitting in for Johnny Carson on *The Tonight Show*, Flip Wilson debuted his variety show in September 1970. For the next two years, it was the No. 2 program in the nation and won two Emmys.

The Flip Wilson Show had the usual complement of musical talent, but most viewers would have happily ditched the supporting cast and settled for an hour of Flip and his one-man repertory company. Although characters such as the Reverend Leroy (pastor of the Church of What's Happening Now) and Sonny, the White House janitor (the best-informed man in

Although Flip Wilson brought big-name guest stars like Sammy Davis, Jr. *(opposite)* onto his program, viewers really watched because Flip was outrageous. Nothing he did was more outrageous than Geraldine *(above* with bodybuilders and *left,* with Cher).

Although many viewers thought he was just as funny as Flip, Richard Pryor's comedy show aired for just five weeks in 1977. Pryor ran afoul of network censors right from the start. In his first episode, he wanted to appear nude from the waist up and clad only in a body stocking from the waist down, but the sequence didn't make it past Standards and Practices. After that, he and NBC never could resolve serious censorship issues about his brand of comedy. At the heart of the matter was the conflict between his insistence on presenting adult humor and the network's desire to air material it deemed appropriate to the "family hour" (8:00–9:00 p.m.) time slot. The all-too-public feud between Pryor and NBC ended with his removal from the schedule in October 1977.

Washington) had their moments, head and shoulders above them all, I'm tellin' you, honey, was America's favorite smart-ass, Geraldine. Sassy, liberated, and outrageous, Geraldine Jones was devoted to her boyfriend, Killer, but "didn't take no stuff"—not from him, not from nobody. She also didn't give no stuff. In-your-face honest, Geraldine was the originator of "what you see is what you get," a phrase that has long outlived

the show, and whose acronym has been institutionalized in computer terminology as WYSIWYG. With her arch falsetto, the wisecracking Geraldine also mainstreamed at least two other expressions into contemporary speech: "When you're hot, you're hot," and the infectious, bullet-proof excuse for all manner of personal indulgence: "The Devil made me do it."

A perfectionist who did much of his own writing for

the show, Wilson successfully navigated one of the toughest tightropes in television—even though he made Geraldine uproariously funny, he was careful to make certain that her image and her humor were never demeaning to black women or inaccessible to white audiences. As a result, she and Wilson's other characters were a gentle but giant step forward in bridging the chasm between races and social classes on television.

LIVE FROM NEW YORK— IT'S SATURDAY NIGHT!

The baby boom generation was the first to be raised on television. But by the time "boomers" reached young adulthood, there wasn't much for them to watch. That was until a thirty-one-year-old television producer named Lorne Michaels created a new variety show to replace Saturday repeats of *The Tonight Show*. On October 11, 1975, NBC's *Saturday Night*—later renamed *Saturday Night Live*—brought a revolutionary kind of comedy to television that was bold enough to make the show a lasting institution.

"Most of what was interesting to me wasn't happening on television," remembers Michaels. "There was a lot of stuff that was much more happening in music, movies, theater...in just about every other place except television, which was still being essentially done and run by people who'd grown up working in radio."

A Toronto native, Michaels worked in Hollywood in the late 1960s as a writer on *Laugh-In*. He also produced several innovative ABC specials for Lily Tomlin in Los Angeles. That work earned him an Emmy and a ticket east to 30 Rockefeller Plaza—courtesy of a young NBC executive named Dick Ebersol—to launch an NBC late-night experiment that would become a pop-culture touchstone for years to come.

NBC President Herb Schlosser said he wanted a program that reached urban young adults, but several NBC executives had something more traditional in mind for *Saturday Night*. They suggested that Rich Little and the USC Marching Band be included on the premiere. But Michaels's vision prevailed. His plan was to offer smart humor that tapped into the shared experience of the first TV generation, of which he was a tube-obsessed member. And his show would be live (so the network overseers would have little chance to meddle) and from New York (to give it an edgy, urban, improvisational quality that would rely on TV production veterans used to the rigors of a live show).

WILD AND CRAZY *(Left)* The two Czech Festrunk brothers—Steve Martin and Dan Aykroyd—had difficulty impressing "American chicks" (Gilda Radner, Laraine Newman, and Jane Curtin). "We're two wild and crazy guys!" was probably *SNL*'s most popular catchphrase. *(Above, left)* A close second was "I'm Chevy Chase and you're not," from the unpredictable "Weekend Update" anchor; Chase, the show's first breakout star, was also first to leave. *(Above, right)* Emily Litella ("Never mind"), a well-meaning if befuddled commentator, was based on Radner's childhood nanny.

FROM FRANCE (AND OTHER PLACES)
The original Not Ready For Prime Time Players turned out a flurry of brilliant characters during their five-year run, such as John Belushi's samurai *(left)*, seen here in the classic "Samurai Deli"; *(above, left)* the never-very-happy Killer Bees; *(above, right)* Garrett Morris's "bery-bery good" ballplayer, Chico Escuelas; and *(circle)* the Coneheads, a family from the planet Remulak who drank massive quantities of beer and claimed they were from France.

WEEKEND UPDATE
(Right) After Chevy Chase left *SNL* early in its second season, Jane Curtin became anchor on "Weekend Update," and was later joined by Bill Murray. Dan Aykroyd and Curtin would frequently team up for "Point-Counterpoint," in which Jane would argue one side of a topic and Dan the other. (The recurring sketch produced Aykroyd's highly anticipated opening retort, "Jane, you ignorant slut.") *(Left)* Don Novello, an *SNL* writer, played Father Guido Sarducci, the hip, cigarette-smoking priest who served as the show's Vatican correspondent.

Isn't That Special!

B y the end of the seventies, *Saturday Night Live* had become a certified ratings smash, continually testing the limits of comedy on broadcast network television and creating a bevy of new stars—most of whom, unfortunately, seemed on their way out the door. Dan Aykroyd and John Belushi were gone by 1979,

on their way to making *The Blues Brothers*, the first *SNL*-based movie hit. The rest of the cast—and producer Lorne Michaels—departed by 1980. Despite the early eighties breakouts of Eddie Murphy and Joe Piscopo, the years that followed saw *SNL* struggle for relevance and a seventies-sized audience.

In 1985, NBC asked Lorne Michaels to return to *SNL*;

the show seemed directionless, and Brandon Tartikoff was on the verge of cancelling it. But in 1986, Michaels started to turn the show around with yet another set of brilliant newcomers, eventually introducing a new generation of talent (Mike Myers, Chris Rock, Adam Sandler, Dana Carvey, Nora Dunn, Phil Hartman, Jon Lovitz, Jan Hooks, Dennis Miller, Julia Sweeney, and Chris Farley, to name a few) who would infuse the show with great comedy and classic characters. By 1991, *SNL* was in a renaissance period with its largest audience ever.

CAN WE TAWK? *(Above)* Linda Richman, the Streisand-worshipping kibitzer on "Coffee Talk," introduced the joys of Yiddish to late-night television ("I'm getting a little verklempt!"). Mike Myers (here, with Glenn Close) based the character on his real-life mother-in-law. *(Circle)* Ed Grimley, Jr. (Martin Short), perhaps the world's biggest Pat Sajak fan, seen here in his usual state of well-meaning cluelessness. *(Right)* Eddie Murphy played Gumby as a bitter, wizened claymation figure and ex-kiddie star ("I'm Gumby, dammit!").

YOU LOOK MAH-VELOUS *SNL*'s early-eighties fortunes steadily improved under the supervision of producer Dick Ebersol, who oversaw a cast of talented newcomers that included Eddie Murphy, Joe Piscopo, Mary Gross, and Julia Louis-Dreyfus. However, in the 1984–85 season, Ebersol put together a one-year-only "all-star" cast that included Martin Short, Christopher Guest, and Billy Crystal, who played "mah-velous" talk-show host Fernando *(right)*. Here he interviews one of his (and *SNL*'s) crew members after guest Barry Manilow had "backed out."

EXCELLENT! *(Left)* "Wayne's World," the most excellent cable-access show, hosted by teenagers Wayne and Garth (Mike Myers, with hat, and Dana Carvey), went on to become the biggest theatrical film based on an *SNL* franchise so far. *(Below, left)* Julia Sweeney's androgynous Pat kept co-workers, acquaintances, and fans guessing her true sex for years. *(Below, right)* Carvey's Church Lady, seen here interviewing Phil Hartman as disgraced evangelist Jim Bakker, frequently wondered aloud if her guests were under the influence of…SATAN!

LORNE MICHAELS

"The show we now think of as *Saturday Night Live* wasn't quite there at the beginning. I think we had the ingredients, but we didn't quite have the recipe. But I kept saying, 'By show ten, we'll know what it is.' And show ten that season, which was hosted by Elliot Gould, won the Emmy. Not because I was so prophetic, but because it really did take us about ten shows.

"We weren't thinking of ourselves as 'antiestablishment' in 1975. What I did was assemble the smartest, funniest, most talented people I could find. And whatever we thought was cool at the time, we put on the air. We weren't thinking, 'That'll show them.' It was much more, in a baby boomer sense, self-involved. I hoped the people I brought together would be considered much more as artists than as anything else.

"So I don't think we were revolutionaries then, as much as I don't think we're establishment now. The politics are less and less important to me. Though I still think whoever's in power probably shouldn't be trusted."

LITTLE HOUSE ON THE PRAIRIE: FOLKSY FARMERS AND FAMILY VALUES

"Home is the nicest word there is."
– LAURA, IN THE FIRST EPISODE,
"A HARVEST OF FRIENDS"

Amidst the screech of police car tires and howls of laughter emanating from most other TV shows of the seventies, *Little House on the Prairie* was an oasis of gentle homilies, solid family values,

and sweet social harmony. NBC—thanks to *Bonanza*—understood the strong appeal of family values and noted the new CBS series *The Waltons* beating *The Flip Wilson Show*. The network suggested to Michael Landon (who had played Little Joe Cartwright on the Ponderosa) that novelist Laura Ingalls Wilder's *Little House on the Prairie* might have potential as a television series. Landon proved them right with a two-hour pilot that paved the way for this successful show, which debuted in 1974 and lasted nine seasons.

The pilot followed the story of the Ingalls family up to their arrival in Walnut Grove, Minnesota, a farming community in the late 1870s. Landon was executive producer of the series, wrote and directed many episodes, and played the role of homesteader Charles Ingalls, the father of the clan. Caroline, his wife, was played by Karen Grassle. Laura, the

central character and narrator through whose eyes we experienced the stories, was played by Melissa Gilbert. Eventually, Laura met and married Almanzo Wilder (played by Dean Butler), and from 1980 to the end of the series, they were at the center of events in Walnut Grove.

In its warm, sentimental themes and its serial style of

continuing story lines, *Little House* adapted successful techniques from the daytime soap operas. Many of the early episodes concerned intimate love affairs and friendships within the small town. Others dealt with natural disasters and incidents with farm animals or troubles that the Ingalls daughters had at school. As the show progressed, Laura's sister Mary became blind, Charles and Caroline adopted several other children, and various cast members moved out of

Walnut Grove to make room for other characters. At the beginning of the 1978–79 season, the Ingalls and all their friends abruptly moved to the city of Winoka, Dakota, because Walnut Grove had been hit with a depression. City life didn't suit them, and Walnut Grove miraculously revived, so everyone moved back later in the season.

Landon left the cast in 1982 (although he continued as executive producer), and for the ninth and final season

the title was changed to *Little House: A New Beginning*. Fans enthusiastically greeted three two-hour specials based on the series—"Little House on the Prairie: Look Back to Yesterday" (1983), "Little House: The Last Farewell" (1984), and "Little House: Bless All the Dear Children" (1984)—but the series itself was never revived. The next series Landon produced, *Highway to Heaven*, featured a guardian angel named Jonathan Smith (Landon) who was sent to

Earth to help people. Assisted by ex-cop Mark Gordon (Victor French, who had portrayed Mr. Edwards in *Little House*), he continued to touch viewers' hearts for five more years.

(Opposite, right) Charles and Caroline Ingalls (Michael Landon and Karen Grassle) arrived in Walnut Grove, Minnesota, with their three daughters, Mary (Melissa Sue Anderson), Laura (Melissa Gilbert), and Carrie (twins Lindsay and Sidney Greenbush, alternating), but it was Laura *(opposite, left,* on horseback) who was the show's narrator. *(Above)* As the series progressed, more characters were added, including former Los Angeles Rams lineman Merlin Olson as Jonathan Garvey (with the beard), and Grace, yet another daughter in the Ingalls household, played by twins Wendy and Brenda Turnbeaugh *(circle, top)*.

STAYING UP LATE – THE MIDNIGHT SPECIAL

(*Top, left*) The Spinners were a Motown group from Detroit that had climbed high in the charts with songs such as "I'll Be Around," "Could It Be I'm Falling in Love," and "Then Came You," with Dionne Warwick.
(*Top, center*) The stage of *The Midnight Special*.
(*Top, right*) Commander Cody and the Lost Planet Airmen.
(*Right*) The Bee Gees, from Australia, looking neo-Edwardian.
(*Circle*) Host Wolfman Jack howled at the moon and generated audience enthusiasm.

In the early seventies, kids wanted to do two things: stay up late and go to rock concerts. Producer Burt Sugarman saw a golden opportunity to meet both demands. With no network programming at 1:00 a.m. on Friday nights, there was no competition, and Johnny Carson, who was averaging better than a 50 share every night with *The Tonight Show*, was an ideal lead-in. When NBC turned down his pitch for a post-Carson show, Sugarman made a deal in which he sold the commercial air time himself, created a live ninety-minute rock concert show called *The Midnight Special*, and signed Chevrolet to sponsor it. The show was an instant hit in February 1973.

In addition to pioneering late-late-night television, *The Midnight Special* presented an extraordinary mixture of rock, pop, soul, disco, and even heavy metal to a national viewing audience. Gravel-voiced deejay Wolfman Jack brought a manic energy to his duties as host, and an impressive array of musical talent—from established veterans to the hottest new groups—shared the stage. Guests included Ray Charles, Jerry Lee Lewis, Alice Cooper, Linda Ronstadt, Elton John, Aretha Franklin, Prince, Diana Ross, Steppenwolf, Van Morrison, Helen Reddy, the Bee Gees, Santana, Etta James, Fleetwood Mac, Chubby Checker, Kenny Rogers, Dolly Parton, Rod Stewart, the Jacksons, Chuck Berry, Billy Joel, Donna Summer, Johnny Rivers, the Village People, James Brown, Aerosmith, Marvin Gaye, Sly and the Family Stone, Jim Croce, Joan Baez, and many more.

Sugarman was an astute showman who encouraged performers to sing and play together in this "live" concert format, and he sometimes used *The Midnight Special* to present events outside of the regular weekly format. For example, David Bowie gave his last performance as Ziggy Stardust in an elaborate cabaret show that was taped over three days at the Marquee Club in London. Titled "The 1980 Floor Show," it was shown on November 16, 1973, and featured Bowie in several theatrical settings with Marianne Faithfull, The Troggs, and other guests.

The Midnight Special howled late into the night each week until May 1981.

Ray Charles *(top)* and Chuck Berry *(above, left)* were typical of the established pop music stars who appeared on *The Midnight Special*. Steely Dan *(above, center)* was formed by two young musicians from Bard College: Donald Fagen on vocals and keyboard and Walter Becker on bass, guitar, and vocals. Loretta Lynn *(above, right)*, of "Coal Miner's Daughter" fame, was one of many country singers who joined the rock 'n' roll guests on *The Midnight Special*.

THE GENESIS OF REALITY TV: *REAL PEOPLE*

Reality TV is thought of as a relatively recent television genre. Yet the concept of putting in prime time the kind of people who gladly let their friends, neighbors, and countrymen see just how adventurous, uninhibited, and "real" they are was first developed in 1979. Producer George Schlatter, of *Laugh-In* fame, put weird, wonderful, and amazing folk from all walks of life on his innovative series *Real People*. "This show speaks to and about the common man," says Schlatter. "It is a look at ourselves." Of course, it was often a look at ourselves through a funhouse mirror. *Real People*

featured segments with midgets, transvestites, and a man who could whistle through his belly button. It also told serious stories, such as the one about an all-black World War II fighter squadron.

The ratings were good and the show was inexpensive to produce, but the critics were appalled. Under the headline "TV Sends in the Freaks," *Newsweek* magazine accused the show of cruelly exploiting vulnerable people: "*Real People* combines the exhibitionism of *The Gong Show*, the voyeurism of *Candid Camera*, and the freaky fascination of *Ripley's Believe It or Not*, but the total effect is unlike anything that has ever come

down the tube." Hosts Fred Willard, Sarah Purcell, John Barbour, and Skip Stephenson solicited opinions from studio audiences about issues of the day, a feature that was spun off as a short-lived show called *Speak Up America*. "I like to describe it as Phil Donahue meets Howard Beale," jokes Schlatter.

Once *Real People* caught on with viewers, it ran successfully for six seasons. It spawned many imitators, including *That's Incredible*, and paved the way for contemporary shows such as *Jerry Springer*, *Survivor*, and *Fear Factor*. Compared to today's "reality" shows, *Real People* appears gentle and dignified, but for its time, it was a shocker.

REAL PEOPLE OF AMERICA

HELP BRING HOME 2,447 MIA's

GEORGE SCHLATTER TALKS ABOUT *REAL PEOPLE*

"To do a TV show using non-famous people was totally revolutionary in 1979. We looked for people who had a story and just started shooting them with Betacams. We would go into a town and find interesting people. Some of them were bizarre and some of them were eccentric. Some of them were average people who did extraordinary things. For example, there was a farmer in Minnesota who had rolled the largest ball of string in the world. It was a story high. It was amazing. But he was just an ordinary farmer.

"We let people tell their own stories. If a guy had built a perpetual-motion machine, we let him explain it. The fact that it didn't work was something the audience found out. The woman who had been visited by aliens just explained what they looked like. And, of course, this was often funny stuff.

"Yes, we did eccentrics. Yes, we did zanies, and included unusual, bizarre things. But we also did heroes. We also did stories that made you feel good about yourself even if you didn't look like Tom Cruise. And that, probably, changed television as much as *Laugh-In*, because it proved that ordinary people were interesting."

(Circle) Sarah Purcell goes over the rail in a segment on roller derby queens. *(Opposite, top)* Skip Stevenson mimics Sarah as Byron Allen *(left)*, Fred Willard *(center)*, and Bill Rafferty *(right)* join the clowning. *(Opposite, bottom)* The cast tries the old collegiate telephone booth trick. *(Top)* The show also championed causes, such as bringing home missing soldiers from Vietnam. *(Above)* Skydiving cast members; Willard with triplet New York City cops. *(Right)* Arizona welcomes *Real People* and Hub Cap Annie.

BIG EVENTS, BIG STARS

SHOGUN

Broadcast in September 1980, "Shogun" plunged viewers into the unfamiliar world of feudal Japan, as seen through the eyes of marooned English pilot, Major John Blackthorne. Based on James Clavell's complex bestseller, the five-part, twelve-hour miniseries won that year's Emmy for Outstanding Limited Series. In a role that served to cement his crown as "king of the miniseries," Richard Chamberlain starred as Blackthorne, a man who abandons the trappings of Western civilization to become a samurai in service to Lord Toranaga, the shogun of the title. Revered Japanese actor Toshiro Mifune co-starred as Toranaga. In a television innovation, Mifune and other Japanese actors spoke Japanese when conversing with one another. Viewers were able to deduce the content of conversations through gestures and visual clues.

Video spectaculars (in the classic, Weaver-esque sense of the word) are a thing of the past, but "event program-ming"—expensively shot, extensively developed, filmed dramas that are either one-shot movies or miniseries—continues to be an important, exciting, and vital part of the TV landscape. These events frequently attract big Hollywood names willing to take on a

project, as opposed to a series.

NBC aired the first ever made-for-TV movie on October 7, 1964, with "See How They Run," a chase thriller (based on Michael Blankfort's *The Widow Makers*) starring John Forsythe and Senta Berger. By then, the network had already acquired a strong reputation for big-time Hollywood fare with *Saturday Night at the Movies*, which aired previously released blockbuster

films. (Although this strategy is common today, it was a big event back then, when networks tended to show only B-grade, or even C-grade, movies.) But not until the mid-seventies did networks begin to commission their own movies in earnest. ABC's two miniseries "Rich Man, Poor Man" and "Roots" were high-profile smash hits. In response, NBC began to air heavily promoted *Big Events*. One was the first television

Though the NBC *Big Events* "umbrella" disappeared in the early eighties, the legacy of brilliant made-for-NBC miniseries and "event" movies is long and noteworthy. Farrah Fawcett starred in "The Burning Bed," which focused on domestic violence and was nominated for eight Emmys. In 1985, "An Early Frost" was a groundbreaking and controversial drama about AIDS, the first of its kind. More lighthearted fare, such as "Merlin" and "Gulliver's Travels," has been extraordinarily popular with viewers as well.

airing of "The Godfather," which attracted eighty million viewers—and many protests from Italian-Americans. Another was the made-for-TV "Jesus of Nazareth," seen by ninety million people. Perhaps the most notable of the *Big Events* was "Holocaust," a stunning and powerful film that ran over four nights in April of 1978. The nine-and-a-half-hour series was seen by an audience of 107 million and featured Emmy Award-winning performances by Michael Moriarty and Meryl Streep. The series won eight Emmys overall.

(Opposite) "Shogun" starred Toshiro Mifune as warlord Toranaga, and Richard Chamberlain as John Blackthorne, with Damien Thomas as missionary Father Alvito, and Yoko Shimada as Blackthorne's lover, Lady Mariko. "Holocaust" was for many the first opportunity to see Meryl Streep *(top and circle)* on TV. Michael Moriarty *(above, left)* played an ambitious Nazi officer; James Woods and Fritz Weaver *(above, right)* played camp internees.

THE GAME THAT TRANSFORMED SPORTS TELEVISION

Baseball fans will forever celebrate the 1975 World Series between the Cincinnati Reds and the Boston Red Sox as one of the greatest ever, with Game 6 as the ultimate moment. Indeed, the entire Series, highlighted by heart-stopping plays, fantastic finishes, and a revolving cast of heroes, riveted millions of TV viewers to their seats. However, it is NBC's left-field camera shot of the dramatic final at-bat of Game 6 that lingers nonpareil.

The batter was Carlton "Pudge" Fisk, the hard-nosed catcher for the Red Sox. He had just mashed a long fly ball to lead off the bottom of the twelfth inning, with the score tied, 6-6. Sparky Anderson's "Big Red Machine" led the Series, three games to two, so it was do-or-die once more for the Bambino-cursed Red Sox, who hadn't won a world championship since 1918— two years before selling Babe Ruth to the New York Yankees.

Midway through the 1970s, baseball's long-held grip on TV audiences had loosened. Fans remained stung by the first-ever players' strike in 1972 and the bloated, free-agent salaries that followed. NBC felt mixed emotions as its coverage of the National Football League

overtook the national pastime in the ratings. The network cherished its relationship with baseball. But it couldn't ignore football's popularity, which it had helped establish since the 1950s, including coverage of the inaugural World Championship Game (later called the Super Bowl) in 1967. Ironically, an NBC gaffe demonstrated viewers' growing gridiron appetite.

It occurred on November 17, 1968, when NBC, under

standard procedure to begin prime-time programming at 7:00 p.m. ET, cut away from the last sixty-five seconds of the New York Jets-Oakland Raiders game—part of its American Football League package— with the visiting Jets up, 32–29. Except on the West Coast, stations cut to their "regularly scheduled program," the movie "Heidi,"—while the Raiders scored fourteen points in nine seconds for the win. NBC's

switchboards were deluged with complaints, and "The Heidi Game" marked the last time a football game wasn't aired to completion.

So on October 21, 1975, as Pudge's hit arced toward Fenway Park's "Green Monster" in left field, baseball's keepers, as well as NBC's, cheered the ratings-rich Fall Classic. But what 66 million viewers watched, instead of the typical flight of the ball, was Fisk, bounding down the first-base line, waving his arms and willing the ball to stay fair. When it bounced off the foul pole for a game-winning home run, he had done more than guarantee a Game 7 in unbelievable fashion. He, along with NBC's ingenious director Harry Coyle, forever refocused baseball on television—some might say television on baseball— with the lens squarely on the players and their spontaneous emotions.

Coyle began revolutionizing baseball coverage in the late 1940s, using multiple cameras to capture not only the nuances of the game but also viewers' rapt attention. The oft-replayed images of the flailing Fisk's body English caught by a camera the prescient Coyle had mounted in the left-field scoreboard symbolize the sea change that still influences how games are produced.

Fisk himself admits as much. "I don't think I realized at the time its [Game 6] significance, particularly in how games are viewed," he said not long after being inducted into the Baseball Hall of Fame in 2000. "From then on, it seemed there were twice as many cameras to catch every emotion that goes on in a game. I didn't realize it would be a turning point in the popularity of the game, how it's watched, and to some extent how it's played."

In the grand scheme of things, it almost didn't matter that the Red Sox lost Game 7, a 4–3 barn-burner watched by nearly 76 million people— except to Fisk and generations of long-suffering Boston fans. "It was a big moment," he mused. "I just wish it had been in the seventh game."

THE MAN WHO WROTE THE BOOK

"Television got off the ground because of sports," said the late Harry Coyle, NBC's longtime dean of directing, noting the meteoric rise of TV sales after the network began broadcasting the World Series and other sporting events in 1947. Just as sports today remains a programming cornerstone, Coyle's influence on the medium is rock solid.

Producers and directors still go by the book, actually a ten-page manual known as "Harry's Bible," which begat the dos and don'ts of baseball coverage. Do have cameras strategically trained on specific players; don't cut to a tight shot of the runner on a play at the plate.

What set Coyle apart until his retirement in the late 1980s was his keen sense of the viewer. "I've always felt there's a gap between the people who do television and people who watch it," he said following his work on the NBC broadcast of the 1984 World Series. That philosophy, no doubt, was why his cameras caught so many great World Series moments: the usually stoic Joe DiMaggio kicking up dirt after being robbed of a home run in 1947; Willie Mays's over-the-shoulder catch in 1954; Yogi Berra's leap into pitcher Don Larsen's arms after he threw a perfect Game 5 in 1956; and, of course, Carlton Fisk doing the home run wave in 1975.

Besides his Bible, Coyle's legacy includes the introduction of the centerfield camera, close-ups, and handheld cameras— plus the untold millions of eye-witnesses to Coyle's behind-the-scenes genius.

(Opposite) In one of the most famous shots in sports, Carlton Fisk waves emphatically toward fair territory as he tries to will the ball's path inside the foul pole. The camera angle that changed the way sports is viewed came about because of a rat. Until this point, cameramen were directed to follow the flight of the ball so the viewer could stay with the action of the game. This time, just as Fisk hit the ball, the rat appeared at the feet of the cameraman stationed inside the "Green Monster"—the big green left field wall that is synonymous with Fenway Park. The man froze, leaving his camera trained squarely on Fisk at home plate. Coyle had the presence of mind to stay with Fisk's reactions, then followed him as he jumped up and down, clapped, and leaped onto home plate *(above)*.

THE SECOND GOLDEN AGE

In 1980, Ronald Reagan's presidential campaign proclaimed it was "Morning in America." Whether the phrase was Republican party hype or not, it felt to many like a new beginning as he took office. Many Americans were more than ready to wake up from a decade of dashed expectations, punctuated by rampant inflation, gas shortages, a hostage crisis, presidential scandals, and increasing crime, poverty, and drug use. The "have a nice day" era—which ironically coincided with a mass reevaluation of the American dream—was about to become a very nice decade.

If it seemed like "Morning in America" as the Reagan years began, it also seemed like "Morning at NBC." Grant Tinker and Brandon Tartikoff took hold of the struggling network's future, and the network found itself in a position it hadn't been in since the early fifties: at the top. Through savvy programming choices—reflecting an upbeat, newly responsible (and newly cynical) American mood—Tinker and Tartikoff made NBC into a winner.

Saturday Night Live continued to bring ironic humor into the mainstream; questioning, satirizing, and undercutting anything and everything in American society became the norm. Old-school comedian Milton Berle tanked when he hosted *SNL*; the gap between Berle's vaudevillian humor and the cool irony of the Not Ready for Prime Time Players was far too wide.

Meanwhile, a comedian named David Letterman applied a heavy dollop of

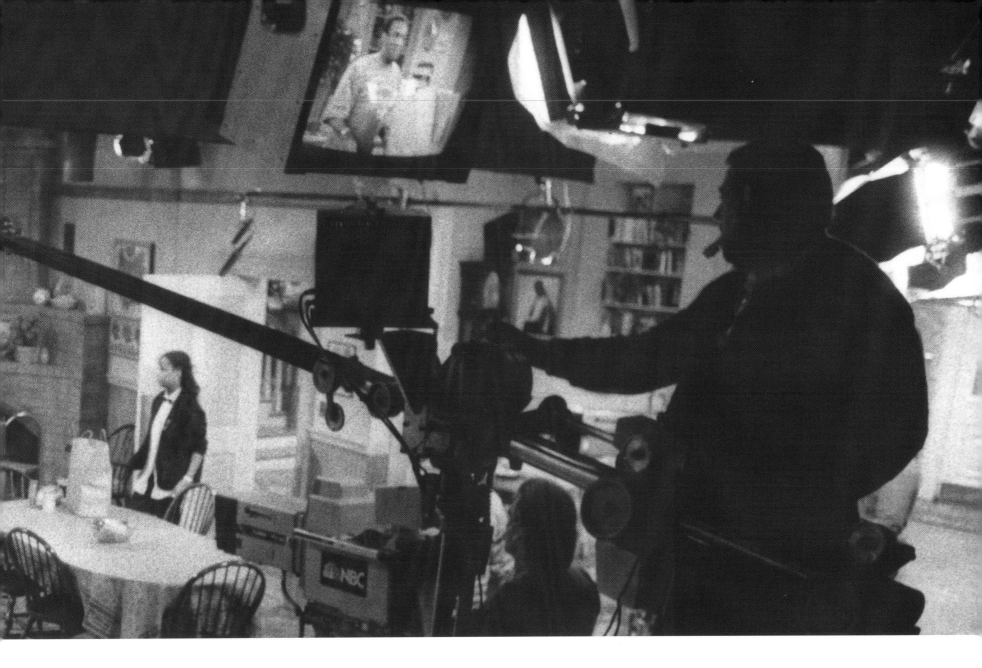

post-*SNL* irony to the classic late-night talk show formula and made it work brilliantly. *Late Night with David Letterman*, a talk show that constantly made fun of the conventions of the talk show, was proof that NBC could redefine itself in a way that would keep Americans awake (and laughing) long into the night.

The *Cosby Show*, a prime-time sitcom whose family was African-American and successful, made an enormous contribution to race relations in American society with a minimum of proselytizing and a maximum of warm humor. Similarly, *Family Ties* advanced a national dialogue about the collision of sixties idealism with eighties yuppiedom—within the deceptively calm confines of a smart sitcom.

Sometimes NBC's hits were more about surface than substance (such as the pastel *Miami Vice* and cartoonish *The A-Team*.) Other times the network wisely stuck with deeper, initially low-rated shows, such as *Hill Street Blues* (with its startling reevaluation of the crime drama) and *Cheers* (with its funny yet unsentimental take on friendship and romance).

Despite the high ratings and high-fives in the hallways at 30 Rock and in Burbank, NBC's future was far from rosy. Parent company RCA was in trouble. Penetration of VCRs and cable TV was growing at an astonishing pace. Many at the company hoped that by becoming the best network in the land—which NBC had certainly done—the worrisome future would take care of itself. Only time would tell.

DEFENDERS OF QUALITY

At age thirty-one, Brandon Tartikoff was the youngest head programmer in television. As a boy of seven or eight, he once watched *Dennis the Menace* on television and complained to his mother that Jay North was miscast as Dennis—an anecdote that sheds light on Tartikoff's rapid rise through the entertainment ranks.

In 1981, NBC was on the ropes, and RCA chairman Thornton Bradshaw knew that he needed a talented broadcasting executive to save the company. He found one in Grant Tinker, the president of highly successful MTM Enterprises. Tinker had started his career in 1949 as NBC's first management trainee, had rejoined the network as head of West Coast programming in the sixties, and was famous as "Mr. Quality TV." Tinker recalls just how dire the outlook was when he agreed to serve as chairman and CEO of NBC: "At the first RCA board meeting I ever attended, Edgar Griffith, who was RCA chairman before Bradshaw, actually proposed selling NBC.

I thought it was a little rude of him, since I had just arrived."

Sweeping aside the conventional wisdom that he had to fire the program guy who had not succeeded, Tinker reaffirmed his faith in Brandon Tartikoff. "I felt that Brandon had never really been at bat," he recalls. "I respected his instincts and we made a pretty good team." That's putting it mildly. Tartikoff's instincts sent him in creative directions that were the genesis of programs such as *The Cosby Show* and *Hill Street Blues*. Fighting separate battles with frustrated affiliates and with his own Hodgkin's disease, Tartikoff took heart from Tinker's strong support. Tinker and Tartikoff showed exceptional courage and patience by renewing

shows such as *St. Elsewhere* and *Cheers* despite discouraging first-season ratings. The extra breathing room allowed audiences time to find the shows and get hooked.

Patience and faith in quality were rewarded in August 1983, when Tartikoff learned that NBC had received 133 Emmy nominations, the most the network had ever received and more than the other two networks combined. Even better, the shows were hits in the ratings. The following season, NBC placed three shows in the Nielsen Top 10 for the first time in a decade. The Peacock network dominated the ratings with Tinker and Tartikoff shows through the rest of the 1980s. There was plenty of celebrating at

(Left) Taking a break at an NBC Affiliates Convention, (left to right) Bob Wright, Brandon Tartikoff, Suzanne Wright, Lilly Tartikoff. *(Middle)* Although Tinker and Tartikoff were separated by twenty years of age, they were an unbeatable team that combined youth, energy, and a dedication to high-quality storytelling. *(Right)* Tartikoff and *Fresh Prince* star Will Smith. *(Opposite, top)* Tartikoff at a party celebrating the 100th episode of *Hill Street Blues*.

30 Rock and in Burbank, but Tinker was philosophical. "I think there is simply a kind of cumulative effect that happens in programming: one good show begets another," he says. "What was most satisfying to me was seeing shows like *Cosby*, *Elsewhere*, *Hill Street*, and *Cheers* on the air. There was just a little more that stuck to your ribs after you'd watched one of those, rather than some witless forgettable comedy or inane drama. I used to get as much satisfaction out of the quality or the character of our shows as I did out of the numbers success."

After Tinker left NBC in August 1986, new CEO Bob Wright convinced Tartikoff to stay on. Wright taught Tartikoff about business, and Tartikoff taught Wright about television. "Brandon was one of the most talented people I've ever worked with," says Wright. "He was a true child of television, familiar with practically every show that had ever aired. He programmed NBC from his heart, and that made all the difference."

Tartikoff left NBC in May 1991 to head up Paramount Pictures. When he lost his long battle with Hodgkin's disease in 1997, the entertainment world lost one of its brightest stars.

"As a kid, Brandon wanted to live inside a television more than anything," says Brandon's wife, Lilly Tartikoff. "NBC made it possible for this boy to live out his dream."

LET'S BE CAREFUL OUT THERE

(Below, left to right): Top row: Ed Marinaro, Betty Thomas, Joe Spano; middle row: James B. Sikking, Taurean Blacque, Rene Enriquez, Bruce Weitz; bottom row: Michael Conrad, Barbara Bosson, Daniel J. Travanti, Veronica Hamel, Michael Warren.

(Right) The ensemble cast shares a typical scene depicting the grittiness of urban life. *(Far right)* Dennis Franz as Lt. Norman Buntz. *(Opposite, left)* Sgt. Phil Esterhaus (Michael Conrad) presides over the morning briefing. *(Opposite, right)* Betty Thomas as Officer Lucy Bates with her partner, Officer Joe Coffey, played by Ed Marinaro.

For better or worse, every cop show since *Dragnet* had played off the conventions of the genre that Jack Webb had established—until *Hill Street Blues*. Created by Steve Bochco and Michael Kozoll, and produced by Grant Tinker's MTM Enterprises, *Hill Street Blues* changed the face of TV drama during its seven-year run (1981–87). Twenty-six Emmys and ninety-eight Emmy nominations later, it remains TV's most honored drama series.

The idea for the show sprang from NBC's then-President Fred Silverman, who was looking for a realistic urban police series. The idea was proposed to Kozoll and Bochco, but they balked—been there, done that. But Silverman and Brandon Tartikoff continued to woo them, so they demanded a degree of autonomy that was unprecedented in network television. They got it—in part because NBC was then a distant third in the three-way ratings race with CBS and ABC. Even before any scripts had been written, Bochco and Kozoll put the network on notice that they intended to break all the rules. That's exactly what they did.

Hill Street Blues took every *Dragnet* convention and stood it on its head. Suddenly, cops were fallible. They behaved badly both on the job and off it. They didn't always go by the book. They had personal lives—messy, stressful personal lives—which carried over into their work on the street. They lied. They drank. They swore. They talked about bodily functions. And the bad guys? Often enough, they walked, and sometimes we never even found out whodunit.

You had to pay attention if you wanted to watch *Hill Street*.

Conventional wisdom had it that viewers couldn't follow more than three plot lines in any one episode. *Hill Street*'s plot threads sometimes approached double digits. Moreover, these intricate threads carried over from one episode to another, and sometimes from one season to another. Conventional wisdom also said that audiences wouldn't care about or follow more than a half-dozen major

the unintentionally hilarious, ramrod reactionary Lieutenant Howard Hunter (James Sikking), head of the SWAT team; and streetwise Lieutenant Norman Buntz (Dennis Franz).

Commanding officer Captain Frank Furillo (Daniel J. Travanti) was perhaps the straightest arrow of the bunch, but even he was hounded by his ex-wife for alimony and was "sleeping with the

conversations, and deliberately grungy setting established the feel of *Hill Street Blues* even before the opening credits (and Mike Post's memorable theme) aired. The roll call reintroduced the primary characters, and Esterhaus's survey of old cases and notes on what might be coming prepped not just the cops but the audience as well.

The series was anything but an instant success. Coming in

characters. *Hill Street Blues* fielded a core ensemble of thirteen the first season, fourteen after that.

The characters were like nothing out of Central Casting. The Hill Street precinct house was staffed by a memorable collection of oddballs. There was the disheveled Detective Mick Belker (Bruce Weitz), who somehow never cut the maternal apron strings but still managed to growl at his suspects;

enemy"—public defender Joyce Davenport (Veronica Hamel). Then there was paternal, thesaurus-mouthed Sergeant Phil Esterhaus (Michael Conrad), who presided over the morning briefing and always sent the team off with "Let's be careful out there."

The morning briefing was the touchstone of *Hill Street*. The "shaky cam," overlapping

eighty-third out of ninety-seven series, *Hill Street* had the distinction of being the lowest-rated program ever renewed for a second season. Working in its favor, however, were strong ratings with the affluent 18–49 demographic and a slew of Emmys for its abbreviated first season. The fact that in July 1981, Grant Tinker left MTM and slid into Silverman's chair at NBC also didn't hurt.

ST. ELSEWHERE

St. Elsewhere did for medical shows what *Hill Street* did for cop shows. In fact, it was often called "*Hill Street* in a hospital." Running from 1982 through 1988, its ensemble cast (including a young Denzel Washington) struggled with personal and professional crises while treating patients at St. Eligius (aka St. Elsewhere), Boston's chaotic public hospital.

The innovative MTM Enterprises program shattered the doctors-as-God tradition set by *Dr. Kildare* and other medical programs. *St. Elsewhere* was a revolving door of life and death for both patients and staff. On staff at one time or another were a serial rapist/physician, a nurse/murderess (who killed the rapist), and a bumper crop of philanderers. Viewers learned that there were no guarantees, and even beloved regular characters were written out of the show. Both in terms of character complexity and plot development, the IV drip runs straight and true from *St. Elsewhere* to *ER*.

The show tackled serious subjects, including the first treatment of AIDS in a dramatic program, but also had a sense of humor. In an episode dubbed "A Moon for the Misbegotten," Chief of Staff Donald Westphall (Ed Flanders) resigned when St. Eligius was acquired by a profit-hungry private medical conglomerate. Before leaving, he dropped his pants and mooned the incoming new corporate head administrator. The last fatality in the show's final episode was the small white kitten that had always meowed as end credits rolled in every MTM production.

(Circle) Cliff (John Ratzenberger) appears on *Jeopardy!* with Alex Trebek. *(Top, left to right)* Rebecca (Kirstie Alley) gets carried away; Diane (Shelley Long) finds plenty of unintended humor in something Sam (Ted Danson) said; sometimes Carla (Rhea Perlman) feels that working as a career waitress is like spending life in jail. *(Opposite, top)* Sam, Woody (Woody Harrelson), Cliff, Norm (George Wendt), and Carla share a story. *(Opposite, bottom)* Toga party!

WHERE EVERYBODY KNOWS YOUR NAME

It all started when NBC wanted a series that reflected the atmosphere of the era's popular Miller Lite commercials. What the network ended up getting was *Cheers.*

NBC's longest-running comedy series, *Cheers* first aired in September 1982. After nearly being cancelled in its first season, the show found its audience and became one of the most beloved sitcoms ever made. During its eleven seasons, *Cheers* earned 26 Emmys and a record 111 Emmy nominations. The show became a Thursday night refuge for millions of viewers, happy to drop in on a place "where everybody knows your name."

Based on an actual Boston bar, the Bull & Finch, *Cheers* was created by Glen and Les Charles and James Burrows, and they filled it with witty dialogue, acerbic putdowns, and comic situations that avoided social issues and never preached. Some soap-opera aspects of the show—Would Sam and Diane become involved? Would Rebecca marry Robin?—were kept in play for entire seasons, but the series preferred irreverence over sentimentality; emotionally poignant scenes were invariably subverted by someone's caustic observation.

Cheers reveled in its disregard for political correctness. Bar owner Sam (Ted Danson) was an unregenerate, albeit charming womanizer. Diane (Shelley

Long) was convinced she was only waitressing until she became a famous author, but her intellectual pretensions were obvious. Sam and Diane had an on-again, off-again romance that finally ended with Diane rejecting his marriage proposal in the fourth season. During the third season, Diane took a hiatus from Sam, and she and psychiatrist Frasier Crane (Kelsey Grammer) became an item. Frasier was supercilious, insecure, and snooty—himself a case study in neurosis.

In 1987, Rebecca (Kirstie Alley) replaced Diane after Shelley Long left the show. To the delight of viewers, Sam and Rebecca eventually took up where the first couple left off.

Bar patrons Cliff (John Ratzenberger) and Norm (George Wendt) traded one-liners and enjoyed the sardonic putdowns of career waitress Carla (Rhea Perlman). Tending bar with Sam were Coach (Nicholas Colasanto) and, later, Woody (Woody Harrelson) who took over the role after

Colasanto passed away in 1985. In their naiveté, both were perfect foils to the bar's sharper-tongued patrons, with Woody especially setting new standards in dimness.

Cheers not only introduced the world to a cast of talented actors, but is credited with advancing the serialization of sitcoms and being the first comedy to perfect the use of the cliffhanger. No wonder *Entertainment Weekly* put it at No. 4 in a list of the greatest 100 TV shows of all time.

FAMILY TIES

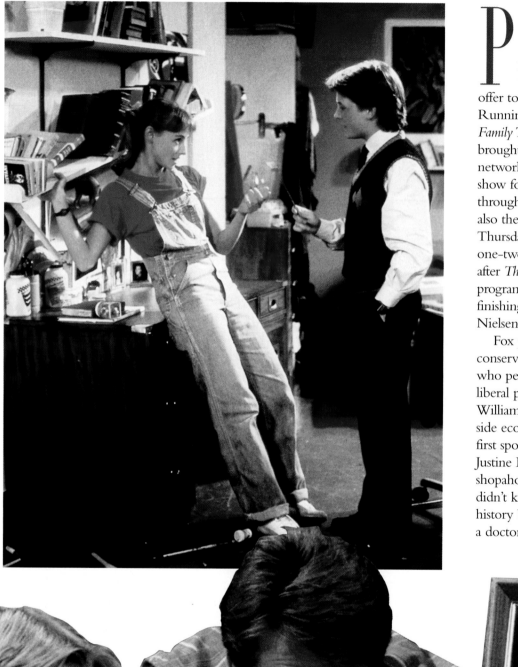

President Reagan said it was his favorite TV series. (The show's producers declined to take him up on his offer to appear in an episode.) Running from 1982 to 1989, *Family Ties* was the series that brought Michael J. Fox to network television. A Top 20 show for six of its seven years, through the mid-1980s it was also the second half of NBC's Thursday night knockout one-two punch, airing right after *The Cosby Show*, the No. 1 program in the nation, and finishing just behind it in the Nielsen ratings.

Fox played the role of conservative teen Alex Keaton, who perpetually dismayed his liberal parents with his love of William F. Buckley and supply-side economics—a child whose first spoken word was "Nixon." Justine Bateman played his shopaholic sister Mallory, who didn't know much about history but could have written a doctoral dissertation on lip gloss. The two of them were enough to make their idealistic, formerly tie-dyed parents, played by Meredith Baxter Birney and Michael Gross, suspect there was a rogue gene or two loose in the family tree. Younger sister Jennifer (Tina Yothers) simply wanted to be a kid, while baby brother Andrew (Brian Bonsall) learned from big brother Alex, as their parents looked on in disbelief.

Series creator Gary David Goldberg, an ex-hippie, considered the show semi-autobiographical. He had originally intended for the show's story lines to emphasize the older Keatons—one-time flower children struggling to reconcile the activism of their youth with their daily parental duties. But the focus shifted, as the cheerily capitalistic Alex Keaton became a 1980s icon and Michael J. Fox became a star. (Matthew Broderick was originally intended for the part, but he was unwilling to move from New York to do the show.)

(Above) Tracy Pollan and Michael J. Fox share an intimate moment. After Meredith Baxter Birney became pregnant in real life, her character Elyse gave birth to a second son, Andrew *(Brian Bonsall, left)*, who idolized Alex (Fox). In the Keaton living room, *(opposite page, left to right)* Michael Gross, Meredith Baxter Birney, Michael J. Fox, Tina Yothers, and Justine Bateman.

Courteney Cox, who had been spotted by the show's producers in the Bruce Springsteen video, *Dancing in the Dark*, portrayed Lauren Miller, Alex's second serious romance. His first, Ellen Reed, was played by Tracy Pollan. Pollan left the show in 1986, but she stayed involved with the show's star, Michael J. Fox—by marrying him.

One episode ("A, My Name is Alex") broke away from the usual format, with Fox on an almost-bare stage, grieving for a friend killed in a car crash. The episode would go on to win an Emmy, a Writers Guild Award, and a Humanitas Award for Goldberg and producer/writer Alan Uger.

What could have been a bitter clash of values and political opinions was played for laughs within the safe harbor of a warm and loving family. The chasm between the values of Steve and Elyse Keaton and those embraced by their children provided an ironic and effective mirror of the ways our nation was changing and questioning itself in the heyday of yuppies and the Me Generation.

Cool Cops, a Suave Impostor, and a Private Army on the Run

Miami Vice, Remington Steele, and *The A-Team* were not just hit TV shows but cultural phenomena. While the cool *Vice* and *Steele* defined eighties male fashion, the overheated *A-Team* turned macho theatrics into prime-time fun—and made a superstar out of a guy who growled "I pity the fool!" at regular intervals.

According to network lore, *Miami Vice* sprang from just two words on a napkin in Brandon Tartikoff's high-concept short-hand—"MTV cops." Created by award-winning *Hill Street Blues* writer Anthony Yerkovich and executive-produced by Michael Mann (who would go on to produce feature films *Last of the Mohicans* and *Ali*), and airing from 1984 to 1989, *Miami Vice* starred Don Johnson as Sonny Crockett and Philip Michael Thomas as Ricardo Tubbs, and for the second half of the 1980s, the show was the epitome of hip. There was nothing cooler than Crockett and Tubbs flying past Miami's art deco hotels in Crockett's Ferrari in hot pursuit of any of the numerous drug dealers who were the program's favorite bad guys. There were other regular characters, most notably Edward James Olmos as brooding Lt. Martin Castillo. The steamy, overripe, and borderline deca-dent Miami backdrop deserved an Outstanding Supporting Actor nomination for its contribution. If film noir had been shot in color, it would have looked like *Miami Vice.*

Miami Vice had a powerful influence on men's fashions, nudging a generation of men out of their earth tones and into tropical pastels. Suddenly, three-day stubble was in vogue. *Miami Vice*'s distinctive Jan Hammer soundtrack helped carry out Tartikoff's vision by making extensive use of rock music in each episode. It also put rock musicians, including Glenn Frey, Ted Nugent, and Phil Collins (who was perfect as a sleazy game-show host) on display in non-singing guest appearances. Stars, fashion, music, the locale—everything about the show was hot. As a result, it was a winner with the younger demographic coveted by advertisers, although the program never ranked higher than ninth overall.

Before he became James Bond, Pierce Brosnan was *Remington Steele.* Stephanie Zimbalist co-starred as the financially struggling private investigator Laura Holt, whose business really picked up after she rechristened her failing agency Remington Steele.

Perpetually explaining to her clients that the fictitious Steele was off on assignment, imagine her surprise when a tall, dark, handsome stranger arrived at the agency and identified himself as the man with his name on the door. Thereafter Steele and Holt solved cases together, but their real specialty was the snappy repartee—behind which always lurked the possibility of romance. She was feisty; he was suave. Together they made a great couple, a Nick and Nora Charles for the 1980s. *Remington Steele* aired for five seasons, beginning in the fall of 1982.

The A-Team was mad, bad, and dangerous. The series was produced by the ingenious and prolific Stephen J. Cannell, whose television credits include *Baretta*, *The Rockford Files*, and *Baa Baa Black Sheep*. The band on the run consisted of four Vietnam vets fleeing a bum rap that had landed them in the stockade at Fort Bragg. Always just a half-step ahead of reincarceration, they kept body and soul together by

hiring themselves out as soldiers of fortune, often in service to the downtrodden. Headed by Colonel Hannibal Smith (played by George Peppard), the rest of the squad consisted of a smooth-talking hustler (played by Dirk Benedict, and dubbed "Faceman"), a quasi-certifiable pilot who could fly anything (Dwight Schultz as "Howlin' Mad" Murdock), and B. A. Baracus, a brawny and ill-tempered mechanic who had a white-knuckle fear of flying.

B.A. (which stood for "Bad Attitude") was the most fear-some of the four-some. Played by the formidable Mr.

T, with his forbidding scowl, Mohawk haircut, powerful build, and massive gold jewelry, he became a bona fide celebrity, and his popularity enabled NBC to spin off a Saturday morning cartoon called *Mister T*.

Audiences loved the *The A-Team*'s many catchphrases and the ingenuity that allowed the team to build whatever they needed out of the most unlikely spare parts. Yet, from time to time, *The A-Team* drew fire as one of the most violent programs on television. Critics missed the point that fans understood completely. Despite all the bullets, crashes, and explosions, there were few fatalities, and the show kept its tongue squarely in its cheek from January 1983 through the series finale in June 1987.

(Opposite, top) Johnson (left) and Thomas showed how cool white suits, no socks, and even pink ties could look—especially if you were driving a Testarossa. *(Opposite, bottom)* Hot boats, hot cars, hot women, hot music and hot weather all blended perfectly. *(Above)* Mr. T had the most notoriety in the A-Team army and its over-the-top schemes. *(Below)* Peppard and "Faceman" (Dirk Benedict) corner a bad guy with their "gun." *(Above, left)* The guy who made the ladies swoon was Pierce Brosnan as Remington Steele, later to become famed secret agent 007.

BASEBALL'S SHOW OF SHOWS

League Baseball series, featuring Lindsey Nelson and color analyst Leo "The Lip" Durocher in the booth. The groundbreaking *Gillette Cavalcade of Sports*—TV's first all-sports program—aired weekly from 1944 to 1964, covering an array of events, including baseball, boxing, and football. But, in 1966, the network negotiated for the rights to the venerable *Game of the Week*. It would become a Saturday afternoon alternative to mowing lawns and taking out the trash for the next twenty-three seasons.

Curt Smith, in his history of baseball broadcasting, *Voices of The Game*, declares *Game of the Week*—which debuted in 1953 on ABC and two years later shifted to CBS—"the most transforming baseball series." Behind the microphone, NBC replaced the folksy Dizzy Dean with Curt Gowdy, who, writes Smith, "emerged for an entire generation of listeners as the national signature of baseball broadcasting." Until 1975, Gowdy called play-by-play for every All-Star Game, every World Series game and virtually every regular-season game on the network.

Through the eighties, *Game of the Week* remained a weekend treasure, as well as a showcase for broadcasters who joined Gowdy as familiar voices of baseball: Lindsey Nelson, Vin Scully, Joe Garagiola,

From its infancy, television presented an ideal medium for bringing baseball into the lives and living rooms of millions of Americans, and no network was as identified with groundbreaking coverage of the national pastime as NBC. The friendly confines of sun-lit ballparks fit nicely in the small screen, and viewers were already intimately familiar with the game's nuances. By the late forties, team owners started getting over their fear that television would keep fans from coming to the ballpark. They realized that, as with radio, airing games actually generates a wider fan base and a lucrative new revenue source through sales of broadcast rights and advertising. So began the Grand Old Game's love affair with television.

This thinking was not lost on the baseball owners of the late fifties, nor on NBC, when it launched its Saturday *Major*

Dick Enberg, Tony Kubek, and Bob Costas. "When you did *Game of the Week*, you were visiting with your friends," Garagiola told *The Arizona Republic*, reflecting on the broadcast's influence beyond major league cities. "They really took you into their home. We'd have big audiences in the Phoenixes, the Des Moineses, the New Orleanses. We were it. You wanted to watch a big-league game, you had to tune into *Game of the Week*."

Costas, ideally teamed with Kubek from 1982 until 1989, represented the new breed of sportscasters—astute, sophisticated, and appealing enough to handle most any assignment. He melded perfectly with NBC Sports' growing strategy of securing rights to broadcast premier events, which during the eighties included the World Series, Super Bowl, and Summer Olympic Games.

Honored as Sportscaster of the Year by the National Sportswriters & Sportscasters Association a record seven times—initially in 1985, at age thirty-three, becoming the youngest recipient—Costas would eventually enrich the network's telecasts of the NFL, NBA, and the Olympics. Yet baseball, which he approached with a unique combination of historical perspective, command of the language, irreverant humor, and a willingness to speak out forcefully on issues surrounding the game, remained his first love. "There's a romance and mystique to baseball that nothing else can match," he once claimed.

In *Voices of The Game*, Smith admires Costas's ability, during his debut season as *Game of the Week*'s play-by-play announcer, "to drape the pastime with a warmth and insight that eclipsed the bare and statistical."

Eventually, American weekends became too hectic for even the most ingenious excuse-makers to sit at home in front of the television on a Saturday afternoon. Costas and Kubek called the Baltimore-Toronto game on September 30, 1989, and turned out the lights in the *Game of the Week* booth for good.

(Opposite) Curt Gowdy and Joe Garagiola pose for a *Game of the Week* promotion. *(Above)* Bob Costas and Tony Kubek. *(Below, left to right)* Gowdy and Kubek in the booth; Garagiola and Vin Scully.

INSOMNIACS' DELIGHT

Not everybody went to bed when Johnny Carson signed off. NBC had learned from the success of *Tomorrow* and *The Midnight Special* that many people—mostly in their twenties and thirties—stayed awake into the wee hours of the morning. To increase viewership in this coveted demographic, the network expanded its late-night programming by taking yet another approach.

The *Late Night* show, airing from 12:30 a.m. to 1:30 p.m., began in 1982. Its host was David Letterman, who cultivated a following of devoted fans with his offbeat humor and smart-alecky style. Letterman was nothing if not unpredictable. Surprise guests materialized on the show, including Jack Paar and Johnny Carson (bearing a check for $1,000,000 from Publishers' Clearinghouse). In one memorable segment, Letterman donned a Velcro suit, ran across the stage, hurled himself at a wall, and stuck there. In another, he put on a suit made of Alka-Seltzer tablets. His goofy recurring skits—elevator races, "Top Ten Lists," "Stupid Pet Tricks," and "Nightcap Theatre" (clips from old movies, much like the fare available on other networks at that hour), as well as his peripatetic wanderings beyond the studio onto the streets of Manhattan—unnerved some of his celebrity guests, especially those who arrived on the set expecting a more conventional talk show. Sir Alec Guinness found himself

faced with a hard act to follow. He came on just after Letterman had scrambled a dozen eggs by hurling them through a jumbo electric fan.

When Letterman left NBC in 1993, Conan O'Brien stepped in as *Late Night* host. The network also discovered that people stayed up even later than *Late Night*. So, beginning in 1988, *Later*

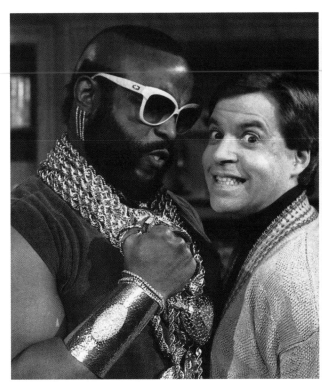

with *Bob Costas* followed *Late Night* to appeal to this audience of night owls. Unlike Letterman or Leno, Costas was not a comedian but a sports-caster. Teamed with former Yankee Tony Kubek, he had done the play-by-play for the baseball *Game of the Week* beginning in 1982. (Eventually, he went on to become NBC's Olympic anchor for the 1992, 1996, 2000, and 2002 Games.)

Later showcased Costas's interviewing skills by presenting just one guest in each half-hour program. The guests, who came mostly from entertainment and sports, were profiled in a film montage before sitting down for a conversation. *Later with Bob Costas* won an Emmy for Outstanding Informational Series in 1993.

In 1994, Costas left *Later* to take on new duties at NBC News, including contributing segments for *Dateline NBC*

and *Today*. Greg Kinnear, who had previously hosted *Talk Soup* on E! Entertainment, stepped in as host and remained with the program until 1996. After he departed to pursue his acting career (*As Good As It Gets*, *You've Got Mail*), Kinnear was replaced by a series of rotating hosts. In January 2002, however, MTV's Carson Daly became the new host of NBC's 1:35 a.m. time slot, rechristened *Last Call with Carson Daly*.

Unpredictable zaniness was part of Letterman's formula for success, and if he had to get on a horse *(above, right)* or wear a suit of marshmallows *(below, middle)*, he was ready to do it. Dave also attracted top celebrities, such as Sonny and Cher (in a famous reunion) *(below, right)* and Eddie Murphy *(below, left)*. Costas talked with Sting *(opposite, lower left)* and joked with Mr. T. *(above, left)*. Kinnear focused on entertainment interviews, such as *ER*'s Noah Wyle *(opposite, lower right)*.

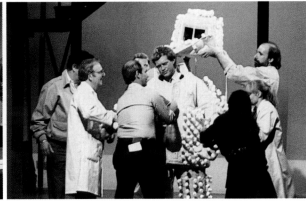

WHAT A DIFFERENCE *TODAY* MAKES

(*Below, left to right*) Gene Shalit, Willard Scott, Tom Brokaw, Jane Pauley. (*Opposite, top*) April 1, 1985: A breakthrough moment, arranged by NBC News Vice President Tim Russert, as *Today* has an audience with Pope John Paul II at the Vatican—a TV first. (*Opposite, bottom*) Pauley and Gumbel on the set of *Today*, live from Beijing.

In 1976, when Barbara Walters left NBC to become network news's first million-dollar anchor at ABC News, she vacated one of the most important chairs in television. The nationwide search for her replacement was conducted in the most public way imaginable: on-air auditions by some very seasoned female broadcasters. The winner had barely four years of experience in broadcasting, and was just twenty-five years old. NBC News had found Jane Pauley anchoring the news in Indianapolis and had tapped her to be Chicago's first evening anchorwoman, at WMAQ, only one year before giving her the tryout for *Today*.

Perhaps to lower the stakes for herself, Pauley would say Barbara Walters's replacement was Tom Brokaw, not her. "Most of the pressure was on him," she says even now. Brokaw had been NBC News White House correspondent and, as Pauley remembers, "was just off the Watergate beat, and still had adrenaline pumping in his veins."

Brokaw and Pauley emerged as an excellent *Today* team. Along with resident wit Gene Shalit, the mustachioed movie critic (then and now), the show achieved solid ratings against the first significant competition *Today* had ever had: ABC's *Good Morning America*, with David Hartman and Joan Lunden.

The team was joined in 1980 by a weatherman with a homey persona: Willard Scott. "My plan is to fill the void left by J. Fred Muggs," he quipped to journalists at the time. Behind the scenes, Scott

fretted that his lovable shtick was too unsophisticated for the show. "I was an instant disaster," he recalls. But when a 30 Rock technician informed him, "My grandmother in Brooklyn loves you," Scott realized he would be all right. "That's perfect," he recalls telling the technician. "As long as your grandmother in Brooklyn loves me, I'm in."

When Tom Brokaw left the show to anchor *NBC Nightly News* in 1982, he was replaced by Bryant Gumbel, a well-regarded NBC sportscaster. Despite having little news experience, Gumbel quickly took to the job, demonstrating a flair for asking aggressive and intelligent questions. "The success of our partnership was in part that I didn't take any guff from Bryant," says Pauley. "He respected me for that.

There was a very strong chemistry between us. I've likened it to sibling rivalry. Bryant and I had a very close relationship, and we're very good friends, even today."

The show had fallen to second place behind *Good Morning America*, but by the mid-eighties *Today* stole the lead back again, winning great acclaim for its spectacular worldwide remotes from locations such as the Great Wall of China, the Kremlin in Moscow, the Roman Coliseum, and the deck of an aircraft carrier, the USS *Coral Sea*.

Pauley, who feels like she grew up on *Today*, looks back at her years there with a great deal of fondness and only one regret. "I wish someone had told me that I would have a thirteen-year tenure on *Today*," she laughs. "It would have made life a great deal easier!"

HAPPY 100TH!

There must be something about Willard Scott and longevity. *Today*'s traveling ambassador, who started at NBC's Washington station in 1950, has long cornered the market on saying "Happy birthday!" to America's one-hundred-year-olds.

"I'd like to say the birthday thing started when we brainstormed for ideas," laughs Scott, "but somebody just sent a card one day, said their uncle was gonna be one hundred. So what the hell? Did it once. Never gave it a thought. Now it's turned out to be my job."

Each week, Scott receives well over a hundred birthday announcements, but has time to mention only twelve. He always mentions the most senior of his seniors, trying to include as many men in the mix as possible—there are usually far more women who break the magic barrier.

"We are now the largest clearinghouse in the country for centenarians," says Scott proudly. "Colleges and researchers all over the world come to us for information about these folks. So that's that story."

LAWYERS IN LOVE

(Above) Sheila Kelley and Michael Cumpsty. (Below) Arnie Becker (Bernsen) in a copyright infringement case. (Opposite, left) Douglas Brackman (Rachins) on Wheel of Fortune with Vanna White. (Opposite, right) Michael Kuzak (Hamlin) and Grace Van Owen (Dey) were adversaries in court and lovers in private. (Opposite, bottom) Jonathan Rollins (Blair Underwood) was the first African-American lawyer to join the firm, and for better or worse, was taken under Arnie's wing.

With intricately interwoven courtroom and human dramas, *L.A. Law* drew viewers into the tangled world of lawyers, much as *Hill Street Blues* and *St. Elsewhere* had us captivated by the worlds of cops and doctors, respectively. The series debuted in 1986, produced by Steven Bochco (who had produced *Hill Street*) and Terry Louise Fisher (a former assistant D.A. and *Cagney & Lacey* producer). It deployed the *Hill Street/St. Elsewhere* approach of an ensemble cast and multiple story lines in the elite firm of McKenzie, Brackman, Chaney & Kuzak.

From his corner office, senior partner and paterfamilias Leland McKenzie (Richard Dysart) tried to ride herd on his unruly band of attorneys, but they didn't make it easy for him. Much like the opening briefing in the squad room of *Hill Street*, viewers sat in on the petty bickering and power struggles in the morning partners' meeting, chaired by the insufferable Douglas Brackman, Jr. (Alan Rachins), managing partner, clock-watcher, and avid bean-counter. Chaney, the third name on the masthead, was found dead at his desk in the first episode, which prompted Machiavellian divorce lawyer Arnie Becker (Corbin Bernsen) to stake his claim to Chaney's office space even before the body had been removed.

There were plenty of office romances—tax lawyer Stuart Markowitz (Michael Tucker) and fellow partner Ann Kelsey (Jill Eikenberry); litigating partner Michael Kuzak (Harry Hamlin) and Assistant D.A. Grace Van Owen (Susan Dey), against whom he appeared in court from time to time; and lecherous Arnie Becker and just about everybody, including numerous clients and eventually his much-put-upon secretary, Roxanne Melman (played by Susan Ruttan).

The Markowitz/Kelsey romance yielded one of the most famous—or infamous—moments of the series. Mousy Stuart didn't strike anyone, not even Ann Kelsey, as a guy loaded with sex appeal, until one of his sleazier clients, a bigamist, let him in on the secret of a technique called the "Venus Butterfly." Despite a flood of mail from curious viewers, the specifics were never divulged, but Stuart and Ann were married in the second year of the run. Another memorable story line dealt with the arrival, then abrupt departure, of new

HOMICIDE: LIFE ON THE STREET

Running from 1993 through 1999, *Homicide: Life on the Street* was a gritty, hard-hitting series centered on the homicide detectives who worked the very mean streets of Baltimore. Overworked cops dealing with burgeoning body counts kept score on a white board in the squad room as cases came and went—red marker for the open ones, black for those that were closed, not all of which were solved or "cleared." Noteworthy as Oscar-winning director Barry Levinson's first venture into television, the program featured handheld camera work, down-to-earth Baltimore realism, and a cast of veteran actors that included Richard Belzer as Detective John Munch, André Braugher as Detective Frank Pembleton, Yaphet Kotto as Lt. Al Giardello, and Ned Beatty as Detective Stanley Bolander. *Homicide* had an umbilical link to *Law & Order*, with a number of story threads that played out on both shows; as the investigation progressed, cast members from one program would appear on the other—an innovative technique that helped both shows. Although *Homicide* struggled in the ratings and is no longer on the air, that link continues to this day: for the past three seasons, the caustic Detective Munch—uprooted from Baltimore to New York—has been part of the *Law & Order: SVU* cast, partnered with Detective "Fin" Tutuola (Ice-T).

partner Rosalind Shays (Diana Muldaur). Brought in as a rainmaker, Shays quickly proved to be a piranha, maneuvering for position while wooing, and eventually pushing out, Leland as senior partner. She met her untimely demise by stepping into an open elevator shaft in a March 1991 episode.

Although the private lives of *L.A. Law*'s attorneys played a prominent part in the show, the series counterbalanced its soap-operatic tendencies by presenting well-crafted legal plotlines pulled from contemporary news stories. Cases dealt with outing homosexuals, corporate responsibility for defective products, Tourette's syndrome, discrimination against fat people, and even dwarf tossing. In 1987, *L.A. Law* broke new ground with the

introduction of office boy Benny Stulwicz (Larry Drake). Benny was one of the first developmentally challenged characters seen in a recurring role on television. Drake won back-to-back Emmys for his portrayal.

Drake's Emmys were just a small part of the Emmy bonanza harvested by the show. It raked in twenty nominations in its rookie season (one less than *Hill Street*'s record haul), and nineteen in its second season. It was named Outstanding Drama Series in its first year on the air, and again for three consecutive seasons beginning with the 1988–89 season.

Although *L.A. Law* always posted respectable Nielsens, the show never made it into the Top 10. As it turned out, a lot of sponsors didn't care—its cachet with affluent

young professionals made its reputation. For better or worse, many observers ascribe the surge in law school applications in the late 1980s and early 1990s to the popularity of *L.A. Law*.

LIVING IN A DIFFERENT WORLD

But beyond that were poignant insights into the difficulties that confront prosperous African-Americans in an overwhelmingly white social environment.

Since starring in *Fresh Prince*, Smith has become a major movie star with blockbusters such as *Independence Day* and *Men in Black*, as well as continuing his award-winning music career.

In 1990, *The Fresh Prince of Bel Air* introduced television audiences to Will Smith. The music world already knew him as half of the rap duo D. J. Jazzy Jeff and the Fresh Prince. In the TV series, Smith portrayed himself, sort of—a streetwise teen from Philly named Will Smith, a rap artist sent out of the 'hood for safety's sake to live with his well-heeled aunt and uncle in their Bel Air mansion.

Produced by Quincy Jones, the show derived its comedy from the clash of cultures. Aunt Vivian (initially Janet Hubert-Whitten, later Daphne Maxwell Reid) and Uncle Philip (James Avery) even had a snootier-than-thou liveried butler, Geoffrey (Joseph Marcell). The rest of the family included terminally preppy son Carlton (Alfonso Ribeiro), self-absorbed daughter Hilary (Karyn Parsons), and Ashley (Tatyana M. Ali). A fourth child, Nicky, was later added.

Audiences responded to the show's broad comedic premise.

dying wish by taking in her two sons, Willis (Todd Bridges) and Arnold Jackson (Gary Coleman).

Coleman's wisecracking Arnold caught fire with audiences almost immediately, and the actor was largely responsible for the show's success. *Diff'rent Strokes* also dealt with important issues, including child molestation and drug abuse (the latter featuring an appearance by First Lady Nancy Reagan).

(Opposite page) Sports stars such as Muhammad Ali and Kareem Abdul-Jabbar made guest appearances on Diff'rent Strokes. (Left) Will Smith was a fish out of water in Bel Air, not just in the kitchen. (Above) Sinbad and Dawnn Lewis dance around on A Different World. (Opposite, left) Todd Bridges and Gary Coleman.

A Different World was that rare phenomenon—a spin-off from a hit sitcom that reinvented itself and became a success on its own terms. The "different world" of the title was university life—the original premise had Denise Huxtable (Lisa Bonet), the second daughter from *The Cosby Show*, leaving home to attend predominantly black Hillman College.

When Bonet left after the first season, producer/director Debbie Allen revamped the show around a new ensemble cast. Continuing characters

included spoiled rich girl Whitley Gilbert (Jasmine Guy), divorcee Jaleesa Vinson (Dawnn Lewis), dorm director Walter Oakes (Sinbad), and hip New Yorker Dwayne Wayne (Kadeem Hardison). Joining the cast were New Age environmentalist Freddie Brooks (Cree Summer), pre-med student Kim Reese (Charnele Brown), and ROTC commander Clayton Taylor (Glynn Turman).

A Howard University graduate, Allen drew on her own experiences to add depth to the show. She also took her

writing team on annual trips to Morehouse and Spelman colleges. As a result, what might have begun as formulaic became something far more significant. In its debut season, 1987–88, and in the following three years, the show finished in the Top 10.

Diff'rent Strokes (1978–86), like *The Fresh Prince*, plunked down streetwise kids in an affluent household and made humor out of the ensuing chaos. The household belonged to white business tycoon Philip Drummond (Conrad Bain), who fulfilled his housekeeper's

GOLDEN GIRLS — AND BOYS

Shy and retiring they were not. A new class of heroes and heroines started to appear on American TV screens just in the nick of time—when many of the Moms and Dads who witnessed the Golden Age of Television firsthand were in their golden years themselves and baby boomers began noticing their own first gray hairs.

For many years, older people were the great invisible men and women of television. When portrayed at all, they typically were either pleasantly helpful or harmlessly irascible, and they were usually defined in terms of their children or grandchildren. Several hit shows changed that stereotype forever.

Premiering in 1985, *The Golden Girls* was both an immediate success and an important breakthrough. Initially, the very idea of presenting a show with four lively, independent, and sexy women over the age of fifty was considered a long shot.

Set in south Florida and nicknamed "Miami Nice," the show featured a quartet of brilliant comediennes—gravel-voiced Bea Arthur as substitute teacher Dorothy Sbornak, Betty White as slightly ditzy grief counselor Rose Nylund, Estelle Getty as Dorothy's mother, salty Sophia Petrillo,

(Circle and below) Ben Matlock (Andy Griffith), an Atlanta lawyer, charged $250,000 to defend a client—expensive for 1986. Miraculously, he seemed to find clients who were all innocent. *(Right)* Quincy (Jack Klugman) makes another startling forensic discovery, as assistant Sam Fujiyama (Robert Ito) looks on. The show began as one-fourth of the rotating *NBC Mystery Movie* and was so popular it became a separate weekly series in 1977.

who always spoke her mind, and Rue McClanahan as oversexed southern belle Blanche Devereaux. Created by Susan Harris, *The Golden Girls* was the surprise hit of the 1985–86 season, attracting an audience that cut across generational lines, and finishing seventh overall for the year. Teens particularly responded to Estelle Getty's Sophia. The antithesis of the mild-mannered granny, Sophia dissed everyone—ostensibly as a result of a stroke that destroyed the part of her brain responsible for tact and diplomacy.

Quincy, M.E. and *Matlock* were two crime shows that featured older main characters whose personalities were at least as engaging as the whodunits they solved. Veteran actor Jack Klugman, who had played Oscar Madison to Tony Randall's Felix Unger in *The Odd Couple* through 1975, portrayed Quincy, the

cantankerous medical examiner, from 1976 through 1983.

Never one to suffer fools, he specialized in second-guessing police officers and district attorneys based on his forensic examinations. The most memorable episode may be "Next Stop, Nowhere," an examination of the dangers of "punk rock" that's become a kitschy cult favorite. And, no, trivia fans, Quincy never had a first name—although aficionados of the series believe his first initial to be "R."

Quincy, M.E. began as one of four rotating *NBC Sunday Night Mysteries* in 1976, but Quincy proved to be such a likable hero that the show was given a weekly time slot.

If you crossed Raymond Burr's Perry Mason with Watergate committee chairman Sam Ervin, Jr., you'd pretty much get *Matlock*. Andy Griffith, a star on television for twenty-five years before the

show's debut in 1986, played Harvard-educated defense lawyer Ben Matlock. He used his well-developed hayseed personality as a smokescreen to conceal formidable skills as both an investigator and a courtroom lawyer. Criminals

who underestimated him did so at their peril.

The Golden Girls, *Quincy*, and *Matlock*—mature, smart, and very-much-alive heroines and heroes—proved that America's television generation could grow old gracefully.

(Top) Dorothy (Bea Arthur) gets married, with her mother Sophia (Estelle Getty) by her side. *(Above, left to right)* Lloyd Bochner and Blanche (Rue McClanahan) dance it up; all four girls sit around the kitchen table, as they often did—and look at Rose (Betty White) in amazement at something she said, as they often did; Dorothy and Rose at the piano.

GUESS WHO'S COMING TO PRIME TIME: BILL COSBY

The Cosby Show changed the face of television, rocketed Bill Cosby into superstardom, and altered the perception of African-American families forever. In early 1984, Brandon Tartikoff watched Bill Cosby doing a standup comedy routine on *The Tonight Show* and felt the comedian could have a winning sitcom. About the same time, producers Marcy Carsey and Tom Werner were in discussions with Cosby about a series. Because of

their status as former ABC executives, Carsey and Werner first offered the show to ABC, which passed. But Tartikoff persuaded a nervous NBC to try six episodes. The first, on September 20, 1984, astonished the industry by beating out *Magnum, P.I.* with a 43 share in the overnights. The next five episodes continued to earn stellar ratings, and for the following five consecutive seasons, *The Cosby Show* was the No. 1 television show in the nation.

The Cosby Show set up the powerhouse Thursday-night lineup that included *Family Ties*, *Cheers*, *Night Court*, and *Hill Street Blues*, and began the NBC turnaround—at last—for Tinker and Tartikoff. It was not only a giant in the ratings, but the kind of classy, witty television that Tinker advocated. With its focus on the Huxtables, *The Cosby Show* revived the family sitcom and continued the television tradition of exploring the meaning of family life in all of its facets. In that groundbreaking

first episode, son Theo (Malcolm-Jamal Warner) told his father he wasn't interested in having a career. "Dad," he smiled, "can't you just accept me and love me 'cause I'm your son?" After a thoughtful pause, Cliff Huxtable responded, "That's the dumbest thing I've ever heard." As the audience roared and applauded, Cosby would later remember, the show had found its voice: a loving yet tough family dynamic that was funny, real, and responsible.

What made this show

(Above, left) Cliff and Claire are interrupted by one of the children, annoying him and amusing her. (Above, middle and right) Kids—and parents' relationships with their kids—were some of the most important aspects of *The Cosby Show*. (Opposite, top; clockwise) Malcolm-Jamal Warner (Theo), Phylicia Rashad (Clair), Keshia Knight Pulliam (Rudy), Bill Cosby (Cliff), Lisa Bonet (Denise), Tempestt Bledsoe (Vanessa), Sabrina LeBeauf (Sondra).

went. He broke Radio City Music Hall's 53-year-old attendance record in 1986. In the same year, his book, *Fatherhood*, set records as the fastest-selling hardcover book of all time. It has sold more than four million copies. His next book, *Time Flies*, had the largest first printing in publishing history—1.75 million copies. His twenty-one comedy albums have earned him eight Gold Records and five Grammy Awards. *The Cosby Show* has proven to be one of the most financially successful shows in television history. Despite all of his extraordinary achievements, however, Bill Cosby is still most beloved for his comic sense of ordinary life.

extraordinary for its time, of course, was that the Huxtables were upper-middle-class African-Americans: a doctor and a lawyer with a daughter at Princeton University. As funny and lighthearted as the show was, it also presented an undisguised challenge to widely held assumptions about African-American families: the Huxtables were everything—educated, stable, professional, affluent— a bigoted white perspective (say, Archie Bunker's) would think an African-American family couldn't be. This positive image opened the door for other shows, including the Lisa Bonet spin-off, *A Different World*.

Mainly, however, *The Cosby Show* was a showcase for Bill Cosby's talent. As the star and co-producer, Cosby shaped the show through his personality and earned the top TVQ rating every year the show was No. 1. Born in a poor neighborhood in Philadelphia, Cosby came through the Navy and Temple University to perform stand-up comedy in Greenwich Village nightclubs. In 1963, he was invited to appear on *The Tonight Show* with Johnny Carson, and his career took a huge jump. In 1965, he co-starred with Robert Culp in *I Spy*—the first African-American to star in a dramatic series on television—and won three Emmys. Cosby became one of the most active and visible performers in the business, starring in movies, such as *Hickey*

and Boggs, Uptown Saturday Night, and *Mother, Jugs and Speed,* and TV shows, including a sitcom, *The Bill Cosby Show* (1971), a children's cartoon series, *Fat Albert and the Cosby Kids* (1972–84), and two variety shows, *The New Bill Cosby Show* (1972), and *Cos* (1976). At the same time, he was pursuing graduate studies, earning his doctorate in education from the University of Massachusetts in 1977.

In the late 1980s, he became one of those rare show-business figures, like Frank Sinatra or Elvis Presley, who created excitement everywhere he

A NEW ERA IN BROADCASTING

Change was the name of the game for the broadcasting industry as NBC celebrated its sixtieth anniversary in 1986.

All three of the major broadcast networks had new ownership that year. Led by Tom Murphy and Dan Burke, media company Capital Cities acquired ABC for $3.5 billion. NBC became property of one of its original founders, General Electric Co., which purchased parent company RCA for $6.3 billion. Investor Laurence Tisch became the major shareholder in CBS, after a takeover attempt by cable mogul Ted Turner.

The corporate shifts were a sign that the hegemony of the Big Three was nearing an end. Cable television, offering viewers a wider variety of choices, had gone from a promise to a reality—with 50 percent of U.S. homes wired in 1986. The broadcast networks' share of audience was slipping as cable continued to expand. At Turner Broadcasting, a young programming whiz named Scott Sassa would launch and program a number of new cable networks over a seven-year period. He would eventually be hired by NBC to head up the network's West Coast operations.

The three major networks had begun to move into cable in the eighties. But General Electric's Bob Wright, named president and chief executive officer of NBC after the acquisition, became the most aggressive advocate of broadcasters' diversification into new technologies, which didn't always make him popular with traditionalists inside the company or with the network's affiliates.

While NBC worked at expanding its shelf space across the cable dial during the nineties, it also faced new challenges on the broadcast side. Australian media mogul Rupert Murdoch launched a fourth broadcast network, Fox, which became a major competitor for NBC's young-adult audience. In 1995, Paramount and station group United Television launched UPN, while Time Warner and the Tribune Co. signed on with the WB Network.

During the early years of GE's ownership of NBC, critics sniped that the company's management didn't grasp the nature of the broadcasting business, which was different from manufacturing turbine engines or appliances. But Capital Cities and Tisch turned out to be transitional owners who sold out to larger entities. Capital Cities/ABC was acquired by the Walt Disney Co. in 1996, and CBS was acquired by Westinghouse, which was eventually merged into Viacom in 2000. GE flirted with potential partners and buyers but ultimately recognized that NBC was in fact a unique and irreplaceable GE business with enormous value. GE's resources have helped NBC adapt to the future while sticking to its core mission of entertaining, inspiring, and informing millions of viewers with quality entertainment programming, comprehensive broadcasts of national and global events such as the Olympic Games, and reliable and comprehensive news and analysis from some of the nation's most trusted broadcast journalists.

THE WRIGHT STUFF

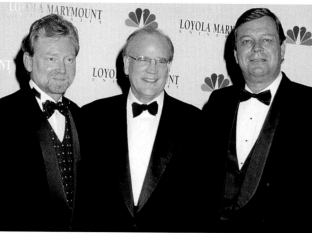

(Top, left) Bob Wright with (left to right) Courteney Cox, wife Suzanne, and Brooke Shields at the 1997 International Radio & Television Society Foundation awards dinner where Wright received the Gold Medal Award for industry leadership. *(Top, middle)* Bob poses with (left and right) Warren Littlefield and Don Ohlmeyer at Loyola Marymount University's Hal Roach Entertainment Award ceremony for NBC. *(Top, right)* Bob with (left to right) his daughter Maggie, Jerry Seinfeld, and Jay Leno at the 1998 NBC Affiliates Convention in Los Angeles. *(Opposite)* Wright stands in front of the complete history of NBC logos, in his office at 30 Rock.

When General Electric acquired RCA in July 1986, CEO Jack Welch worked hard to persuade Grant Tinker to remain at the helm of NBC. But, after five years of a bicoastal commute, Tinker was ready to move on. Fortunately, Welch had a backup plan: Bob Wright, a GE executive with a broad background, who at the time was serving as head of GE Capital, GE's financial services arm.

Wright and his wife, Suzanne, were no strangers to the media business, Bob having interrupted his GE career for a three-year stint as executive vice president of Cox Broadcasting and president of Cox Cable Communications. Nonetheless, the announcement that Wright would replace Tinker unnerved many NBC veterans, who felt that GE's rigorous financial discipline would ill-suit

a creative enterprise like broadcasting. NBC's late-night host David Letterman had a field day with lightbulb jokes.

To say the skeptics have been proven wrong is an understatement. In an industry where constant turnover in the upper ranks is expected, Bob Wright has become one of the most successful network chiefs in history, presiding over the evolution of NBC from a television network with an outdated business model to a global media powerhouse, with leadership in broadcast network television, cable programming, station ownership, and television production. While corporate parent GE applauds NBC's business achievements, what viewers see is a continuation of the same legacy of quality that has distinguished the network for decades. NBC has garnered the most Emmy awards of any broadcast network

for eight consecutive years, and the consensus among critics is that series such as *ER*, *Frasier*, *Friends*, *Law & Order*, and *The West Wing* constitute the high-water mark of network entertainment programming.

Under Welch, GE became famous for its impatience with bureaucracy and its ability to move with breathtaking speed. The company is renowned for driving its managers to reach for—and meet—seemingly impossible goals. Wright has proven that these values are not only transferable to a creative business like NBC but essential for its long-term success. Welch says, "Bob brought exactly the right qualities to NBC. He knew the business, but he also had the empathy you need to work well with the creative talent at the network."

Wright came to NBC with his agenda already set: get NBC

into cable, and streamline costs. Neither item was popular. NBC was on a roll, having just finished its best season in years, behind Tartikoff's Bill Cosby-led Thursday-night lineup, so it came as a shock to employees when instead of being patted on the back, they were challenged to embrace radical change. From Wright's perspective, he was merely pointing out the obvious.

"Brandon had done a terrific job on the programming side. But the reality was that cable was growing, network audiences were declining, and costs were out of line."

The transformation was soon under way. By the early nineties, NBC boasted a cable portfolio that included stakes in networks such as Bravo, American Movie Classics, and Court TV. But its most significant cable property was CNBC, which would eventually become the world's leading financial-news network. In 1996, NBC teamed with Microsoft to launch MSNBC, a twenty-four-hour cable news network and Internet site.

At the same time, Wright remained true to NBC's legacy as a network broadcaster and station owner. Under his watch, NBC has acquired an additional seven NBC-affiliated television stations around the country, bringing its total to thirteen. NBC's broadcast presence has also been extended by its significant investment in Paxson Communications and its acquisition of Telemundo, the nation's No. 2 Hispanic broadcaster. This acquisition—the largest in NBC's history—will make NBC the only major broadcast network dedicated to developing and airing Spanish-language programming.

One of Wright's most important talents is knowing how to build a strong executive team. Key to NBC's success during the Wright era have been leaders and producers such as Don Ohlmeyer and Warren Littlefield, who in 1993, following the acclaimed Brandon Tartikoff, made "Must See TV" a part of the nation's lexicon as they piloted a resurgent NBC to unprecedented success. Andrew Lack also came to NBC in 1993 and, with executive producers Neal Shapiro at *Dateline* and Jeff Zucker at the *Today* show, remade NBC News into the most-watched news organization, with a business model that is the envy of the competition. Today the significant costs of news production are amortized across three platforms: NBC, CNBC, and MSNBC. (Lack is now NBC's president and chief operating officer. Shapiro is president of NBC News. Zucker is president of NBC Entertainment, and Wright is NBC's chairman and CEO.) NBC Sports has been led since 1989 by another highly successful producer, Dick Ebersol, among whose achievements was the stunning preemptive strike that resulted in NBC's securing the exclusive rights to every Olympics broadcast through 2008. NBC Television Network president Randy Falco, with more than twenty-five years at the network, has played an important role in areas ranging from broadcast operations to affiliate relations to NBC's Olympics broadcasts.

In our current era of hundreds of cable networks tailored to every imaginable taste, the greatest challenge for a broadcaster such as NBC is to remain, in a literal sense, a *broad*-caster, reaching the largest and most diverse audience possible. NBC will continue to lead the way in serving a mass audience, even as it looks toward new digital technologies to enable it to deliver customized programming for more narrowly focused audiences. One sure thing, as Wright says, no matter how the business evolves in the years to come, "The viewer wins every hand in this game."

Business News, Consumer Tips, and a Rough Start

Even before Bob Wright had settled into his new office at 30 Rock, he knew it was essential to get NBC into cable television. In 1980, 15 million homes were wired for cable; by 1986, the number had swelled to 40 million, with nearly 10,000 more homes wired each day. Although some network veterans still thought of cable as television with training wheels, the new CEO recognized the folly of ignoring cable's dramatic growth.

In 1989, with the cable network business still reasonably uncrowded, Wright and his business-development manager, Tom Rogers, teamed up with Cablevision Systems' chief Chuck Dolan and launched the Consumer News and Business Channel—CNBC, for short. Business news seemed to be a good bet for a new cable network, as there was only one competitor: FNN, the Financial News Network, a financially struggling outfit catering to the professional investor. FNN had tiny audiences, but it was an invaluable place for a new breed of broadcast journalists to learn—or invent—their craft: specifically, friends and colleagues Ron Insana, Sue Herera, and Bill Griffeth. None had any business background—never mind on-air experience—when they were hired at FNN. "We were lucky we could take the time to break in the act before the big spotlight hit us," says Griffeth.

Herera was the first to be wooed to the new operation. "I didn't know it at the time, but I was the first employee!" she laughs. "There was no studio, no walls, there was nothing. It was a construction site. And we were two months from air. I kept saying, 'This is never going to work, this is never going to work!'"

Somehow the network struggled onto the air, launching on April 17, 1989, with *The Money Wheel*, an uneasy blend of financial news and consumer stories. In the beginning, the network was convinced that audiences needed a hefty dose of supermarket tips and garden facts with their market coverage. "They had reports from the produce desk," remembers Insana, "tips on animal husbandry, all this kind of stuff in the morning as the market was opening."

The network had more than a few obstacles in the early days. For one, despite Wright's fervent support, many at NBC weren't yet sold on the idea of cable. "We were the stepchild," recalls Herera. "It was very hard to build the brand." For another, not many viewers were interested in the stock market back then. Only 29 percent of American households owned stock in 1989, compared to more than half today.

Other factors played in CNBC's favor—principally, the network's No. 1 fan: GE's CEO Jack Welch, who not only was a regular viewer but was among the first to recognize CNBC's growth potential. Welch strongly supported NBC's purchase of FNN for $155 million in 1991 (culminating in a preemptive strike to outbid Dow Jones and Westinghouse). The acquisition greatly expanded the CNBC audience and improved the business-news coverage, especially by reuniting Herera with Griffeth and Insana.

After the FNN merger, CNBC jettisoned the consumer tips (but kept the CNBC acronym) and found the right balance of market analysis and viewer-friendly explanations. Even so, the first half of the nineties continued to be tough going, first with the 1991 recession, and then with the diversion of the O. J. Simpson trial. Although CNBC's prime-time programs (Geraldo's *Rivera Live*, Chris Matthews's *Hardball*, and Charles Grodin's quirky talk show) attracted some notice, business news was no match for the "trial of the century." "Our daytime audience went away," Insana recalls. "Nobody would ever come to us to watch O. J."

It wasn't long, however, before CNBC began riding the tide of a booming stock market. It has become the world's leading name in financial broadcast news and a true cultural phenomenon, demystifying the financial markets with good humor, intelligence, and a touch of irreverence.

> "I thought we had great people, we had a very good idea, but we knew we were going to have to struggle."
>
> — BOB WRIGHT

(Opposite) The three mainstays of CNBC, Bill Griffeth, Sue Herera, Ron Insana. *(Above, left to right)* Ted David and Doug Ramsey anchor the desk of CNBC/FNN, as it was called directly after the acquisition; Sue Herera on the floor of the New York Stock Exchange; Ted David and Leslie Cardé at the desk of the Consumer News Business Channel, possibly reporting the latest in animal husbandry tips.

DATELINE NBC

Dateline NBC debuted in spring of 1992 against formidable odds. Michael Gartner, who had joined NBC as president of NBC News in 1988, had done much to control costs while increasing efficiencies and production capabilities. But a winning prime-time newsmagazine had eluded the network. Indeed, NBC had been trying to find success in this genre since the Nixon presidency, but the network was batting 0-for-17.

Among *Dateline NBC*'s cancelled precursors were *First Tuesday*, *Chronolog*, *Weekend*, *Prime Time Sunday*, *NBC Magazine*, *Monitor*, and *First Camera*. What *Dateline NBC* had going for it was the appeal and experience of anchors Jane Pauley and Stone Phillips. Phillips had been a news correspondent for a decade before coming to *Dateline NBC*. Pauley was familiar to most viewers—and beloved by many—after thirteen years as co-anchor of the *Today* show. Still, more than one critic snickered that NBC was about to be 0-for-18.

Then NBC News was hit with any news organization's worst nightmare. Airing on

November 17 was a program called "Waiting to Explode," a segment about gas tank safety on General Motors pickup trucks. Certain models were alleged to have design defects that caused the fuel tanks to explode in an accident. To illustrate its point, the report included footage of crash demonstrations that showed dramatic explosions. The demonstrations were conducted with the aid of "sparkers" on the bottom of the vehicle chassis. Although sparking devices are sometimes employed in government tests, *Dateline* did not tell viewers of their use in the footage. GM objected loudly and publicly. With the credibility of NBC News on the line, Pauley and Phillips issued

an on-air apology, and, in the aftermath, Gartner retired from the network.

NBC brought in Neal Shapiro from ABC's *Prime Time Live* as the show's new producer—and last hope. "Coming to *Dateline* was like walking onto a ship that had just run aground on a sandbar," remembers Shapiro. "But when I got here I said: 'You know what? That was a mistake... but there are a lot of smart people here, and if we reinvent the show and try to do some different things, we'll get past it.'"

Bob Wright then brought in Andrew Lack, a seasoned and outspoken CBS News producer, as the new top news executive. Shapiro and Lack shared a passion for news as compelling, story-telling television, and both men agreed that *Dateline* was a valuable asset. They grew the show—first to two nights, then to three, eventually to as many as five nights a week. "I thought it was lunacy,"

recalls Pauley. "But it was brilliant. We created a brand."

Under Shapiro's direction, *Dateline NBC* became the most-honored news program in television. With an outstanding complement of correspondents and producers, *Dateline* has served NBC extraordinarily well as something of a time-slot SWAT team, ready at a moment's notice to meet programming needs anywhere on the schedule.

Pauley's reputation for probing the human dimension has brought *Dateline* compelling stories such as that of downed pilot Lt. Scott O'Grady, whose survival in Bosnia and daring rescue brought him home to a hero's welcome; and the two-part saga of Olympic figure skater Nancy Kerrigan, first, when she was nearly crippled in an assault associated with her rival Tonya Harding, and later, returning home with a silver medal to an avalanche of criticism that she had been a poor sport.

Among Phillips's more

noteworthy stories was his interview with Lisa Beamer, wife of one of the heroic passengers aboard United Flight 93 on September 11, 2001, who sacrificed their lives to prevent terrorists from flying the plane into their intended target in Washington, D.C.

From the start, Shapiro's goal was to expand the limits of nonfiction television, to find interesting real stories and tell them in a way that makes them just as compelling as a fictional drama. For example, one of the traditionally dullest subjects turned out to be the most fascinating. In 2000, *Dateline* aired "The Paper Chase," a one-hour investigation on fraud in the insurance industry, a seemingly certain recipe for boredom. The report won eleven journalism awards— more than any other individual show in the history of TV news.

Success begets success. In June 2001, Shapiro became president of NBC News and Lack was named president and chief operating officer of NBC.

(Above, left) Stone Phillips and Commander Scott Waddle in his first television interview. Waddle captained the *Greenville*, the Navy submarine that collided with a Japanese fishing boat near Honolulu, killing nine people. *(Above, middle)* Jane Pauley with Attorney General Janet Reno. *(Above, right)* Phillips and Bernard Goetz after his release from prison. Goetz was thrust into the national spotlight in 1984 for shooting four African-American teens on a New York City subway. *(Opposite, left)* Phillips reviews scripts in the control room. *(Opposite, right)* Pauley in front of the *Star Trek*-inspired set.

FRIENDS AND FAMILY

On Madison Avenue, the decision makers buying advertising time on television pay a high premium to reach the young-adult demographic. Just starting out in life, young adults are developing the new habits and tastes that advertisers want to influence. But while the members of Generation X— as they were called in the early 1990s—made a desirable target audience, network television rarely tried to portray how they lived.

"Whether it's Portland or New York or Atlanta, there are young people who are having firsts," Warren Littlefield recalls telling his program development team at NBC Entertainment. "First job, first love, first loss— all those first things. And they can't afford in any of these cities to live in great places. Where is the show that deals with that?" After rejecting a number of scripts, programming executive Jamie Tarses came to Littlefield with a pitch from David Crane and Marta Kauffman, who had

created the racy sitcom *Dream On* for HBO. Along with executive producer Kevin S. Bright, they developed a show loosely based on the writers' own experiences as just-out-of-college New Yorkers.

That pitch evolved into *Friends*, which went into NBC's Thursday-night lineup in the fall of 1994. In their new season previews, many television critics called *Friends* a knockoff of *Seinfeld*, which was hardly the case. Jerry Seinfeld and his pals disdained romantic commitment and were happy to indulge in their many neuroses. On *Friends*, the humor was derived from the vulnerabilities of Rachel, her roommate Monica, Monica's brother Ross, Chandler and his roommate Joey, and Phoebe. All were struggling to make it in the

grown-up world and needed each other's support when they failed in love or at work.

The connection between the attractive cast—Jennifer Aniston, Courteney Cox Arquette, Lisa Kudrow, Matt LeBlanc, Matthew Perry, and David Schwimmer—and the audience built slowly during the first few months. But by the spring of 1995, *Friends* was a ratings powerhouse. The power-pop *Friends* theme, "I'll Be There for You" by the Rembrandts, was in heavy rotation on Top 40 radio stations, and young women were going into hair salons clutching magazine photos of Aniston and asking for the "Rachel."

The success of the show not only attracted the people on Madison Avenue who bought commercials, but the ones who made them as well. *Friends* cast members appeared in Diet Coke spots and were recruited to wear milk mustaches for the American Dairy Association's "Got Milk" campaign. The heavy added exposure might have burned out other shows, but the public likely picked up on how real the bond was between these friends. Off the set, they were close. They supported each other during personal crises, and even banded together when negotiating their contracts. Maybe it was because they were experiencing their journey to fame together.

"Before I got *Friends*

I was selling my furniture in order to eat," LeBlanc told *TV Guide* in 1995.

Other networks tried to imitate the unattached-singles-living-together formula. Viewers rejected most of them, from *Townies* (*Friends* in a blue-collar town) to *Dweebs* (*Friends* in a computer company). The imitators missed the point. "It has nothing to do with a bunch of pretty singles," Kauffman said in 1995. "It has to do with characters you care about." After eight seasons, viewers still care as the relationships on the show continue to evolve. *Friends* remains the top-rated sitcom in prime time.

The sextet of friends on *Friends* are both lovers and buddies who have seen one another through marriages (Chandler and Monica, *opposite, top,* and *above, right*), birthdays *(above, left)*, and simple everyday living (the gang on the couch at Central Perk, *opposite, bottom*). The cast *(below, left to right;* Kudrow, LeBlanc, Cox Arquette, Schwimmer, Aniston, Perry) is in effect a self-selected family, remarkable both in its longevity as an intact unit and in its staying power at the top of the ratings.

TOSSED SALADS AND SCRAMBLED EGGS

Former NBC Entertainment President Warren Littlefield still remembers the phone call he received from *Cheers* star Ted Danson in early 1993. "Ted said, 'I've got to find Ted. And I can't be Sam Malone anymore,'" Littlefield recalls. "And I was like 'Does that mean you're not going to come back to *Cheers*?' The phone receiver at that moment weighed a thousand pounds."

Once he snapped out of the catatonic state that programming executives fall into after losing a top-rated show, Littlefield started looking within *Cheers* for a replacement. Sequels to long-running hits were highly uncertain (anyone remember *AfterMASH*?), especially when the writing team that created the original—in *Cheers'* case Les and Glen Charles—had moved on. But *Cheers* was

creatively solid to the very end, and NBC was able to turn to the writer-producer team of Peter Casey, David Lee, and David Angell to mine a new show from the series' rich ensemble of characters.

Angell, Casey, and Lee believed that Kelsey Grammer's Frasier Crane, the pompous, erudite psychiatrist who hung out with Sam Malone's crowd, had the range needed to carry a

series of his own, even though he was not a main character on *Cheers*. The team pitched *Frasier* as a family comedy, but not in the traditional prime-time sense of a husband and wife with a couple of kids. Instead, after *Cheers*, Frasier would move to Seattle, become a radio shrink, and take in his gruff ex-cop father, Martin (John Mahoney) who was disabled after being shot in the line of duty. Added

to the mix was David Hyde Pierce, who impressed NBC executives on a short-lived political sitcom *The Powers That Be*. The stage veteran was cast as Frasier's snooty brother Niles, also a psychiatrist, who had an icy wife viewers only heard about through her husband's arch commentaries.

The tension between Frasier, Niles, and their father has rung true to a generation of adult viewers faced with caring for aging parents. Frasier's world is classical music, good food and wine, and an ultrachic apartment straight out of *Architectural Digest*. Blue-collar Martin's world is Ballantine beer in a can and a tattered Barcalounger repaired with duct tape. Rather than pro-vide unconditional love, Frasier sees his father as a burden. ("I asked Dad to pass me a bran muffin," he told Niles over coffee at their hangout Café Nervosa in an early episode. "You know what he said to

me? 'What's the magic word?' He didn't think it was very amusing when I said 'rest home.'") Martin, on the other hand, is frustrated that he is dependent on two sons he doesn't completely understand.

The show's edginess made NBC executives somewhat uncomfortable at first. "It scared everybody a little bit," says Littlefield. "Then I was reminded that the things that we had a little fear over always had the biggest upside."

That was certainly the case with *Frasier*. Scheduled on Thursday behind a red-hot *Seinfeld* in the fall of 1993, it became a Top 10 hit in the Nielsen ratings and was immediately regarded as the most sophisticated, intelligent comedy in prime time. The series has won twenty-four Emmy Awards, including five consecutive trophies for Outstanding Comedy Series. The strong ensemble cast, including Peri Gilpin

as Roz Doyle, Frasier's sassy, man-hungry producer, and Jane Leeves as Daphne Moon, Martin's whimsical physical therapist (and more recently Niles's love interest) is still intact after nine seasons. While *Frasier* has made Grammer one of the best-paid performers in prime time, he takes more pride in being part of what many consider the best-written sitcom ever, once telling *TV Guide* "You could probably pay me nothing and I'd still do this job."

(Opposite) A Crane family portrait that captures a familiar family dynamic. (Top, left to right) Niles and Frasier talk by the Barcalounger that is almost another character, a silent but visible witness to much of the trials and tribulations; Daphne and Niles share a moment while Frasier tries to look busy; one of many moments of tension between Frasier and Roz in the studio at the radio station. (Above) Martin in his tattered and taped Barcalounger, which he loves and his sons detest. (Left) Daphne and Niles share a tender moment.

MASTERS OF THEIR DOMAIN

(Circle) In the show, as in real life, Jerry's job is stand-up comedy. *(Below, left to right)* George spends another disconnected moment with his parents; like *Cheers* and the Boston pub it was modeled after, there really is a take-out soup shop on New York's West Side (although there may not be a "Soup Nazi" there). Here, a delighted Elaine gets a chance to tell off the Soup Nazi; Jerry sits on the couch with his nemesis Newman. *(Top)* George, Kramer, and Jerry light up Cuban cigars over Kramer's latest scheme—sneaking Cuban cigar-rollers into the country to make classic hand-rolled cigars. *(Opposite)* Kramer makes one of his famous entrances.

The more typical sitcom scenes of Jerry and his friends at common day locations were negatively received. As one viewer put it, "You can't get excited about going to the Laundromat"… No segment of the audience was eager to watch the show again.

That's what a test audience had to say about a 1989 NBC comedy pilot called *The Seinfeld Chronicles*. Stand-up comedian Jerry Seinfeld pitched it as a series about his off-stage life and how he turns it into material. NBC executives had concerns as well (Brandon Tartikoff's famous reaction was "Too New York, too Jewish.") They didn't put it on the fall schedule but were intrigued enough to not want to let it go. Programming executive Rick Ludwin, who first suggested the idea of giving Jerry Seinfeld a series, took money allotted for specials that season to make four more episodes.

Based on such a small commitment, Seinfeld didn't believe the show had much of a future. (It was even offered to Fox before NBC finally decided to pick it up.) So he and his partner, Larry David, neither of whom had ever done a sitcom before, threw mass appeal aside and did the kind of show they wanted to do. At the network's suggestion they also added a female character, which led to the casting of Julia Louis-Dreyfus in the role of Elaine.

The four episodes drew strong enough ratings in the summer of 1990 for NBC to give the retitled *Seinfeld* a pickup for thirteen more episodes, which began airing in January 1991. Slow to become a ratings hit, it was an immediate cult favorite with its memorable sight gags and catchphrases ("Not that there's anything wrong with that," "sponge-worthy"). It also took solipsism to new heights—or depths. Jerry and his circle of friends— brittle Elaine, hapless George (Jason Alexander), and eccentric

neighbor Kramer (Michael Richards)—stuck to David's guiding principle of "no hugging, no learning," whether they were spoofing *Schindler's List* or competing over who could go longest without self-gratification.

Often referred to as the "show about nothing," *Seinfeld* became known for its depiction of mundane experiences. Although based in New York City, the show was popular in large and small markets. It was considered young and hip, but Jerry Stiller and Estelle Harris as George's overbearing parents, joining Barney Martin and Liz Sheridan as Jerry's parents, provided stories that brought in older viewers as well. When *Seinfeld* took over the Thursday 9:00 p.m. time period from *Cheers* in 1993, it exploded into a ratings and pop-culture phenomenon that had critical acclaim to match. The bizarre multiple plots were usually the leading topic around watercoolers everywhere on Friday mornings.

NBC tried to dissuade Jerry Seinfeld from calling it quits at the end of the 1997–98 season. But he knew from years onstage as a stand-up that he wanted to bow out while his show was still No. 1. "There's one moment where you feel the audience is still having a great time and if you get off right there, they walk out of the theater excited," he told *Time* magazine in 1998. "If I get off now, I have a chance for a standing ovation. That's what you go for."

MAD ABOUT YOU

(Above) Beloved dog Murray. Many segments took place in the Buchmans' Greenwich Village apartment and focused on the details of everyday life. One episode took place exclusively in their bathroom. *(Near right, top)* Paul and Jamie with baby Mabel; the cast *(left to right)*: Anne Ramsay (Lisa Stempel), Helen Hunt (Jamie E. Buchman), Paul Reiser (Paul Buchman), Leila Kenzle (Fran Devanow), John Pankow (Ira Buchman).

It was far from being the first sitcom about a happily married couple. America loved Rob and Laura Petrie in their twin beds and blissful suburban domesticity, but three decades later America was ready for an updated, more contentious romantic relationship that flourished amid the urban jungle of Manhattan. Seldom before had a popular series celebrated the kiss-and-make-up escapades of a young,

career-oriented twosome who were not ashamed to confront each other over the most intimate details of their personal life.

Mad About You was the brainchild of former *Roseanne* writer Danny Jacobson and Paul Reiser, a stand-up comic and film actor (*Diner*), who starred in NBC's *My Two Dads*. Both considered themselves guys who would never experience

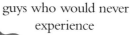

matrimonial bliss. When it happened, they were eager to do a show that would tell grown-up stories about how their marriages worked, showing the passion and the anger.

Warren Littlefield remembers being underwhelmed by the script for the pilot—until Helen Hunt read for the part of Jamie, and he saw how she played off overbearing, neurotic Paul. "You believed they had a lot of stuff they had to work out," he recalls. "And you felt great for them as a couple."

When NBC moved *Mad About You* to Thursdays at 8:00 p.m. in 1993, it grew into a major hit, despite its adult themes and occasionally risqué story lines. "We were into a world where the average household had twenty-five channel

choices," says Littlefield of the early nineties. The network realized that in an era of expanded viewing options, the traditional conventions governing "family viewing" could be redefined.

(Above, left) A close shave. *(Above, right)* One episode involved Paul's dream sequence and an erotic close encounter with supermodel Christie Brinkley.

NIGHT COURT

Night Court was in session from 1984 through 1992, and its loopy denizens attracted a dedicated audience that followed the show through no less than fourteen time-slot changes. Presiding over the shenanigans was Harry Anderson as Judge Harry T. Stone, a jeans-wearing, hang-loose Mel Tormé aficionado. Other stalwarts of the cast included John Larroquette as smarmy skirt-chasing Assistant D.A. Dan Fielding, Markie Post as public defender Christine Sullivan (who spent a lot of time defending her skirt from Dan), and Richard Moll as bailiff-cum-tree-stump Nostradamus "Bull" Shannon.

Judge Stone's Manhattan courtroom was little more than a backdrop for the amorous adventures and misadventures of the cast and for the parade of off-the-wall characters having run-ins with the law, including nudists, hookers, clowns, and prestidigitators. In *Night Court*, the surreal was normal, and bawdy innuendos and double entendres were always on the docket.

FAMILY VALUES FOR A NEW GENERATION

(Opposite, top) The extraterrestrial cast of *3rd Rock from the Sun* included (left to right) Kristen Johnston, John Lithgow, French Stewart, and Joseph Gordon-Levitt. (Top, right) The earthbound family in *Providence* features (left to right) Paula Cale (holding baby), Melina Kanakaredes, Mike Farrell, Seth Peterson, and Concetta Tomei.

(Top, left) Debra Messing (Grace Adler in *Will & Grace*) is having a little trouble with her new water bra, despite the efforts of Will Truman (Eric McCormack) to assist. (Circle) Jack McFarland (Sean Hayes) dances it up with devilish Karen Walker (Megan Mullally).

(Opposite, below) George Segal, as millionaire publishing tycoon Jack Gallo, is not impressed by editorial assistant Dennis Finch (played by David Spade), who desperately wants to impress the boss on *Just Shoot Me*.

In the late nineties, the biting and contemporary social humor of *Will & Grace, Just Shoot Me*, and *3rd Rock from the Sun* was balanced by the down-home comfort of a traditional family trying to find its way in the toasty drama, *Providence*.

Described by creators Terry and Bonnie Turner as "Carl Sagan meets the Marx Brothers," *3rd Rock from the Sun* was a bit of inspired lunacy that encouraged us to see our world from an extraterrestrial point of view. John Lithgow (who won three Emmys as Outstanding Lead Actor in a Comedy Series for the role) starred as Dr. Dick Solomon, who posed as a physics professor at Pendelton University in a fictional Ohio town but was actually High Commander of an alien mission sent to study our planet—the "third rock." The show opened with a bang. As *TV Guide* put it: "We dare anyone to watch this 'Rock' with a stone face." Kristen Johnston played Sally Solomon, who didn't really enjoy being a girl, since she was actually a male lieutenant and second in command. Despite their superior intelligence, Dick, Sally, and the other "Solomons"—Harry (French Stewart) and Tommy (Joseph Gordon-Levitt)—were often befuddled by human life, but not as confused as Dr. Mary Albright (Jane Curtin), Dick's paramour and professorial colleague, who grappled with her madcap lover's idiosyncrasies. Airing from 1996 through May of 2001, *3rd Rock* garnered eight Emmy Awards under the aegis of the Turners and legendary producers Marcy Carsey, Tom Werner, and Caryn Mandabach.

After Ellen came out on the ABC sitcom *Ellen* and was met with a widely publicized ratings decline, the last thing industry observers expected to see was another network prime-time comedy with a gay lead character. Yet just a few months after

Ellen's cancellation in the spring of 1998, the groundbreaking series *Will & Grace* burst on the scene. The two titular Manhattan best friends share the same passions, antipathies, and psychoses. Friends for years, they could be mistaken for the perfect married couple, except for one small difference—attorney Will Truman (Emmy Award winner Eric McCormack) is gay and interior designer Grace Adler (Debra Messing) is straight. Will and Grace are a matched, if flawed, set, and their abiding closeness sustains them through their respective romantic entanglements. The comedy, from creators Max Mutchnick and David Kohan, with the legendary James Burrows serving as executive producer and director, also derives its edge and bite from its two supporting cast members—Emmy winner Megan Mullally (as self-absorbed socialite Karen Walker and Grace's underachieving assistant) and fellow Emmy winner Sean Hayes (as flamboyant Jack McFarland, Will's hyperkinetic pal). The series, which has won six Emmys, including Outstanding Comedy Series, gained the coveted 9:00 p.m.

centerpiece time period on "Must See TV" Thursday night and quickly became a major draw for many stars who made rare guest appearances.

The New York offices of a tacky fashion magazine are home to a collection of staffers whose personal lives are lampooned on *Just Shoot Me*, a staple of NBC's "Must See TV" comedies. Quasi-respectable at best, *Blush* magazine is owned by lothario Jack Gallo (George Segal), a dollars-and-cents publisher who vigilantly guards his profit margins. His more-principled daughter Maya (Laura San Giacomo) came to work for her father after being canned from her TV newswriting job for trying to take the moral high road—only to find that at *Blush*, the high road is not only unpaved but off the map entirely. Rounding out the staff are high-strung beauty editor Nina Van Horn (Wendie Malick); photographer Elliott DiMauro (Enrico Colantoni); and Dennis Finch, Jack's blundering Machiavellian assistant (*SNL* alum David Spade). The series, created by Steven Levitan (who earned fame on *Frasier* and *The Larry Sanders Show*), premiered in March 1997.

Providence came out of nowhere when it debuted in January 1999 to become an immediate Friday-night hit from former *St. Elsewhere* producer/writer John Masius. In this family drama, Dr. Sydney Hansen (Melina Kanakaredes)—fed up with the nose jobs, collagen implants, and liposuctions that filled her life as a Los Angeles plastic surgeon—moves back to her hometown of Providence, Rhode Island. Once there, she finds more fulfilling work in a shoestring-budget clinic catering to the medically indigent, but also is pulled back into messy relationships with her quirky family: her disconnected dad Jim (Mike Farrell), a veterinarian who gets along better with animals than with people; her perky sister Joanie (Paula Cale), an unwed mother; and her trouble-prone brother Robbie (Seth Peterson), who can't resist a quick-buck scam. Caring about her family is emotionally taxing, but Syd finds that the family tie that binds the most is the one from the hereafter in the spirit of her recently deceased but still domineering mother, Lynda (Concetta Tomei), who is compelled to share her acerbic expertise from beyond the grave.

THAT WAS THE DECADE THAT WAS

I f ever there was an ideal time to be an armchair sports fan, it was the 1990s. The Big Three—baseball, basketball, and football—along with Summer and Winter Olympics telecasts dominated the networks' airwaves, and with the proliferation of regional cable and satellite broadcasters, everything from Olympic archery to minor league baseball found a television home. ESPN's maturation in the 1980s proved the viability of a 24-hour sports smorgasbord, but not even Marshall McLuhan could have predicted that the medium would give rise to The Golf Channel, Speedvision, and the Outdoor Life Network.

The decade will also be remembered for NBC Sports' embarrassment of riches. Take 1996, for example. NBC broadcast the Atlanta Olympics, the World Series, the Super Bowl and the NBA

Finals. Throw in Wimbledon, U.S. Open golf and Notre Dame football and it's no wonder NBC Sports Chairman Dick Ebersol was named by *The Sporting News* as the most powerful person in sports that year.

The 1990s opened with NBC taking over the rights to the NBA from CBS. The timing could not have been better for NBC, as Michael Jordan won the first of his six championship rings with the Chicago Bulls. *The NBA on NBC* became a prime-time hit, helping propel the league to unprecedented growth during the Jordan Era.

But in 2001, as sports rights fees spiraled out of control, NBC chose to walk away from the NBA—just as it had with football and baseball—rather than accept hundreds of millions of dollars in losses.

The NBA on NBC had a great run, and Jordan's breath-taking, last-second shot to beat Utah in Game 6 of the 1998 NBA Finals for the Bulls' sixth title provided one of the decade's indelible images. Another scene captured on NBC, just as triumphant, if haunting, was of a different kind of last shot by Payne Stewart to win his second U.S. Open, in June 1999. After sinking a clutch putt to save par on 16 and birdieing 17, Stewart edged Phil Mickelson by a shot with a dramatic 15-foot putt on the final hole. Stewart pumped his fist in celebration and embraced Mickelson.

In September 1999, on NBC, Stewart and his U.S. teammates won a scintillating Ryder Cup match in England. A month later, his private jet mysteriously crashed in South Dakota, killing the 42-year-old golfer and his fellow passengers.

"All I wanted to do was give myself a chance," the colorful Stewart remarked after his winning putt at the Open. "I never gave up. I got the job done."

OLYMPIC GOLD

In 1967, an ambitious Yale student dropped out to accept a plum assignment with ABC Sports as its first-ever Olympic researcher, before the 1968 Winter Games in Grenoble. Dick Ebersol eventually graduated from Yale and went to work full time at ABC, joining Roone Arledge, Jim McKay, and other Olympic TV pioneers.

With his passion for the Olympics, it's no surprise that Ebersol says his greatest accomplishment as chairman of NBC Sports has been to establish the network as the home of the Olympic Games. It took two rounds of globetrotting wheeling and dealing to win this designation for NBC.

It began with a surreptitious New York-to-Sweden-to-Montreal-to-New York odyssey in August 1995, during which he outmaneuvered the competition for not only the 2000 Sydney Summer Games ($705 million), but also the 2002 Winter Olympics from Salt Lake City ($545 million)—marking the first time the IOC had sold more than one Olympics. Four months later, in a stunning coup, NBC secured the rights to the Summer and Winter Games through 2008 for an equally stunning $2.3 billion.

"Other than family, there's nothing I love more than the Olympics," Ebersol says. "The Olympics are different from anything else in sports. It isn't really about results. It's about the athletes, who for ten seconds or two minutes of glory, are willing to give up four years of their lives without much more ahead of them than the possibility of a medal."

(Opposite, below) Bob Costas, the signature voice of NBC Sports, hosted Olympic coverage and worked on Major League Baseball, NBA, and NFL telecasts. *(Opposite, left to right)* Breakfast at Wimbledon on NBC is an annual Saturday and Sunday morning television event and one of sports television's great traditions. Pete Sampras won seven Wimbledon titles from 1993 to 2000; Michael Jordan launches the game-winning shot in Game 6 of the 1998 NBA Finals to give Chicago its sixth title; Payne Stewart celebrates his U.S. Open victory after sinking a difficult uphill putt. *(Above)* Three legends of the broadcast booth, left to right: Bud Collins (arguably the "voice" of tennis), John McEnroe (the most unabashed voice in tennis), and Dick Enberg (the classiest voice in tennis).

BOB HOPE: A LEGEND IN LAUGHTER

Superlatives fail to do justice to Bob Hope. He is a star of vaudeville, Broadway, radio, television, and motion pictures. He entertained audiences all over the world in nine out of ten decades of the twentieth century. He has received more than two thousand awards and citations for humanitarian and professional efforts, including fifty-four honorary doctorates. President John F. Kennedy called him "America's most prized ambassador of goodwill throughout the world" when he presented Hope with the Congressional Gold Medal.

Bob Hope's relationship with NBC, which began in 1933, is in the *Guinness Book of Records* as the longest continuous contract between a performer and a television network. The show, "Bob Hope: Laughing with the Presidents," which aired in November 1996, was his 284th television special for NBC. Many of those shows were staged in war zones around the world, where Hope tirelessly entertained American troops for six decades. In May 2000, he officiated at the opening of the Bob Hope Gallery of American Entertainment at the Library of Congress in Washington, D.C.

HOPE WITH GEORGE BURNS AND MICKEY ROONEY *(Right)* No member of this legendary trio—George Burns, Bob Hope, and Mickey Rooney—was primarily famous as a dancer, but they all were famous hoofers. They came from an era when all performers were expected to do a little song, a little dance, and a lot of comedy. Nathan Birnbaum, Leslie Townes Hope, and Joe Yule, Jr., changed their names and set off to conquer the worlds of vaudeville, motion pictures, and television—and all three of them did.

HOPE WITH FRANK SINATRA *(Left)* Hope's second television special of 1950 featured Frank Sinatra's first appearance on television. On TV, Hope continued the tradition of entertaining American troops that he had begun on radio in 1941. His specials were always highly rated, averaging a 40 share. In 1954, he began a series of Christmas specials with American soldiers around the world, which continued for five decades. He won an Emmy for his 1966 Christmas special from Southeast Asia, and his 1970 Christmas special was the highest-rated program in television history to that date.

HOPE WITH BRANDO AT OSCARS (Left)
When Marlon Brando won the Oscar for Best Actor in *On the Waterfront* at the *27th Academy Awards* on March 30, 1955, Hope was already an old hand at hosting the annual event. He started in 1940, when the Oscars were broadcast on radio from the Cocoanut Grove in Los Angeles, and he was the host of the first televised *Awards* on March 19, 1953, from the RKO Pantages Theatre. RCA paid $100,000 for the TV rights to be broadcast on NBC, even though there were only twelve awards presented. Hope holds the record as Oscars host, with seventeen visits to the podium.

"When vaudeville died, television was the box they put it in." — BOB HOPE

HOPE WITH BING (Below)
Hope and Crosby first performed together in 1932 at the Capitol vaudeville theater. They made *The Road to Singapore* (1940) with Dorothy Lamour and were a hit team from then on. In six more *Road* movies, including *The Road to Morocco* (1942), nominated for two Oscars, they sang, danced, and joked their way to movie immortality. Their infectious camaraderie spilled out of the big screen. They were discussing a *Road* reunion picture in 1977 when Bing collapsed from a heart attack and died.

HOPE WITH BERLE (Above)
NBC tried to lure Hope into television in 1949, but he wrote back: "It was nice to receive your vote of confidence with regard to television, but Berle can have that medium to himself for the next year. Then, I shall have my head blocked and we'll all go back to vaudeville." Hope and Berle were friends from the vaudeville circuit and never really competed on television. Hope didn't feel his own brand of humor would sustain a weekly show. The following year, the nation's top motion-picture box office star would begin his series of monthly specials for NBC. The first Hope special, in April 1950, featured Beatrice Lillie, Douglas Fairbanks, Jr., and Dinah Shore. The ninety-minute extravaganza was also the most expensive TV program produced to that date, costing $1,500 per minute.

HOPE WITH BIG BIRD IN CHINA (Above)
When Hope visited the Forbidden City in Beijing for "On the Road to China," he quipped, "What opulence! It looks like Caesars Palace without the slot machines!" The 1979 special featured Mikhail Baryshnikov, Crystal Gayle, and Big Bird from *Sesame Street*. Big Bird was a hit in China because one didn't need to understand English to get the joke. One segment actually featured musical guests Peaches and Herb doing a disco number on the steps of the gold-encrusted Temple of Heaven.

LAST HURRAHS

Television series were once like old soldiers: they never died; they just faded away into eternal repeats in syndication. That changed as the medium matured and producers and writers brought more realism to the home screen. When a show ended its run, they wanted it reflected in the last episode. So did viewers. In 1967, the final episode of *The Fugitive* on ABC was the most-watched entertainment program up to that time. The finale of *M*A*S*H*, which aired on CBS in 1983, still stands as the record holder for the largest audience for an entertainment program, with 106 million viewers. Those success stories were not lost on NBC when it had to part ways with its biggest hits. The network understood the powerful bond that developed between audiences and their favorite stars. Saying good-bye has not only meant big ratings, but has also made for some memorable pop-culture events.

MAY 1992 • JOHNNY CARSON

Johnny Carson gave NBC a year's notice that he would be leaving *The Tonight Show* after thirty years as host. So no one expected the emotional response of the press, studio audiences, guests, and Carson himself when May 22, 1992, finally came. "My God, the Soviet Union's end hasn't received this kind of publicity," Carson cracked in his last monologue. Between the laughs, the man often described as cool and aloof had trouble holding back tears in his final week. Carson's penultimate show included one of television's most memorable performances when his final guest, Bette Midler, who got her break on *Tonight* twenty years earlier, serenaded him with "You Made Me Love You," and "One for My Baby." The Emmy-winning moment not only marked the end of an era for *Tonight*, but also for the clubby bonhomie that existed among performers of Carson's generation. The final sign-off came the following night, as 41 million viewers joined Carson as he sat on a stool in front of a studio audience of family and friends, joking with Ed McMahon and Doc Severinsen and showing highlight clips from his thirty-year reign. His only stated regret was that his son Rick, who had died the previous year in a car accident, couldn't be there. He closed the show with a Rick Carson photo of a California sunset.

MAY 1998 • SEINFELD

Social critic Neal Gabler described the buildup leading to the finale of *Seinfeld* as "a national Irish wake." Plans were made to show it on the thirty-five-foot Astrovision screen in Times Square. Plot scenarios were floated over the Internet (George becomes a TV critic; Jerry marries Elaine). There was even news coverage of which commercials, purchased for $1.7 million each, would be seen on the seventy-five-minute episode. The audience of 76.3 million was huge, with the finale ranking fourteenth on Nielsen's list of most-watched TV shows of all time, but the anticipation inevitably led to a mixed reaction from critics and fans. Unlike the comforting series send-offs viewers were used to, the series ended with Jerry and his pals thrown into jail for their years of callousness. Yet aficionados of *Seinfeld* should have known that after having dispensed with many sitcom conventions over the previous nine years, the show's producers would try to confound viewers in its farewell. Jerry Seinfeld, true to the spirit of his creation, was sentiment-free when he appeared on *The Tonight Show* after his last show aired. "What the hell," he coolly told a cheering audience, "I'll do one more season."

MAY 1993 • CHEERS

When Ted Danson decided his days as Sam Malone were over, *Cheers* became the first sitcom since *M*A*S*H* to end its run while still in the Nielsen Top 10. So when it came time to permanently close the barroom door, NBC promoted the ninety-minute *Cheers* finale as a major television event, complete with a Bob Costas-hosted special reviewing highlights of the series. Advertisers paid a Super Bowl-like rate of $650,000 for commercials on the show. The plot became subject matter for the supermarket tabloids. President Clinton was even lined up for an appearance, but backed out at the last moment. The climactic scene, when Sam and Diane Chambers (Shelley Long) call off a half-baked plan to get married, was shot on a closed set in order to preserve the suspense. But the final moment stayed true to the show's previous 274 episodes, showing the *Cheers* regulars sitting around the bar, smoking cigars, and musing about life. Eighty-five million viewers watched on May 20, 1993, and many stuck around to see several tipsy cast members celebrate afterward on *The Tonight Show* with Jay Leno, which aired live from the Bull & Finch Pub, the Boston bar on which *Cheers* was based.

APRIL 1992 • THE COSBY SHOW

When the final episode of *The Cosby Show* aired on April 30, 1992, 54 million viewers made the hour the most-watched NBC series finale up to that time, a testament to the series' stunning eight-year run. But the last *Cosby*, in which Theo Huxtable graduates from college, is better remembered for how it almost didn't air that night. The previous day, four white Los Angeles policemen were acquitted in the videotaped beating of unarmed black motorist Rodney King. The verdict sparked the worst urban violence in the nation's history with more than fifty dead and two thousand injured in Los Angeles. NBC had considered postponing the *Cosby* finale's airing in the city, which would have been an odd coda to a series that many believed was prime time's most progressive portrayal of an African-American family. At the request of Los Angeles Mayor Tom Bradley, the episode went on with the hope that it would calm a city in turmoil. Bradley even got Bill Cosby to tape a public service announcement that was shown afterward. The beloved TV star asked viewers to "pray for a better tomorrow, which starts today."

A NEW CENTURY

At the end of the twentieth century, some might have said that network broadcasting was a thing of the past. Despite the perennially top-rated NBC's lineup of veteran shows that were healthier than ever (*Today, Tonight, Saturday Night Live, Meet the Press, Days of our Lives*), and newer shows that continually redefined their

genres (*Dateline NBC, ER, Friends, Late Night with Conan O'Brien*, and *Law & Order*, to name a few), one often heard that network TV was dying; that the shared experience no longer mattered; that "new media," with its promise of entertainment, commerce, and information all delivered over a personal computer, handheld device, or even cellular phone, would eclipse the need for

broadcasting; and that the art of casting a broad net of entertainment and information for the widest possible audience was doomed to irrelevance.

Yet as the Internet bubble continued to grow (and then to burst), and as viewers' tastes continued to shift, NBC didn't act like it was in a declining industry. Far from it. For one thing, Bob Wright's NBC had never been afraid of cable, and

by the late nineties CNBC was reaching unprecedented new audiences by documenting the rise and fall of the great 1990s bull market, and by helping its viewers gain control of their own financial destinies. Meanwhile, MSNBC and MSNBC.com succeeded in presenting an exciting new paradigm: a television/Internet "synergy" that actually worked, combining NBC News'

breadth and legacy with Microsoft's know-how and Internet savvy. NBC was now truly a twenty-four-hour entity, a button-click away for a smart new audience.

As the national audience (familiar with low-cost MTV-style programming) showed a sudden and seemingly insatiable desire to watch real people dare to be humiliated, triumphant, or greedy on the small screen, NBC responded with shows like *Fear Factor* and *Weakest Link*, revealing NBC to be a network willing to grow, to take risks, and to have some fun.

Then came September 11, 2001. NBC News would provide a steady, calming voice while reporting the greatest national tragedy America had ever seen. As the *New York Observer*'s Jason Gay wrote in early 2002, "And then suddenly there we were, riveted, like we thought we'd never be again.... Television felt as important as ever; the vaunted 'shared experience' had returned."

As the National Broadcasting Company looks back over seventy-five years of being America's premier broadcaster, its commitment to do what it does best is stronger than ever. "We have to look forward and backward at the same time," says Bob Wright. "The greatest challenge we have is trying to serve the broadest audience. It is easier to serve a narrow audience. What's hard is to continue doing what is the core of our business: being broadcasters. But when you're working with the best news, information, and entertainment professionals in the business, the challenge is very exciting."

IN THE CRIMINAL JUSTICE SYSTEM...

"…The people are represented by two separate yet equally important groups: the police, who investigate crime, and the district attorneys, who prosecute the offenders. These are their stories."
— Preamble to *Law & Order* (voiceover)

Few viewers are likely to remember a short-lived 1963 drama on ABC called *Arrest and Trial.* Twenty-five years later, it served as the basis for the most durable drama series in the history of television.

Arrest and Trial was a ninety-minute drama divided into two halves. One half followed police who investigated a crime and made the arrest. The other half focused on the lawyers who represented the criminal. Barry Diller, head of Fox Television in 1988, was a fan and told executives at Universal Television, which owned the show, to look at reviving it.

Dick Wolf, a screenwriter and former writer/producer for *Miami Vice,* jumped at the idea when Universal presented it. He had been looking to develop an hour-drama that could be split into half-hours for syndication.

Wolf adapted the concept to suit the national mood. The old series aired at a time when legal shows often had defense lawyers springing the wrongly accused. In 1988, crime was on the rise and politicians were defined by their stance on the death penalty. Wolf made the prosecuting attorneys the lawyer-heroes on his show. Even his title, *Law & Order,* was a nod to more conservative times.

Law & Order was also a throwback in other respects. TV dramas in the 1980s emphasized character development and serialized stories

(Above) Sam Waterston as Assistant District Attorney Jack McCoy. *(Right)* Jerry Orbach as Detective Lennie Briscoe, and Jesse L. Martin as Detective Ed Green. *(Opposite, top)* Detective Robert Goren (Vincent D'Onofrio) gets serious with murder suspect Henry Talbott (Griffin Dunne) in *Law & Order: Criminal Intent. (Opposite, in circle)* Waterston and Elisabeth Rohm as Assistant District Attorney Serena Southerlyn.

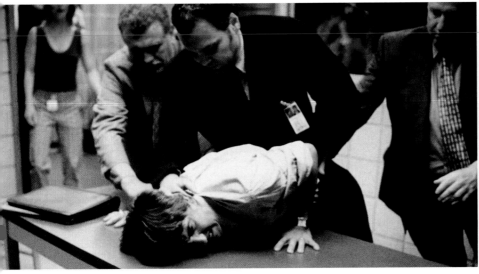

(Above, right) The cast of *Law & Order: Special Victims Unit* *(left to right)* Stephanie March (Assistant District Attorney Alexandra Cabot), Ice-T (Detective Odafin "Fin" Tutuola), Christopher Meloni (Detective Elliot Stabler), Mariska Hargitay (Detective Olivia Benson), Dann Florek (Captain Donald Cragen), Richard Belzer (Detective John Munch).

aimed at hooking viewers every week. *Law & Order* focused on the process of catching and convicting criminals rather than the personal lives of cops and lawyers. "Where other shows give you character by the glass, we give it by the eye dropper," says Peter Jankowski, who serves as one of *Law & Order*'s executive producers and also as president of Wolf Films. "It's more about the story than the individual characters."

To get a gritty, urban look, Wolf insisted on shooting on location in New York, which had been abandoned by other producers because it was too expensive. To make it affordable, he got concessions from the trade unions.

After CBS passed on the pilot—no female appeal, the network's testing said—*Law & Order* was shopped to NBC, where executives were intrigued. Brandon Tartikoff eventually picked up the series for the 1990–91 season.

Law & Order was a slow

starter in the ratings, finishing outside of the Nielsen Top 30 in its first three seasons. NBC also sustained revenue losses when advertisers steered clear of episodes about abortion clinic bombings and assisted suicide by AIDS patients—the price the series paid for using controversial stories from the day's headlines. But the network's patience was rewarded after repeats of *Law & Order* began airing several times daily on cable network A&E. The self-contained hours were just right for a generation of channel-surfing viewers. The added cable exposure helped turn the show into a major hit.

Law & Order's story-driven nature has made it impervious to numerous cast changes during its run. In the fourth season, Wolf followed a network edict to hire actresses in principal roles. It led to the casting of mainstay S. Epatha Merkerson, an African-American actress who played a cleaning woman on an early episode, as head of the detectives. Ratings have

grown over the years. After seven seasons, *Law & Order* won its first Emmy for Outstanding Drama Series in 1997.

NBC and Wolf turned *Law & Order* into a franchise in 1999 when they introduced *Law & Order: Special Victims Unit*, about a separate unit of detectives and prosecutors who investigate sex crimes. A third iteration arrived in 2001 with *Law & Order: Criminal Intent*, where the story unfolds from the perpetrator's point of view.

NBC is committed to the original *Law & Order* through 2005. By then, it will be the longest-running crime drama series in television history.

"SIR, I AM A COMPLETE UNKNOWN!"

In the thick of the media frenzy over the Carson-to-Leno transition, NBC announced to the press that the replacement host for David Letterman's 12:30 a.m. slot had been found, and his name was…Conan O'Brien.

A self-deprecating, gangly Irish-Catholic writer for both *Saturday Night Live* and *The Simpsons*, O'Brien had very little performance experience—and no name recognition. When asked how it felt to be offered such a high-profile gig as a "relative unknown," O'Brien indignantly replied, "Sir, I am a *complete* unknown!"

He was, however, an unknown with a powerful ally. Lorne Michaels, executive producer of *SNL*, had been tapped to executive-produce this new show, and he needed a host who would appeal to younger viewers. Michaels initially thought of O'Brien as a producer for the show but soon realized that the writer—who had a knack for making his fellow writers crack up—was better suited to be the host. To serve as producer, Michaels tapped *Kids in the Hall* veteran Jeff Ross. And so the announcements were made, a sidekick was chosen (comedian

Andy Richter), a killer band was assembled (led by Bruce Springsteen's drummer Max Weinberg), and *Late Night with Conan O'Brien* debuted on September 13, 1993.

The show had a rough start. NBC initially renewed the show in thirteen-week increments—not exactly a strong vote of confidence. But within a couple of years, *Late Night* found its distinctive style; and O'Brien, with his personal, surreal, sometimes even ridiculous humor, so different from Letterman's ironic style, found a loyal college-age audience.

"The concept of the show,"

says O'Brien, "was that it should almost look like a throwback. I wanted it to look like the 1964 *Tonight Show* with Johnny Carson. I wanted it to appear very conventional. And then I wanted the comedy and the content to be very irreverent and postmodern, sort of like *The Simpsons* or *Pee Wee's Playhouse*, with a lot of counter-cultural nonsense going on."

O'Brien's sense of humor somehow maintains both a childlike innocence and a sharp adult's-eye view of the bizarre realities of life in the twenty-first century. One of the most popular bits on the show is known as "Clutch Cargo," in homage to the cartoon of that name from the early sixties. As O'Brien talks to a still photo of the president, or some other powerful figure, the picture's lips appear to move as the host and the "guest" carry on an absurd conversation. There are also outlandish recurring characters, such as Triumph the Insult Comic Dog—the Don Rickles of dog puppetry that, among other things, led to legal wrangling with Pets.com.

The guest list for *Late Night*

sounds much like that from any other talk show, but the actual appearances often veer off the main road. Jim Carrey sat on the 1964-style sofa debuting clips from his new biopic *The Conan O'Brien Story* (in which Carrey claimed to play O'Brien). Martha Stewart drank malt liquor and ate a bean burrito. Veteran newsman Sam Donaldson shared the sofa with the heavy metal band Motley Crüe. *Late Night* also has taken an ahead-of-the-curve approach to its musical guests. The show has been the network television debut for star acts such as Radiohead, Green Day, Sheryl Crow, Jewel, and Barenaked Ladies.

Since *Late Night*'s first night, a small picture gallery has hung next to O'Brien's desk, with framed photos of Steve Allen, Jack Paar, Johnny Carson, and David Letterman—NBC's historical lineup of New York late-night talk show hosts. "The thing that's made me happiest doing this show," says O'Brien, "is knowing I'm part of this chain."

(Opposite) O'Brien with Mike Myers. (Above, left) In a "Clutch Cargo" segment, O'Brien "talks" with a photo of George W. Bush; when Clinton was president, his photo had a propensity to yell "Neee-Haah!" (Above, right) One year, when Tom Hanks wasn't going to be home for the holidays, *Late Night* brought Christmas to him. (Left) The original lineup: Max Weinberg, Andy Richter (who left the show in 2000), and Conan O'Brien.

No Consolation Prizes, No Lovely Parting Gifts...

Just an icy kiss-off— "You are the weakest link, good-bye," in leather-clad host Anne Robinson's clipped, impeccable British diction. An instant hit since its debut in April 2001, *Weakest Link* is an all-or-nothing fight to the finish that features trivia combat among eight players. Each round of questions is followed by a vote that eliminates one player; first the too dim, then the too smart, and finally the merely inconvenient are voted off by the others. As Machiavellian alliances among surviving contestants evolve and then dissolve, viewers so inclined can enjoy the "dissing" among

opponents, as well as Robinson's cutting commentary on the players' intellectual inadequacies.

This game show for the twenty-first century has its roots in a program that premiered twenty-five years ago— *The Gong Show*. Hosted and produced by Chuck Barris, this parody of talent shows stood Ted Mack on his head and featured three boisterous and at times downright disorderly celebrity panelists (often including Jaye P. Morgan, *Laugh-In*'s Arte Johnson, or *M*A*S*H*'s Jamie Farr) charged

with rating offbeat acts on a scale of 1 to 10. Many contestants didn't stay onstage long enough to be rated. If they were bad enough—and we at home lived for these moments—the judges raucously gonged them off the stage. If all the acts were gonged off, no one won the $516.32 grand prize; but how could you not love the lady in the tutu who spun around upside-down with her head in a teacup, playing "Old Folks at Home" on the mandolin?

The meager grand prize was part of the gag, but it was

also a reminder that the scars from the quiz show scandals ran deep. For decades, the winnings on game shows were deliberately kept small. For example, *Concentration*—created by Jack Barry and Dan Enright in 1958, just as the scandal was about to go public—avoided being tainted by offering low-valued winnings from the start. Contestants had to match fifteen pairs of prizes, displayed on one side of a three-sided wedge; successful matches would then be turned to reveal portions of a rebus puzzle that players had to solve. Hugh Downs was the first emcee of what would become NBC's longest-running game show, which finally left the network in 1973.

The original *Jeopardy!* aired on NBC daytime beginning in 1964 and stayed on for eleven years before going into syndication—produced, then as now, by Merv Griffin Productions. (Merv even wrote the legendary "Final Jeopardy" theme himself.) First hosted by Art Fleming, and memorably announced by Don Pardo, *SNL*'s current announcer and a beloved NBC mainstay with the network since 1948, the program was in the vanguard of "literate" game shows and was known for the difficulty of its questions.

Not so on *The Hollywood Squares*, where contestants simply had to agree or disagree with the often facetious answers offered up by celebrity panelists in order to win at tic-tac-toe. Over the long run of the program, regular panelists—chosen as much for their quick wit as for their notoriety—have included George Gobel, Wally Cox, Cliff Arquette (aka Charley Weaver), and, of course, legendary center square Paul Lynde. Hosted by Peter Marshall, this not-very-serious show was created and produced by Merrill Heatter and Bob Quigley.

From 1936's *Uncle Jim's Question Bee* (the first nationally broadcast quiz show) to today's *Weakest Link*, NBC continues to put real people on the air, competing for cash, prizes, and fifteen minutes of fame and glory.

A NEW "REALITY"

When Jeff Zucker, president of NBC Entertainment, appeared before the Television Critics Association in the summer of 2001 to defend his programming choices of "reality TV," he walked out to the music of "Hit Me with Your Best Shot," wearing a bulletproof vest. To critics who had accused him of tarnishing the legacy of the "quality network" he responds, "Of course, NBC still stands for quality. But, c'mon, we're broadcasters—which means casting a net for the widest audience possible with a variety of programming. We can't just do twenty-two hours of *The West Wing*."

There's no arguing with success. *Fear Factor*, in which six contestants (three women and three men) face their primal fears while performing outrageous stunts, has successfully drawn new audiences to NBC. Hosted by Joe Rogan, this much-discussed program pits real people against each other—and themselves—in the hope of taking home a cash prize of $50,000 at the end of each one-hour episode.

(*Opposite, top*) Anne Robinson rules the set of *Weakest Link*. (*Opposite, bottom*) The colors and atmosphere were quite different on the set of the original *Jeopardy!*, hosted by Art Fleming. (*Above, left*) The guest stars of *Hollywood Squares* sit in a tic-tac-toe board (in this shot, no one has yet to be labeled as a circle or a square). (*Above, right*) Chuck Barris, the creator and host of *The Gong Show*, stands happily with mallet in hand.

PROFITING FROM EXPERIENCE

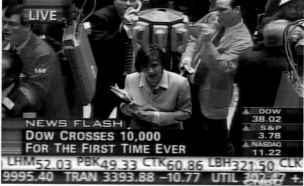

MARIA BARTIROMO

If you doubt CNBC's role as part of America's pop culture, consider the recent career of Maria Bartiromo. After becoming the first person to broadcast live from the floor of the NYSE, Bartiromo—a serious business correspondent with Sophia Loren-esque looks—quickly acquired an avid fan base. In fact, Joey Ramone, the late lead singer for the Ramones, was such a CNBC fan that he wrote a song entitled "Maria Bartiromo."

Bartiromo has played a key role in helping to level the playing field for individual investors everywhere. She shared the following anecdote with *TV Guide Ultimate Cable* in 2000: "I got in a cab one day, and the cabby was a nice guy. I didn't think he recognized me, but just as I am about to get out, he says to me, 'Maria, do you think I should stay in oil stocks?'"

As the 1990s progressed, CNBC—now far from its days as a consumer tips channel—found itself on a dramatic, unprecedented financial boom. Millions upon millions of Americans began to take an interest in their money as the stock market blossomed and the Dow reached ever-headier heights.

CNBC found itself booming right alongside. "We got very lucky," says Sue Herera. "The great bull market helped a lot, and people were interested in stock. It became sexy."

Since the heady days of the late 1990s, through the boom and bust, the sure-things and disappointments, CNBC continues to make financial news matter—for CEOs and for average folk. "Business news impacts every viewer in a uniquely personal way," says Pamela Thomas-Graham, CNBC's president and CEO. "Whether the bulls are charging or the bears have taken over the Street, viewers turn to CNBC for its in-depth coverage and analysis of the information that impacts their financial well-being far beyond their portfolios."

The allure of CNBC is that it consistently presents intelligent financial information in a compelling and under-standable way. "The great thing about business news," says Ron Insana, "is there's always some variation on a theme that you never thought of before. There's a real intellectual, creative problem every day. The level of complexity just continues to increase, then you have to figure out a way to put it into English so that people actually understand what you're talking about."

The real beginning of the CNBC-as-Must See TV era began with the 1995 debut of *Squawk Box*, which coincided with the arrival of the channel's new president, Bill Bolster (who now heads CNBC's international expansion as chairman and CEO of CNBC International). *Squawk Box* was designed from the beginning to, first, prepare viewers with the information that would move the markets and, then, guide them through the trading activity immediately following the opening bell. Hosted by Mark Haines, the program features interviews with CEOs and financial analysts, while David Faber and Joe Kernen contribute savvy reportage without taking themselves too seriously. (In 2001, Kernen started a write-in campaign for himself in *GQ* magazine's Man-of-the-Year contest.)

After the markets close for the day, CNBC provides a complete recap of market activity with Ron Insana's and Sue Herera's *Business Center* (which made history as the first show hosted from the floor of the New York Stock Exchange).

Key to the channel's success is its overall feel: urgent, exciting, inquisitive, but not too difficult for the interested beginner to understand.

With the addition of the real-time ticker, CNBC has become an extremely useful network for a nation of viewers who may want to become rich—or simply want to be responsible and safe with their money. The fact that intelligent correspondents such as Insana, Herera, Bill Griffeth, and Bartiromo have became pop-culture figures was never really a goal. It is just a by-product of a focused channel that's found its voice in the right place at the right time.

"People watch CNBC for one simple reason," says Griffeth. "They want to know how their money's doing. Sure, they're happy when the market's going up, but they still have a portfolio, they're still saving for college. When it goes down, there's still that basic question: 'How's my money doing?' "

(Opposite, left; right) Ron Insana at the NASDAQ; Maria Bartiromo on the floor of the New York Stock Exchange as the Dow hits the 10,000-mark for the first time ever. *(Above)* Left to right: Sue Herera, Bill Griffeth, Bartiromo, David Faber, Tyler Mathisen, Joe Kernen, Kathleen Hays, Mark Haines, Ron Insana, Ted David.

NBC and Microsoft Get Connected

In 1995, as the World Wide Web grew with astonishing speed, Bob Wright's and then–NBC News chief Andrew Lack's hopes of starting a cable news network coincided rather neatly with Microsoft CEO Bill Gates's quest for a definitive online news outlet for Microsoft.

Tom Brokaw was helpful in getting Microsoft and NBC together, since he had become friends with Gates while making a 1995 NBC documentary. Brokaw pointed out to him that NBC News had a surfeit of talent and stories: many quality pieces were seen once (if at all) on the limited airtime available on *Today*, *Dateline*, and *Nightly News*. Integrating a cable network and a news website could be an extension of Wright's and Lack's goal of finding new ways to bring NBC's rich news content to viewers.

So MSNBC was born. From its launch on July 15, 1996, it was in concept both simple (a cable news network in sync with a sister website) and ambitious (a model for a future in which distinctions between the TV and the PC become increasingly blurred). MSNBC.com broke new ground by allowing users to customize the site and receive the specific news most important to them. The integration was a way to bring the latest news to a younger, Internet-friendly audience often averse to news-papers and evening newscasts.

MSNBC was put to the test only two days after launch when TWA Flight 800 exploded over

the Atlantic. MSNBC covered the story, in all its dimensions, with all of its resources, demonstrating the network's trademark ability to thoroughly cover a central story.

Then, on February 4, 1997, President Clinton's State of the Union address was airing on NBC when the O.J. Simpson civil case verdict was handed down. NBC stayed with the president, MSNBC cable covered O.J., and MSNBC.com covered both breaking stories at once—a feat of news distribution no other news organization could do.

Since then, the cable network and website have continued to reach a younger, more "connected" audience, while NBC's network news programs have used the website to add depth to their stories and interviews. Tom Brokaw, Jane Pauley, and Matt Lauer (with his *Headliners & Legends*) are regulars on cable, while *Nightly*, *Dateline*, and *Today* use the Web to expand their stories and interviews.

The News with Brian Williams continues to be at the network's heart, a nightly newscaster's

dream: in-depth, literate, timely, and a full-hour long. *Imus in the Morning*, a televised version of Don Imus's radio show, has become wildly popular among political addicts. And *Hardball* host Chris Matthews has become enough of a pop-culture icon to be parodied on *Saturday Night Live*.

But MSNBC's primary goal is to present breaking news in innovative ways across new platforms of communication. MSNBC.com has long been the nation's No. 1 Internet news site, functioning as the equivalent of the nation's most widely read newspaper. Under the leadership of MSNBC's president and general manager Erik Sorenson, the network continues to bring a new generation of NBC News talent, such as Ashleigh Banfield, Lester Holt, and Norah O'Donnell, to the nation.

"MSNBC was a transforming event for NBC News," says Lack, "because Bob Wright had the vision to see that it wasn't about cable or the Internet. It was about television, and that viewing habits are changing. The Internet is going to

transform that again. It doesn't matter if we call this box a TV or PC. The video and stories NBC produces will continue to affect people's lives the way NBC has for seventy-five years. That won't change."

(Opposite) Left to right: Bob Wright, Jane Pauley, Andrew Lack, Peter Neupert (Microsoft VP and acting general manager of MSNBC.com at launch), and Brian Williams, as they announce the debut of MSNBC cable.

(Top, left to right) Ashleigh Banfield in Pakistan; Brian Williams points at a map to show viewers where TWA Flight 800 went down; Lester Holt reports from the studio. *(Above)* The MSNBC studio in Secaucus, New Jersey, is more advanced than any other in the world. MSNBC debuted in 1996 to more than 20 million homes through major cable and satellite outlets such as AT&T Broadband, Cox Communications, Time Warner Communications, DirecTV, and Echostar. Within five years, under the leadership of David Zaslav, president of NBC Cable, MSNBC could be seen in more than 70 million households in the U.S. and Canada.

SATURDAY NIGHT ALIVE AND WELL

SPARTAN SPIRIT
(Above) Overeager outcast cheerleaders Craig and Arianna (Will Ferrell and Cheri Oteri) were two of the first breakout characters in one of the most cohesive and praised casts in the show's history.

Lorne Michaels, creator of *Saturday Night Live*, has been the show's overseer for twenty-two of its first twenty-seven seasons, making him one of network television's last true impresarios. "I just love the action of it," he said in a recent interview. "Blank page to air in six days, it being 10:23 p.m. and not knowing what the opening is."

While the show was considered antiestablishment in the 1970s, it is now more of a funhouse mirror reflection of public opinion. After Vice President Al Gore gave what many considered to be an overbearing know-it-all performance in his first 2000 presidential debate, his advisors tried to rein him in by showing him a tape of Darrell Hammond's dead-on impersonation. (Hammond had also portrayed President Clinton as an irascible scamp immune to the forces out to get him—not necessarily an exaggeration.) Will Ferrell's impression of George W. Bush as an addled good ol' boy raised more questions about the candidate's readiness for the White House than any negative political ad could. But Ferrell shifted his impersonation away from that image as public confidence in the performance of President Bush soared after the terrorist attacks of September 11—while still keeping it funny.

In 1999, Tina Fey became the show's first female head writer. Fey brought a razor-sharp edge to "Weekend Update" when she joined Jimmy Fallon as co-anchor a year later, and was listed as one of *Entertainment Weekly*'s 2001 "Entertainers of the Year."

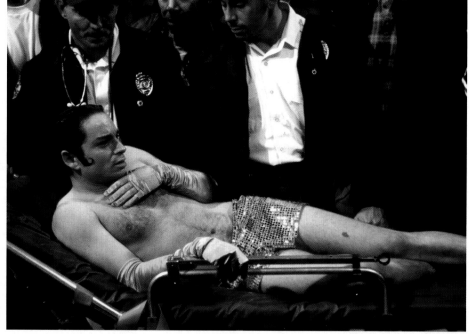

LUST AND FLYING LEAPS *(Above)* Chris Kattan's high-strung exotic dancer, Mango, has been the "fantasy" of many an *SNL* guest host, male and female. *(Left)* Molly Shannon's repressed Catholic schoolgirl, Mary Katherine Gallagher, makes a pit stop at a school dance with the late, great Chris Farley.

MAKIN' COPIES! (*Above*) Rob Schneider's Copy Guy—aka "The Richmeister"—was the office nudge you loved to hate. (*Left*) Bobbi Moughan-Culp and husband Marty (Ana Gasteyer and Will Ferrell) were a fearless duo with unique interpretations of hit songs—when they weren't teaching music at Altadena Middle School.

MARATHON "MAN" (*Left*) Tim Meadows's syntax-mangling sex expert Leon Phelps made it to the big screen with the 2000 release of *The Ladies Man*—the seventeenth *SNL* spin-off film. Meadows put in ten years on the show (1991–2001), the longest yet by any cast member.

MAKING NEWS (*Left*) Darrell Hammond's Al Gore and Will Ferrell's George W. Bush (*left*) became a bellwether of the 2000 presidential election. "I think there are times when it's very important that we're on the air," says Lorne Michaels, "and the election was one of them." (*Above*) Tina Fey and Jimmy Fallon on "Weekend Update," an institution of the show since 1975. Here, former "Update" anchor Colin Quinn (*on the left*) reports on life in New York City after September 11, 2001.

BEHIND THE MEDICINE

Even the turnover of staff during the show's eight-year history mimics hospital life. Original cast members George Clooney, who played pediatrician Doug Ross *(opposite, bottom)*, Eriq La Salle (surgeon Peter Benton, *below right; opposite, top left)*, Julianna Margulies (nurse Carol Hathaway), and William H. Macy (ER head David Morgenstern) are among many who served a rotation and moved on. Recently, Sherry Stringfield (Dr. Susan Lewis) returned to *ER* after a five-year hiatus. Other original regulars, including Anthony Edwards, as Dr. Mark Greene *(circle, right)*, and Noah Wyle (Dr. John Carter, *below, left*) have evolved through personal and professional changes, and have been joined by a new group of regulars, including Laura Innes, as Dr. Kerry Weaver *(opposite, far right)*, Goran Visnjic (Dr. Luka Kovac), Alex Kingston (Dr. Elizabeth Corday), Maura Tierney (nurse Abby Lockhart), and Sharif Atkins (third-year medical student Michael Gallant). We've laughed, cried, and lived with them all, even tyrannical, manipulative chief of staff Robert Romano (played by Paul McCrane), who once made Dr. Corday operate on his dog.

In the spring of 1994, a debate was raging in Washington about the future of health care in America, with First Lady Hillary Clinton leading an initiative for a federally run plan. Across the country at NBC's Burbank headquarters, another heated discussion was going on. The network was considering an emergency-room-based medical series, created by *Jurassic Park* author Michael Crichton, based on a 1974 screenplay Crichton wrote about his own experiences at a Boston hospital. While NBC wasn't sold enough on the script to make a series commitment, and other networks had rejected it before, the network went ahead with a pilot thinking it would at least end up with an original Crichton movie produced by Steven Spielberg to put on the air.

The *ER* pilot was a two-hour shot of adrenaline. Director Rod Holcomb filmed much of it in a documentary style, using a SteadiCam for rapid, winding takes through the corridors of an empty hospital in East Los Angeles. *ER* had eighty-seven speaking parts and forty-five stories, many of which had no resolution. Blood spurted everywhere. Doctors shouted out orders in medical jargon. Patients died. Not everyone at NBC was ready for it. "They thought it was too fast," says executive producer John Wells, "and that it covered too much territory, and that you didn't get involved enough in the individual characters' lives. In everyone's defense, it was very different than any medical show that had been on the air before."

When *ER* was shown to test audiences, however, the response was overwhelmingly positive. Along with the traditional melodrama of doctor shows, the fast pace gave the show the appeal of an action movie.

NBC scheduled *ER* on Thursdays at 10:00 p.m., pitting it against *Chicago Hope*, a more conventional medical drama from *L.A. Law* alum David E. Kelley. Many TV critics and ad agencies

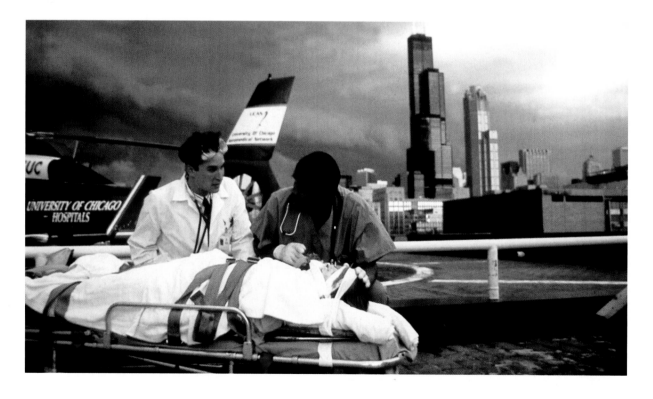

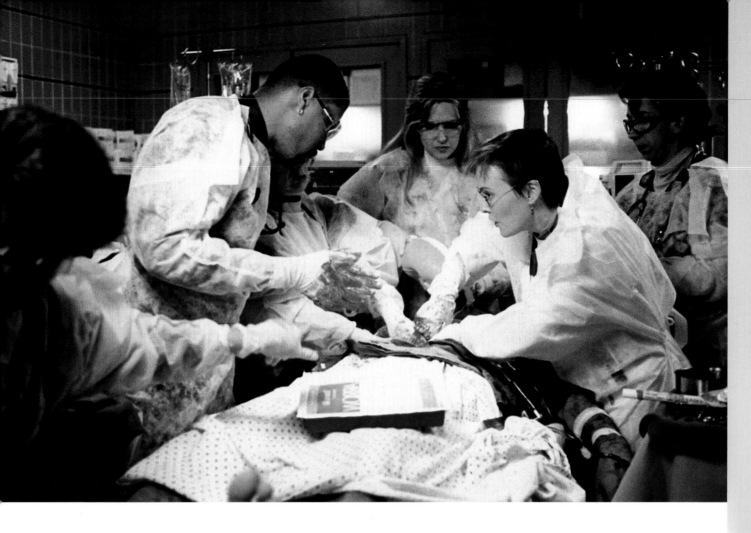

In a rare feat for today's episodic television, *ER* presented a live telecast on September 25, 1997.

"I was directing an episode (of *ER*) in the second season," says Thomas Schlamme, who directed the live telecast, "when I first overheard Anthony Edwards and George Clooney talking about doing a live show. I knew right away we had to do it. It was this great connection to the history of television, and there was a quality to *ER* that I believed deserved that connection. It wasn't just a gimmick or a publicity stunt.

"During the broadcast, the action never stopped for forty-two minutes. If you weren't in a scene, you were still in the background somewhere, living your life on camera. The stage managers were nurses and doctors and technicians wheeling carts with little plugs in their ears, giving cues. I know that people in the audience were watching it for the train wreck, waiting for something to go wrong. But, thank God, it didn't."

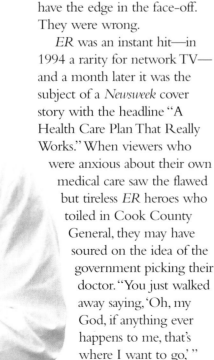

thought the CBS show would have the edge in the face-off. They were wrong.

ER was an instant hit—in 1994 a rarity for network TV—and a month later it was the subject of a *Newsweek* cover story with the headline "A Health Care Plan That Really Works." When viewers who were anxious about their own medical care saw the flawed but tireless *ER* heroes who toiled in Cook County General, they may have soured on the idea of the government picking their doctor. "You just walked away saying, 'Oh, my God, if anything ever happens to me, that's where I want to go,'"

said then-NBC Entertainment President Warren Littlefield.

The massive success of *ER*—the top-rated network drama in all of its eight seasons to date and winner of seventeen Emmy Awards—also affected the way network television did business. When it came time in 1998 for NBC to negotiate a new deal with the series' studio Warner Bros. Television, competitors expressed enough interest to drive the price up to a reported $13 million per episode, the highest price ever paid for an entertainment program. The deal accelerated the efforts of the networks to own more of their prime-time series so they wouldn't find themselves in the same situation.

THIS IS *TODAY*, ON NBC

In 1990, Katherine Couric—who would soon be known by one and all as "Katie"—was offered the job of national correspondent on the *Today* show. It was a turbulent time for the program, and Couric, who had the Pentagon beat at the time, asked her then-boss at NBC's Washington bureau—Tim Russert—about the wisdom of making the move. Russert replied that he thought the producers would soon be asking her to take on a different job: that of co-host. "Couric said, 'Wow,'" remembers Russert. "And then she got up from her chair, went to the doorway, turned around and said, 'I could do that job.'"

Couric was right—and so

was Russert. In 1991, she replaced Deborah Norville in the co-anchor seat next to Bryant Gumbel. Since then, the *Today* "first family"—Couric, Matt Lauer, weather reporter Al Roker, and news anchor Ann Curry—has taken the now-half-century-old *Today* to heights barely imaginable by David Sarnoff, Pat Weaver, or even Barbara Walters. More than six million Americans start their day with the program,

which currently has the longest winning streak (more than 300 consecutive weeks, dating back to 1995) in the history of morning television.

The show's success reflects the talents of executive producer Jeff Zucker, who had an unparalleled knack for anticipating the "water-cooler" topic of the day. (Zucker now serves as president of NBC Entertainment, with former *NBC Nightly News* executive producer Jonathan Wald filling his slot at *Today*.)

Also playing a big role is Studio 1A, the show's "Window on the World." Since 1994, this

widely imitated, but never matched, phenomenon has attracted hundreds of thousands of fans a year to the corner of 49th and Rockefeller Plaza in Manhattan.

After getting used to the new job ("I didn't even know how to turn the page to match my copy to what was happening on the teleprompter"), Couric triumphed early on during a Barbara Bush–led live tour of the White House in 1992.

When President Bush wandered by for what he thought would be a brief, pleasant hello, Couric initiated an impromptu interview. "There were a lot of things to talk to him about, and I was able to get him into my web, if you will. Afterwards I thought, wow, that was good television, and I didn't completely blow it! I didn't become so flustered that I wasn't able to ask legitimate news questions and get some important answers."

Matt Lauer—who began as *Today*'s news anchor in 1994 and replaced Bryant Gumbel in 1997—had a similar journalistic coup. In his January 27, 1998, interview with Hillary Clinton, the First Lady made the highly publicized claim that her husband was the victim of a "vast right-wing conspiracy." By then, it was obvious Lauer had mastered the *Today* host requirements: knowing when to push, knowing when to lay back, presenting (often making) the morning's news in a calm, friendly yet precise manner.

Lauer understands *Today* still has a role quite similar to what Pat Weaver imagined for it in the early fifties. "We keep in the back of our minds that people are not sitting around glued to the television for three hours a morning," he says. "The idea is for *Today* to be a companion in your room, so you can do the things you need to do, and then turn to us when something catches your attention."

Couric adds, "*Today* gives people a good understanding every day they wake up that the world is still around, that life is still going on, and that there are important things happening we need to understand. The show is much greater than the sum of its parts because of its longevity, because it has such a great tradition behind it."

(Opposite, top) Katie Couric and Matt Lauer toast Jennifer Larou and Jeffrey Scott, the winners of the "*Today* Throws a Wedding" contest on September 5, 2001. (Top) Couric interviews Ross Perot at his political apogee in a two-hour special interview in June 1992. (Bottom, left to right) Couric and Lauer in Studio 1A; Lauer in Sydney, Australia, during *Today*'s coverage of the XXVII Olympiad in September 2000; Couric with Michael Shoels and Craig Scott, two days after the shootings at Columbine High School (Couric: "Many people have this energy to get their story out in terribly tragic times. My job is to make those people feel as comfortable as they possibly can."); Lauer interviews George W. Bush in the Oval Office, April 26, 2001.

MEET THE PRESS — THE RUSSERT ERA

(Above, left) Tim Russert with Vice President Dick Cheney after the events of September 11, 2001. (Above, right) The on-air debate between Democratic presidential candidates Bill Bradley and Al Gore was one of those spirited sessions for which Meet the Press has become famous. (Opposite) An interview with then-President Bill Clinton. The set of Meet the Press has evolved since the 1950s to take advantage of advances in technology, and guests now meet only Russert instead of a panel of questioners, but the substance of the show remains the same.

Growing up in Irish-Catholic South Buffalo, New York, Tim Russert watched Lawrence Spivak politely but persistently grill powerful figures on *Meet the Press*, but he never dreamed he would one day be in Spivak's role. Instead, Russert seemed destined for a life as a lawyer after his work in the executive and legislative branches of government.

In 1984, he became a vice president at NBC News, and in 1989 he became Washington bureau chief for the network (a job he still holds). As Russert offered his news analysis during departmental telephone conference calls, he caught the attention of then-NBC News President Michael Gartner. "He called me up and said, 'I'm learning a lot from these conference calls. You should take that information on the air,'" Tim recalls. "And I said, 'Michael, I don't have any of that kind of training.' And he said, 'It doesn't matter. Just go out there and do it.'"

Russert started appearing as a panelist on *Meet the Press* in 1990. After one show, he fretted that he had become too aggressive in his grilling of David Duke, the former Ku Klux Klan leader and Louisiana gubernatorial candidate. (Duke was unable to name the three biggest employers in his state. Shortly afterward he lost the election.) When Russert called his father, worried he had perhaps pushed Duke too far, his Dad told him: "Son, if you go too far, go too far with a Nazi."

Soon afterward, in December 1991, Tim Russert became the ninth moderator of *Meet the Press*. In the years since, he's taken the historic show to its peak of influence and importance, and earned a reputation in Washington as the best-prepared interviewer on television. The exclusive one-on-one interview with Vice President Dick Cheney at Camp David, less than a week after the September 11 disasters, had an audience of fifteen million. "It was very important, not only for *Meet the Press*, but I think for the country," says Russert, "because we had a chance to hear from him in a riveting, informative, and almost comforting way."

Meet the Press has a lively respect for its history, showing weekly excerpts from the show's vast archive (often illustrating that "new" crises are rekindlings of old controversies). Russert notes that politicians in the forties and fifties used to be far more forthcoming and much less guarded than they are today. "People were generally more responsive to a question. They didn't have media consultants, there were not handlers as such. Politicians today are much more trained, more briefed, more skilled in spin."

That's the principal reason *Meet the Press* shifted to a permanent one-hour format in the fall of 1992, with Russert usually grilling the guests himself, follow-up question after follow-up question. The show continues to make headlines by getting interviewees to say much more than they had planned.

Immediately upon being named moderator for *Meet the Press*, Russert telephoned then-ninety-one-year-old Lawrence Spivak. The show's legendary founder had a few words of advice: "Learn everything about your guests' positions on the issues—and take the other side!" This continues to define Russert's approach and the mission of *Meet the Press*, the longest-running and most-quoted television program in the world, and the most-watched Sunday-morning program in America.

" *Meet the Press* is a national institution, a national treasure, and I'm honored to be its temporary custodian." —TIM RUSSERT

A NEW AGE IN SPORTS BROADCASTING

NBC Sports begins its second seventy-five years with a lineup of prestigious sports properties. As America's Olympic Network, NBC will bring sports' most powerful vehicle to hundreds of millions of homes through 2008. NASCAR, America's fastest-growing sport, highlights the NBC Sports calendar from July through November, when the Winston Cup champion is crowned. NBC airs NASCAR's premier event, the Daytona 500, every other year.

In addition, NBC Sports possesses the premier broadcast packages in golf, tennis and thoroughbred racing. NBC's prime golf events include the U.S. Open, Ryder Cup and a PGA Tour lineup that includes The Players Championship and the President's Cup. The revival of interest in thoroughbred racing in 2001 coincided with NBC's successful first year of Visa Triple Crown coverage. Add the Breeders' Cup World Thoroughbred Championships and NBC is the place to see the best horse racing has to offer. Wimbledon, the most important championship in tennis, continues its longtime association with NBC Sports, as does the French Open. NBC is also the home of Notre Dame football, the most powerful brand in college sports. The Gravity Games, launched in 1999 and co-owned by NBC, in 2001 delivered the highest rating ever for an extreme sports telecast.

TRIPLE CROWN FINDS A HOME The Visa Triple Crown moved to NBC in 2001 and the network delivered the series' largest audience since 1992, a stretch which includes three years (1997–99) when a Triple Crown was at stake entering the Belmont. Ratings were 49 percent higher than in 2000, with each race growing by a larger percentage than the one that preceded it. NBC's thoroughbred racing coverage was also critically acclaimed in 2001, winning favorable reviews and a prestigious Eclipse Award for the Breeders' Cup telecast.

NASCAR GROWTH CONTINUES Marked by unprecedented growth in viewer interest, the 2001 NASCAR Winston Cup season was capped by Jeff Gordon joining Richard Petty and the late Dale Earnhardt as the only four-time Winston Cup champions. Along the way, there were dozens of unforgettable moments as nineteen different drivers won races, including Dale Earnhardt, Jr., (seen here with Dale Earhardt, Sr.) in the Pepsi 400 at Daytona, the same track where his father perished five months before. That race was watched by 25 million viewers on NBC, making it the most-watched-prime-time NASCAR event of all time. NASCAR ratings on NBC and TNT were up 34 percent over the comparable second-half races the previous year. NASCAR posted its biggest gains in the Southwest, Pacific and Northeast—outside the traditional NASCAR stronghold of the Southeast.

GOLF'S NEW LEGEND The "Dominator" of golf continues to be Tiger Woods, who completed one of sports' most masterful streaks in 2000, winning ten tournaments, including three majors. Woods won the 100th U.S. Open at Pebble Beach by a major championship record 15 strokes, attracting a U.S. Open record TV audience of 53 million viewers to NBC. Woods had already become the youngest golfer, at 24, to accomplish the career Grand Slam when he ignited a national debate by winning the 2001 Masters to gain possession of all four major titles at the same time. Since his victories were not in the same calendar year, could it be called a true Grand Slam? Conventional wisdom said no, while others dubbed his feat the "Tiger Slam." NBC's golf analyst Johnny Miller summed it up best: "You can call it whatever you want, but the bottom line is the guy has all four major championship trophies on his coffee table and that's pretty special."

NEW-LOOK TENNIS Youth is being served. One of the new breed of power players on the women's circuit, Venus Williams holds court in tennis, smashing her way to her first two Grand Slam titles in 2000, at Wimbledon and the U.S. Open, before capturing the gold medal at the Sydney Olympics. She successfully defended both titles in 2001, dispatching tenacious Belgian teen Justine Henin at the All England Club, shown on NBC, and then younger sister Serena at the Open. On the men's side, Lleyton Hewitt and Andy Roddick stand out among the new breed challenging Pete Sampras and Andre Agassi for supremacy.

AMERICA'S OLYMPIC NETWORK

(Top, left; right) Kerri Strug is held in triumph by coach Bela Karolyi; Rulon Gardner is victorious over a stunned Alexander Karelin. *(Circle)* Kathy Freeman wins in her full-body running suit. *(Right)* Michael Johnson breaks the tape to set a new world record. *(Far right)* The great Ali lights the torch to start the Atlanta Games.

When French Baron Pierre de Coubertin founded the Modern Olympic Games in 1896, in the spirit of uniting the world in sport, art, and culture, he could not have imagined the effect television would have on this effort. The phenomenal growth of the Olympic Movement can be directly linked to television, as the global broadcasts of the Games have made it by far the most-watched event of any kind in the world.

As America's Olympic Network, NBC has broadcast the 2002 Salt Lake Winter Games and every Summer Olympics since 1988—dominating prime time, even in an era when the average viewer has seventy-five channels to choose from. As a television property, the Olympic Games are without equal.

American viewers caught their first glimpse of the Olympics in 1960, when CBS paid the International Olympic Committee $60,000 to air fifteen hours of the Winter Games from Squaw Valley, California. ABC grabbed the Olympic rings at the 1964 Innsbruck Winter Games, and broadcast ten of the next thirteen Olympics before bowing out after the 1988 Winter Games in Calgary. ABC Sports President Roone Arledge

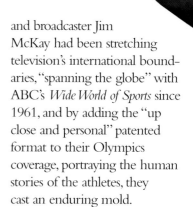

and broadcaster Jim McKay had been stretching television's international boundaries, "spanning the globe" with ABC's *Wide World of Sports* since 1961, and by adding the "up close and personal" patented format to their Olympics coverage, portraying the human stories of the athletes, they cast an enduring mold.

NBC ventured in and out of the Olympics starting with the

1964 Tokyo Summer Games, which featured the first live coverage of the Opening Ceremony, then again at the Sapporo Winter Games in 1972. Beginning with the 1988 Summer Games in Seoul, in a series of innovative deals, NBC won the rights to broadcast all the Summer Olympics through 2008, and the Winter Games in 2002 and 2006.

"NBC has become the home of the Olympics, which is the most important family entertainment platform in American television," says Dick Ebersol, the chairman of NBC Sports and NBC Olympics and the orchestrator of the unprecedented multiyear deal with the IOC. Under Ebersol's leadership, NBC refined the art of storytelling begun at ABC in the early 1960s, while emphasizing event coverage.

Olympic television has transported many of the world's greatest athletes and their amazing performances into our living rooms. From Barcelona in 1992, we witnessed Carl Lewis anchoring the U.S. sprint relay team to a gold medal in world record time; and a triumphant Magic Johnson, beaming as the star-studded Dream Team

received their basketball gold medals. At the 1996 Summer Games in Atlanta, we watched Kerri Strug lead the USA to gymnastics gold; and Michael Johnson, floating on golden running shoes across the finish line of the 200-meter sprint and looking as though even he couldn't believe he had just shattered the world record. The moment became all the more magical thanks to a camera NBC had mounted on a rail alongside the track, which followed Johnson, stride for stride. In a bold move, director Andy Rosenberg used the "rail-cam"—intended as a replay camera—for live coverage of Johnson's historic dash. "We had that look of disbelief, too," says Ebersol, speaking for the TV audience, "because we ran with him."

An estimated 3.7 billion people in 220 countries and

territories watched more than 36 billion combined hours of television coverage during the seventeen days of the 2000 Sydney Olympics. In the U.S., an average of 59 million viewers per night watched NBC's coverage as the network won 103 of 106 prime-time half-hours. Planetwide, we celebrated female track and field stars, from Australia's Aboriginal Cathy Freeman, dashing to gold in the 400-meters, to American Marion Jones, who captured three golds, and her USA teammate Stacy Dragila,

the winner of the first-ever women's pole vault. They saw swimming sensations Ian Thorpe—Australia's beloved "Thorpedo"—and the USA's Lenny Krayzelburg live up to their hype. The universal spirit of the Games shone brightest, though, on the smiling face of Greco-Roman wrestler Rulon Gardner after his improbable defeat of three-time Olympic champion Alexander Karelin, the Russian's first loss in thirteen years. Somewhere, Coubertin was smiling proudly, too.

THE PERSONAL DRAMA OF POLITICS

In 1999, any sensible pollster would have recommended against producing an ensemble show about politics and the White House. At the time, public cynicism toward government abounded. Yet when John Wells, *ER*'s executive producer, asked Aaron Sorkin, "What have you got?" over lunch, Sorkin decided on the spot to make a pitch: "What about the White House?" So with Thomas Schlamme, who at the time was co-executive-producing ABC's *Sports Night* with Sorkin, they took their idea to the networks.

Apparently NBC West Coast President Scott Sassa wasn't a pollster either. Although few others thought a political show would work, Sassa encouraged the trio to make a pilot. After two years, *The West Wing* stands as a critical and ratings success, having garnered a record-breaking nine Emmys in its first season and eight more in its second, including Outstanding Drama Series both times.

The West Wing gives viewers a behind-the-scenes glimpse into the Oval Office as seen through the eyes of its eclectic group of frenzied staffers and the devoted First Family. Far from being the jaundiced, cynical group of common public perception, the White House staff is passionate, dedicated, and out to do the best they can under trying circumstances.

The producers think of *The West Wing* as, in effect, a family drama. Like a family, the staff spends many hours together, while President Josiah "Jed" Bartlet (Martin Sheen) rules as the undisputed patriarch and moral compass. "After all," says Sorkin, "the show takes place in a house."

Sorkin, Wells, and Schlamme give credit to Steven Bochco (*Hill Street Blues* and *L.A. Law*) for opening network doors to shows like *St. Elsewhere, ER,* and *The West Wing*, which focus on many small dilemmas of life at a time, rather than just one large one.

"The premise of *The West Wing* starts with the belief that people want to be challenged," says Schlamme. "We want viewers to understand the moral complexities of life these people face. But more importantly, we want them to see that people can actually hold two emotions at one time; that issues don't have to be black or white, right or wrong. It's usually more complicated."

The West Wing's probing exploration of humanity was well-exemplified by the "In Excelsis Deo" episode during the series' first season. As Christmas Eve approaches, President Bartlet sneaks out of the White House for some last-minute Christmas shopping, while his communications director Toby Ziegler (Richard Schiff) learns more about a forgotten Korean War hero who died alone on the district's cold streets—wearing a coat that Toby once donated to charity. As the nation's capital is draped in its own mantle of snow, and people scurry about while occupied with holiday matters, Toby quietly arranges for a touching and proper military send-off for the castoff veteran.

The West Wing's success has reaffirmed the connection between television and viewers. In the summer of 2001, a survey revealed that America's view of politicians had dramatically changed over the previous years. It cited *The West Wing* as the primary reason for the shift.

(Opposite) The ensemble cast; (left to right) Presidential Aide Charlie Young (Dulé Hill); Deputy Communications Director Sam Seaborn (Emmy nominee Rob Lowe); Press Secretary C. J. Cregg (Emmy winner Allison Janney); President Josiah Bartlet (Emmy nominee Martin Sheen); Communications Director Toby Ziegler (Emmy winner Richard Schiff); First Lady Abby Bartlet (Emmy nominee Stockard Channing); Chief of Staff Leo McGarry (Emmy nominee John Spencer); Deputy Chief assistant Donna Moss (Janel Moloney); Deputy Chief Josh Lyman (Emmy winner Bradley Whitford).

(Left) In the final moments of the second season, President Bartlet stands in church after the funeral service for his beloved assistant and angrily challenges God. (Below, left to right) Lyman and McGarry at the White House; Ziegler at a rally for the President; Seaborn and Cregg at one of their many meetings.

Jay Leno: Keeping *Tonight* on Top

(Above, left to right) Jay Leno hosts L.A. Laker Kobe Bryant; New York Giant Jason Sehorn surprises *Law & Order*'s Angie Harmon with a marriage proposal, as Elton John looks on; Hugh Grant makes his first appearance after a very public indiscretion and is subjected to Leno's famous question, "What the hell were you thinking?" *(Below)* Billy Crystal in the comfort of Leno's arms. *(Opposite, top)* Leno had many celebrities sign this Harley-Davidson, sold it on eBay for $360,000, and donated the money to the Twin Towers Fund. *(Opposite, below)* The O.J.-era Dancing Itos.

James Douglas Muir Leno, part Scottish and part Italian—was born on April 28, 1950, in New Rochelle, New York. The following month, a few miles to the south, the National Broadcasting Company debuted the very first late-night network TV program: *Broadway Open House*, a precursor of *The Tonight Show*, starring Jerry Lester and Morey Amsterdam.

More than a half-century later, both James "Jay" Leno and NBC are at the top of their game. As Leno marks his tenth anniversary as host, *The Tonight Show* continues to be America's favorite reason to stay up late—and an essential next-morning water-cooler topic. *Tonight* is consistently No. 1 against all network competition.

There is more than a little merit to the claim that Leno is, as he is often called, "the hardest-working man in show business." He works relentlessly, spending endless hours crafting the best monologue on TV, doing the show, jetting across the country to do one-nighters and charity gigs, entertaining men and women in the armed forces, maintaining an obsessive hobby with cars and motorcycles, and just generally staying in touch with the American people. The last part is probably why Leno is No. 1: He has an unerring sense of what is on the nation's mind, and what we, as a people, think is worth poking fun at.

His reputation as a hard worker has been around for a while. Leno got his start in the seventies doing 300-plus performances a year on the endless comedy-club circuit. Then he hit the mark every comedian dreams of: his first

you could think of, Leno's monologue has become even funnier and more essential. Now more than ever, viewers rely on the monologue and the rest of the show to get a hilarious take on the day's news.

Leno continues to snag the biggest celebrities and hippest bands in late-night TV. And with his recurring skits—including "Headlines" and "Jaywalking" (where people answer the most elementary questions with the most amazingly dimwitted answers)—*The Tonight Show with Jay Leno* cheerfully maintains NBC's grand tradition as America's premier late-night destination.

shot on *The Tonight Show* came on March 2, 1977. Leno, a soft-eyed, big-jawed "everyman," had a brilliant talent for expounding on the absurdities of daily life, and an inclusive, garrulous style perfect for television. Leno became a permanent guest-host on Carson's *Tonight* in 1987; he also made more than forty appearances on *Late Night with David Letterman*.

The early nineties Carson-to-Leno transition—with Letterman's well-publicized departure to CBS—was big news in the country for a while—proof positive (in case anyone was wondering) of just how important the NBC late-

night slot had become. Leno handled the turbulence with characteristic grace, telling the press the controversy was "good for the world of late-night TV. It'll get some attention to it, cause more folks to stay up late."

In 1994, *The Tonight Show*'s Burbank set adopted a more nightclub-like atmosphere, playing much more to Leno's strengths. The appearance of the first guest was pushed back to give Leno more time to exploit his gift for comedy. The changes worked; before long, he had overtaken Letterman in the ratings race. Since then, thanks to the foibles of just about any politician, celebrity, and famous name

NIGHTLY NEWS, BROKAW STYLE

(Circle) Tom Brokaw reports from the White House lawn during the Watergate era. *(Opposite)* Three pillars of NBC News tradition: John Chancellor, David Brinkley, and Brokaw.

Writer-director Nora Ephron once said, "If Jimmy Stewart were an anchorman, he'd be Tom Brokaw."

For nearly thirty years, Brokaw has been the public face and the soul of NBC News. He was born in 1940 and raised in Yankton, South Dakota, the son of hard-working blue-collar parents. After college and marriage to his high school sweetheart, he moved briskly through TV news jobs at NBC affiliates in Omaha and Atlanta, and became the main anchor at KNBC, the network's owned-and-operated station in Los Angeles, at the tender age of twenty-six. Instead of being just a pretty face behind a desk, he was out chasing stories and developing a reputation as a solid political reporter. Yet when the network tapped him to cover the White House in 1973 in the

midst of the Watergate scandal, he wondered if it was too much, too soon. "There was no hiding place at that level," Brokaw said. "And I just hate to fail." But Brokaw's resourcefulness on the beat earned him praise inside and outside of NBC News.

Brokaw's next assignment was NBC's *Today* show, but with the condition he would not have to do live commercials as other hosts of the morning show had done. He never wanted to be thought of as anything but a journalist. In 1981, Brokaw nearly left NBC, which was in chaos after falling to third place in prime time and losing affiliates to a hot ABC. In fact, ABC News tried to lure Brokaw as well, but NBC countered with an offer to co-anchor *NBC Nightly News* with Roger Mudd. The new role helped, but the decision to stay was mostly out of loyalty to the

network he grew up with.

Brokaw became the solo anchor in 1983, and while *Nightly*'s ratings had their ups and downs during the next decade, his commitment to reporting never wavered (his tireless globetrotting had earned him the nickname "Duncan the Wonder Horse"). He was the only network anchor at the Berlin Wall when it came down, and he broke the story of Nelson Mandela's release from prison in South Africa.

While television news is steeped in its traditions, Brokaw has been willing to embrace change. In the mid-nineties, he knew that the evening newscast could not survive as the "broadcast of record" in a world with twenty-four-hour cable news and the emergence of the Internet. *Nightly News* moved toward a format that went deeper into issues such as health,

technology, and government spending ("The Fleecing of America") and has been an evening-news ratings leader ever since. Brokaw also introduced NBC and General Electric brass to Microsoft founder Bill Gates, whose company became a partner in NBC's cable news network, MSNBC.

Brokaw has prepared for the future while not forgetting the importance of understanding the past. After a visit to the shores of Normandy on the fiftieth anniversary of the U.S. invasion, he was moved enough to want to preserve the stories of the war veterans and others from that era who made sacrifices for their country.

The result was three best-selling books, *The Greatest Generation*, *The Greatest Generation Speaks*, and *An Album of Memories*.

Brokaw says he would like to be remembered simply as a newsman who had "gotten it mostly right and still had his personal integrity." Jimmy Stewart couldn't have said it any better.

(Opposite, bottom, left to right) Tom Brokaw was the only American anchor to report from the Berlin Wall the night the historic barrier fell, on November 9, 1989; Brokaw was the first American anchor to report on the human rights abuses in Tibet and to conduct an interview with the Dalai Lama; in the fall of 1987, Brokaw conducted the first exclusive one-on-one television interview with then-Soviet leader Mikhail Gorbachev.

(Below, left to right) In 1995, as part of an hour-long NBC profile on Bill Gates, Brokaw spoke to the Microsoft chief at that year's Comdex convention and also interviewed him using Microsoft's new video technology; Brokaw covered the release in February 1990 of Nelson Mandela, who had spent twenty-seven years in a South African prison; Brokaw anchored election night, 1976, from NBC's famous Studio 8H. He's been doing it ever since.

SEPTEMBER ELEVENTH

(Circle) Tom Brokaw reports to the world with the World Trade Center towers in flames behind him. *(Above, left to right)* Ashleigh Banfield, covered with dust and rubble from the collapse of the towers, reports live from the scene in lower Manhattan; rescue workers embrace; Jim Miklaszewski reports in front of the Pentagon as it smolders; scenes such as this one of bloodied people and battered cars were conveyed throughout the day to viewers around the world. *(Opposite)* Exhausted heroes of the day walk away from the remaining skeleton of a World Trade Center tower.

The horror of the images television viewers saw on the morning of September 11, 2001, was beyond description or comprehension. For hours, cameras were fixed on the thick cloud of smoke that shrouded lower Manhattan after two hijacked passenger jets crashed into the World Trade Center towers, bringing them down and causing massive casualties. Another hijacked jet damaged the Pentagon, while a fourth came down south of Pittsburgh. "The profile of Manhattan has been changed," NBC anchor Tom Brokaw told viewers after watching the second tower crumble. "There's been a declaration of war by terrorists on the United States."

For more than ninety hours straight, NBC and its counterparts provided continuous, uninterrupted pictures and words that depicted the unfolding tragedy that would have an indelible impact on life on America. There had not been such sustained coverage since the assassination of President John F. Kennedy in 1963. Suddenly the discussion of whether network television was vital in a world of hundreds of channels and the Internet became moot. "Television was the center to find information and to find comfort," said *Meet the Press* moderator Tim Russert. "It was a place for the common experience of a nation mourning and a nation healing."

Talk and variety shows that depended on topical gags had to walk a fine line when they returned to the air the following week. *Tonight Show* host Jay Leno and *Late Night*'s Conan O'Brien seriously addressed the tragic events before trying to make audiences laugh again. *Saturday Night Live* devoted the opening of its season premiere to then-Mayor Rudolph Giuliani and America's new heroes, New York's police and firefighters. *SNL* executive producer Lorne Michaels asked the mayor, "Can we be funny?" to which Giuliani replied "Why start now?" The show's quick return to political humor—most of it aimed at America's new enemy, the Taliban regime in Afghanistan—became a symbol of the country's resilience.

AFTERWORD

ANDREW LACK
President and COO

As so many of the previous pages demonstrate, television, more than any other medium, provides the American public with the closest thing we have to a universally shared experience, whether it be a moment of national trauma such as the terrorist attacks on the World Trade Center and the Pentagon or a period of national celebration such as NBC's broadcast of the Olympic Games. For this reason, the history of NBC is much more significant than the account, fascinating though it is, of David Sarnoff and the rise of a business enterprise boldly calling itself the National Broadcasting Company.

From the start, NBC's history has been created by extraordinarily talented people telling compelling stories, whether they be the comedies and dramas of entertainment programming, the real-life sagas of news reports and documentaries, or the live action of sports broadcasts with their implicit narratives of victory and defeat. Behind everything we do, throughout this company, is an intense love of the well-told tale, and this is as true today as it was in the early years of the medium, when Pat Weaver was inventing new forms of television.

NBC is about more than storytelling, however. It is about personality and about trust. NBC is the faces and voices that Americans turn to every day for knowledge, comfort, and entertainment, whether it be Katie Couric and Matt Lauer in the morning, or Tom Brokaw at dinnertime, or Kelsey Grammer's Frasier Crane each Tuesday evening, or Jay Leno before we go to bed. NBC is based on trust, on a covenant with the viewer that we will be honest and reliable— because great programming and a passion for storytelling are impossible unless you trust the teller, be it the person on the screen or all the people laboring behind the cameras.

What's most wonderful to me about working in television is that in spite of the mysterious (to me) technology that is responsible for the instantaneous transmission of countless televised images in living color, it all boils down to something that couldn't be more essentially human: using words and images to touch the emotions that are the stuff of life, to make you laugh and cry, to make you feel, and think, and experience a world larger and more complex and more amazing than any of us can fully comprehend.

For me and my colleagues past and present, broadcasting's ability to directly touch the heart and mind and spirit of innumerable viewers across the nation always has been— and still is—the essence of NBC. As proud as I am of the contributions we've made over the past seventy-five years, I'm even more excited about what we will accomplish in the years to come, as we continue to serve the nation, feeding our insatiable, and fundamentally human, appetite for a good story, in every form imaginable.

BIBLIOGRAPHY

Archer, Gleason L. *Big Business and Radio*. New York: American Historical Company, 1939.

____. *History of Radio: To 1926*. New York: American Historical Company, 1939.

Auletta, Ken. *Three Blind Mice*. New York: Random House, 1991.

Ball, Rick, and NBC News. *Meet the Press: 50 Years of History in the Making*. New York: McGraw-Hill, 1998.

Barnouw, Eric. *A Tower in Babel*. New York: Oxford University Press, 1966.

____. *The Golden Web*. New York: Oxford University Press, 1968.

____. *The Image Empire*. New York: Oxford University Press, 1970.

____. *Tube of Plenty*. New York: Oxford University Press, 1990.

Bedell, Sally. *Up the Tube: Prime-Time TV in the Silverman Years*. New York: Viking, 1981.

Bergreen, Laurence. *Look Now, Pay Later: The Rise of Network Broadcasting*. Garden City: Doubleday, 1980.

Brooks, Tim, and Earle Marsh. *The Complete Directory to Prime Time Network and Cable TV Shows: 1946–Present*, 7th ed. New York: Ballantine, 1999.

Brown, Les. *Les Brown's Encyclopedia of Television*, 3rd ed. New York: Gale, 1992.

Buxton, Frank, and Bill Owen. *The Big Broadcast, 1929–1950*. New York: Viking, 1966 and 1972.

Cader, Michael, ed. *Saturday Night Live: The First Twenty Years*. New York: Houghton Mifflin, 1994.

Campbell, Robert. *The Golden Years of Broadcasting*. New York: Charles Scribner's Sons, 1976.

Castleman, Harry, and Walter J. Podrazik. *Watching TV: Four Decades of American Television*. New York: McGraw-Hill, 1982.

Davis, Gerry. *The Today Show: An Anecdotal History*. New York: William Morrow, 1987.

DeLong, Thomas A. *Radio Stars*. Jefferson, N.C.: McFarland, 1996.

Douglas, George H. *The Early Days of Radio Broadcasting*. Jefferson, N.C.: McFarland, 1987.

Douglas, Susan J. *Listening In*. New York: Random House, 1999.

Dunning, John. *Tune in Yesterday*. Englewood Cliffs, N.J.: Prentice-Hall, 1976.

Frank, Reuven. *Out of Thin Air: The Brief Wonderful Life of Network News*. New York: Simon & Schuster, 1991.

Halberstam, David. *The Fifties*. New York: Ballantine, 1994.

Harris, Jay S., ed. *TV Guide: The First 25 Years*. New York: Simon & Schuster, 1978.

Jaker, Bill, Frank Sulek, and Peter Kanze. *The Airwaves of New York*. Jefferson, N.C.: McFarland, 1998.

Jennings, Peter, and Todd Brewster. *The Century*. New York: Doubleday, 1998.

Kisseloff, Jeff. *The Box: An Oral History of Television, 1920–1961*. New York: Viking, 1995.

Lackman, Ron. *Same Time Same Station: An A–Z Guide to Radio from Jack Benny to Howard Stern*. New York: Facts on File, 1996.

LaGuardia, Robert. *The Wonderful World of Soap Opera Stars*. New York: Ballantine, 1974.

Lindheim, Richard D., and Richard A. Blum. *Inside Television Producing*. Boston: Focal Press, 1991.

MacDonald, J. Fred. *Don't Touch That Dial!* Chicago: Nelson-Hall, 1979.

Maltin, Leonard. *The Great American Broadcast*. New York: Dutton, 1997.

Marc, David, Robert J. Thompson. *Prime Time, Prime Movers*. Boston: Little, Brown, 1992.

McNeil, Alex. *Total Television: The Comprehensive Guide to Programming from 1948 to the Present,* 4th ed. New York: Penguin, 1996.

Metz, Robert. *The Today Show*. Chicago: Playboy Press, 1977.

Mitchell, Curtis. *Cavalcade of Broadcasting*. Chicago: Follett, 1970.

Nachman, Gerald. *Raised on Radio*. New York: Pantheon, 1998.

National Broadcasting Company. *The Fourth Chime*. New York: National Broadcasting Company, 1944.

National Broadcasting Company History Files, 1922–86. Motion Picture, Broadcasting and Recorded Sound Division, Library of Congress, Washington, D.C.

O'Connell, Mary. *Connections: Reflections on 60 Years of Broadcasting*. New York: National Broadcasting Company, 1986.

Newcomb, Horace, ed. *Encyclopedia of Television*. Chicago: Fitzroy Dearborn, 1997.

Ritchie, Michael. *Please Stand By: A Pre-history of Television*. Woodstock, N.Y.: Overlook, 1994.

Rovin, Jeff. *The Great Television Series*. South Brunswick, N.J.: A. S. Barnes, 1977

Sarnoff, David. *Looking Ahead*. New York: McGraw-Hill, 1968.

Schwartz, David, Steve Ryan, and Fred Wostbrock. *The Encyclopedia of TV Game Shows*. New York: Zoetrope, 1987.

Settel, Irving. *A Pictorial History of Radio*. New York: Citadel, 1960.

Shulman, Arthur, and Roger Youman. *How Sweet it Was*. New York: Bonanza, 1966.

Stark, Steven D. *Glued to the Set: The 60 Television Shows and Events That Made Us Who We Are Today*. New York: Free Press, 1997.

Tartikoff, Brandon, and Charles Leerhsen. *The Last Great Ride*. New York: Turtle Bay Books, 1992.

Thompson, Robert J. *Television's Second Golden Age: From Hill Street Blues to ER*. New York: Syracuse University Press, 1996.

Utley, Garrick. *You Should Have Been Here Yesterday: A Life Story in Television News*. New York: PublicAffairs, 2000.

Weaver, Pat. *The Best Seat in the House*. New York: Knopf, 1994.

Wertheim, Arthur Frank. *Radio Comedy*. New York: Oxford University Press, 1979.

Wilson, Earl. *The NBC Book of Stars*. New York: Pocket Books, 1957.

CREDITS

INDEX